The Doctrine of Atonement

The Doctrine of Atonement

From Luther to Forde

Jack D. Kilcrease

Foreword by Roland Ziegler

WIPF & STOCK · Eugene, Oregon

THE DOCTRINE OF ATONEMENT
From Luther to Forde

Copyright © 2018 Jack D. Kilcrease. All rights reserved. Except for brief quotations in critical publications or reviews, no part of this book may be reproduced in any manner without prior written permission from the publisher. Write: Permissions, Wipf and Stock Publishers, 199 W. 8th Ave., Suite 3, Eugene, OR 97401.

Wipf & Stock
An Imprint of Wipf and Stock Publishers
199 W. 8th Ave., Suite 3
Eugene, OR 97401

www.wipfandstock.com

PAPERBACK ISBN: 978-1-5326-3904-3
HARDCOVER ISBN: 978-1-5326-3905-0
EBOOK ISBN: 978-1-5326-3906-7

Manufactured in the U.S.A.

Dedication

This work is dedicated to my wife Dr. Bethany Kilcrease. Her wonderful support and encouragement has helped me complete this book.

Contents

Foreword | ix
Abbreviations | xii

Chapter 1: Contexts and Methodology | 1
    Introduction | 1
    George Lindbeck's *The Nature of Doctrine* | 2
    Strengths and Weaknesses of Lindbeck's Model | 5
    Thomas Kuhn's "Paradigms" and Heiko Oberman's
        "Tradition I" | 15
    The Confessional Lutheran Paradigm | 23

Chapter 2: Martin Luther's View of Atonement | 26
    Introduction | 26
    The History of Scholarship on Luther's View of Atonement | 27
    Previous Atonement Theologies | 29
    Luther's Early Psalms Commentaries (1515–1513) | 35
    The Freedom of a Christian (1520) | 39
    Luther's Small and Large Catechisms (1529) | 43
    Great Galatians Commentary (1531, 1535) | 45

Chapter 3: Atonement in the Lutheran Confessions and Scholasticism | 51
    Introduction | 51
    The Lutheran Confessors and Scholastics: Philipp
        Melanchthon | 51
    Martin Chemnitz and the Formula of Concord | 55
    The Lutheran Scholastics: Two Developments | 60

CONTENTS

Chapter 4: Modern Rethinking of the Lutheran Doctrine of Atonement: Moderate Revisionists | 66
    Werner Elert | 67
    Gustaf Aulén | 70
    Gustaf Wingren | 74

Chapter 5: Modern Rethinking of the Lutheran Doctrine of Atonement: Radical Revisionists | 79
    Wolfhart Pannenberg | 79
    Robert Jenson | 84
    Eberhard Jüngel | 92

Chapter 6: Gerhard Forde's View of the Law | 101
    Introduction and Sources | 101
    Sources of Forde's Thought | 102
    Forde's General Concept of the Law | 106
    Forde on the Second Use of the Law | 115
    Forde on the First and Third Uses of the Law | 122
    Conclusion | 130

Chapter 7: Gerhard Forde's View of Atonement and Justification | 131
    Introduction and Sources | 131
    Forde's Use of Scripture | 131
    Forde's Critique of Previous Theologies of Atonement: Penal Satisfaction | 139
    "Subjective" or "Moral Influence" Theories of Atonement | 141
    "Classical" or "Conquest" Theories of Atonement | 144
    Forde's Treatment of Luther's Theology of Atonement | 145
    Human Existence under the Hidden God | 150
    The Actualization of Atonement and Justification: The Ministry, Death, and Resurrection of Jesus | 152
    A Confessional Lutheran Assessment and Response | 156
    Conclusion. | 164

Bibliography | 173

Foreword

AT THE CENTER OF the Christian story, and thus of the Christian faith, stands the death and resurrection of Christ. This is shown in the very structure of the Gospels. In 1892, Martin Kähler wrote in his seminal essay "The So-Called Historical Jesus and the Historic Biblical Christ" against the interest of some theologians of his time in writing a biography of Jesus focusing on the development of his self-consciousness: "To state the matter somewhat provocatively, one could call the Gospels passion narratives with extended introductions"[1] and "The fact remains that the decisive thing in all the biblical portrayals is the twofold ending of Jesus' Life, what our forefathers called the 'work' of our Lord, though perhaps in a rather too wooden distinction from his person."[2] But what is the meaning of the passion of Christ, and what is the meaning of the work of Christ? In this book, Jack Kilcrease describes the discussion among Lutherans on the meaning of the cross. For Luther, the cross was central as a salvific event, key for all theology. He was a true theologian of the cross. But in the nineteenth and twentieth century, a dissatisfaction with the view of Christ's suffering as punishment for the sins of mankind, as bearing the curse of God himself, grew in some circles of Lutherans. The doctrine of vicarious satisfaction had never been without its detractors in modernity. Already, in the time of Lutheran orthodoxy, Abraham Calov and Johann Andreas Quenstedt spent considerable effort in refuting the teachings of the Socinians on this point. And after the enlightenment, the doctrine of penal suffering was rejected in many quarters of mainstream Protestantism.

In Lutheran circles, though, the authority of Luther was so great that many sought to find support for their departure from the understanding of

---

1. Kähler, "So-called Historical Jesus," 1964.
2. Ibid., 95.

Christ's death as vicarious satisfaction in the great reformer himself. And thus, beginning with the debate between Albrecht Ritschl and Theodosius Harnack, the dogmatic debate on the understanding of Christ's death among Luther goes hand in hand with a debate on the correct interpretation of Luther. Gustaf Aulén's contention that Luther did not teach the *satisfactio vicaria* put the mantle of authentic Lutheranism on the shoulders of those who rejected the position of Lutheran orthodoxy. Such an aversion to the view of the vicarious atonement was fueled by the waning of the doctrine of the wrath of God. Since the wrath of God is revealed through the law, the issue of the law and its connection with the doctrine of the atonement became also a focus point of the discussion. Ever since the reformation, Lutherans had been involved in recurring debates on the relationship of law and gospel, in a struggle to uphold the predominance of the gospel without falling into antinomianism. The existential tension of the experience of law and gospel in the Christian that are an experience of the wrath and love of God never comes to a resolution in this life. Because Lutherans emphasize the gospel as the revelation of the innermost being of God, and because they do not understand the law as just formally different from the gospel, it is a specific Lutheran danger to disassociate God from law. If this is combined with the Neo-Protestant dislike of the wrath of God, we come to the revisionist theologies described by Jack Kilcrease, where God's wrath and his love, his punishment and his redemption, are resolved by a theory that ignores the seriousness of God's wrath. The cross is not only the supreme revelation of God's love; it is also the supreme revelation of his wrath. That God's wrath over man's sin can only be stilled by God taking his wrath on himself, is the central message of the cross.

In his lectures on Isaiah 53, Luther expressed this message thus:

> But this is truly great: Christ experiences the wrath of God more that you and I. It is not a kind of pretense or feign that is acted in this person. He experiences the wrath of God in such a way, as if he is were forsaken by God and as if he suffered because of the wrath of God, therefore he cries, Ps. 21(22): "My God, my God, why hast thou forsaken me" and Ps. 8: "You have made him abandoned from God for a little while." Certainly he has experienced here the wrath of God, and more so than any man. But indeed, he has experienced the hellish punishment, especially because his tender nature and his innocent conscience, and when God does not help, then follows forsakenness, as here "he was forsaken."[3]

3. *WA* 43 III, 716, 1–9: "Hoc vere magna est: Christus iram Dei plus sensit, quam ego

> The suffering of him who is apprehended among the guilty and is hurried off to death is solely punishment, But Christ's suffering, who is seized among us sinners, is by far another discipline, which is inflicted on him not only because of our sins, but also works peace for us, and takes away not only the guilt of sins, but also accomplishes and bestows peace and salvation to us.[4]

This book, by showing the straight path as well as the meandering paths that lead away from the straight path, sharpens the reader's discernment and helps him or her to a greater appreciation of the biblical and Lutheran teaching on the death of Christ.

Dr. Roland Ziegler
Concordia Theological Seminary,
Fort Wayne, IN

---

et tu, nec est fucus aut simulatum quiddam, quod in hac persona geritur. Iram Dei ita sensit, quasi derelictus a Deo esset et pateretur propter iram Dei, ideo clamat, Psal. 21: 'Deus, Deus meus, quare me dereliquisti,' et Psal. 8: 'Derelictum eum fecisti paulo minus ab Angelis.' Certe hic sensit iram Dei, et magis quam ullus homo. Quin etiam infernalem poenam sensit, praesertim tenerrima natura et concscientia innocens, et quando Deus non adiuvat, sequitur desertio, ut hic: 'derelictus est.'" Ps 22:2; Ps 8:6.

4. WA 43 III, 717, 19–24: "Istius passio, qui inter sontes deprehenditur et ad mortem rapitur, tantum est poena. At Christi passio, qui inter nos peccatores comprehensus est, longe est alia disciplina, quae non solum proter peccata nostra infligatur ei, sed nobis quoque pacem operatur, et tollit non solum reatum peccatorum, verumetiam impetrat et largitur nobis pacem et salutem."

Abbreviations

ANF	*Ante-Nicene Fathers*. Edited by Alexander Roberts and James Donaldson. 10 vols. Peabody, MA: Hendrickson, 2004.
Ap	Apology to the Augsburg Confession
BF	*Summa Theologiae*. Black Friars Edition. 60 vols. New York: McGraw-Hill, 1964–present.
CA	Unaltered Augsburg Confession
CD	Barth, Karl. *Church Dogmatics*. Translated by G. T. Thomason, et al. 4 vols. Edinburgh, Scotland: T & T Clark, 1936–1977.
CT	*Concordia Triglotta: The Symbolical Books of the Evangelical Lutheran Church, German-Latin-English*. Edited and translated by W. H. T. Dau, et al. St. Louis: Concordia, 1921.
Ep	Epitome of the Formula of Concord
FC	Formula of Concord
ICR	Calvin, John. *Institutes of the Christian Religion*. 1559.
LC	Large Catechism of Martin Luther
LW	*American Edition of Luther's Works*. Edited by Jaroslav Pelikan, Helmut Lehmann, and Christopher Brown. 55 vols. Philadelphia: Fortress, 1957–1986.

Abbreviations

NPNFa	*Nicene and Post-Nicene Fathers.* Edited by Philip Schaff. First Series. 14 vols. Peabody, MA: Hendrickson, 2004.
NPNFb	*Nicene and Post-Nicene Fathers.* Edited by Philip Schaff and William Wace. Second Series. 14 vols. Peabody, MA: Hendrickson, 2004.
SA	Smalcald Articles of Martin Luther
SC	Small Catechism of Martin Luther
SD	Solid Declaration of the Formula of Concord
ST	*Summa Theologiae* of Thomas Aquinas
WA	*D. Martin Luthers Werke: Kritische Gesammtausgabe.* 120 vols. Weimar, Germany: Hermann Böhlau and H. Böhlaus Nachfolg, 1883–2009.

1

Contexts and Methodology

Introduction

IN MODERN THEOLOGY, THE work of Christ is a significant point of dispute. The Enlightenment thinkers largely regarded the Patristic, Medieval, and Reformation understandings of the work of Christ to either be crassly mythological or stultifyingly legalistic. In particular, modern theologians have charged that the doctrine of substitutionary atonement makes God into a merciless judge who refuses to forgive sinners apart from the killing of his own son. A related charge is that the doctrine of substitutionary atonement constitutes an act of divine child abuse. Feminist theologians argue that insofar as God the Father abuses his own divine Son, every earthly father, is in some sense, justified in imitating their heavenly father.[1]

Attacks on the doctrine of atonement are particularly problematic for confessional Lutheran theology. All dogmas of the Christian faith are interconnected, and consequently, the rejection of one inevitably causes difficulties with others. Central to the Lutheran understanding of the gospel is the claim that, through Christ's substitutionary act of atonement on the cross, God punished all sins and has made it possible to receive the imputation of righteousness through faith. Therefore, Christ's death as a substitutionary act is the necessary correlate of God's mercy in justification through faith. In the same manner, if it was not necessary for Christ to fulfill the law of God, it would also mean that God's law is not an objective standard

---

1. See this frequently cited article which perfectly embodies this line of argument: Brown and Parker, "For God so Loved the World?", 1–29.

of morality. This would not only call into question the entire moral order of the universe, but would also create the vexing question of why Scripture consistently describes the salvation as necessitated by the gap between an utterly holy God and utterly sinful human beings.

This book deals with this central question of atonement in Lutheran theology and its current challenges. In the coming chapters, I examine the answers the historic Lutheran tradition has offered on the basis of Scripture. From the perspective of these answers, I will then both describe and critique the alternative theologies of its modern detractors, who nonetheless claim the name Lutheran.

In particular, the final two chapters consist of a close examination of the theology of Gerhard Forde (1927–2005). Forde has enjoyed a great deal of influence in North America over the last four decades. Despite Forde's wide influence in certain quarters of Lutheranism (particularly more traditionalist ones), his theology has generated a relatively small amount of secondary criticism.[2] Therefore, it is important to begin the process of testing his theological proposals against the standards of Scripture and the Lutheran Confessions.

But before entering into a discussion of these various theologies and related topics in the history of the Lutheranism, it is important to establish a clear understanding of the nature of Christian doctrine. This will clarify the basis of the following theological critique. To establish a clear understanding of doctrine as a concept, I will first examine a popular contemporary paradigm for describing the nature of doctrine (i.e., George Lindbeck's *The Nature of Doctrine*) and then make a counter-proposal. I will conclude with a description of what I will call the "Confessional Lutheran Paradigm." This paradigm will serve as the basis for the critiques offered in the later chapters of the book.

George Lindbeck's *The Nature of Doctrine*

In order to investigate a particular Christian doctrine (namely the Christian doctrine of atonement), it is important to first define the nature of

---

2. The following reviews and articles represent the bulk of the secondary criticism of Forde's theology. See my articles on the subject: Kilcrease, "Gerhard Forde's Theology of Atonement and Justification," 269–94; Kilcrease, "Gerhard Forde's Doctrine of Law," 151–180. Also see Mattes, "Gerhard Forde on Revisioning Theology," 373–93; and Liefeld, "Killing to Make Alive," 45–51. Both of these articles are very well-written and have many valuable things to say about Forde's theology.

Christian doctrine as a whole. In order to do this, it seems reasonable to begin with George Lindbeck's *The Nature of Doctrine*,[3] a relatively recent and widely received model for how to understand doctrine. In *The Nature of Doctrine*, Lindbeck develops a taxonomy of doctrinal theories gleaned from his study of the history of Christian theology. He identifies three main approaches to the question of what Christian doctrine is. Lindbeck's first theory of doctrine is a "cognitive" or "propositionalist" model. In this view, doctrines are simply propositions to be believed, either true or false. According to Lindbeck, this understanding of doctrine presupposes that Christian theology is similar to philosophy or the natural sciences as they were classically conceived. However, Lindbeck finds this conception of doctrine particularly problematic, because it tends to be very static and inflexible: "For a propositionalist, if a doctrine is once true, it is always true, and if it is once false, it is always false." This inflexibility creates a problem for ecumenism, a major fixation of Lindbeck and many of his disciples: "This [the propositional theory of doctrine] implies, for example, that the historic affirmations and denials of transubstantiation can never be harmonized. Agreement can be reached only if one or both sides abandon their earlier positions."[4]

Lindbeck describes the second approach to doctrine as the "experiential-expressive" approach. This approach has its origin primarily in the thought of Friedrich Schleiermacher in the nineteenth century. It was later picked up in the twentieth century (in a form mixed with the propositionalist model) by Roman Catholic figures like Bernard Lonergan[5] and Karl Rahner.[6] According to the "experiential-expressive" model, doctrine is essentially a way of describing people's experiences of God. Such experiences are shared universally by the human race. As a result, they can be expressed in culturally different ways according to different circumstances. There is, states Lindbeck, "at least the logical possibility that a Buddhist and a Christian might have basically the same faith, although expressed very differently."[7] The primary difficulty that Lindbeck has with this approach is that it presupposes some sort of privileged access to pre-linguistic experience. Since human beings are shaped by culture and language, there is no such thing as a pre-cultural

3. Lindbeck, *The Nature of Doctrine*.
4. Ibid., 16.
5. See, for example, Lonergan, *Method in Theology*.
6. For an example, see Rahner, *Foundations of Christian Faith*.
7. Lindbeck, *The Nature of Doctrine*, 17.

or linguistic experience.[8] Therefore, instead of the outward cultural expressions of inner experiences, Lindbeck observes that "it is the inner experiences which are . . . derivative."[9] This is because inner experiences are always filtered through the language and culture of the person who is having them. There is no such thing as a pure and mediated experience.

The third model of doctrine that Lindbeck identifies is the "cultural-linguistic model."[10] This is the model favored by Lindbeck. It presupposes that religions "resemble languages together with their correlative forms of life and are thus similar to cultures (insofar as these are understood semiotically as reality and value systems—that is, as idioms for construing of reality and the living of life)."[11] Doctrines, according to this model, are conceived of as something like rules for cultural-linguistic practice. Lindbeck gives the example of differing rules which vary by country concerning whether one should drive on the left or right side of the road. When applied to distinctions in Christian doctrine, Lindbeck uses the example of the ecumenically divisive doctrine of transubstantiation. Transubstantiation is the Roman Catholic teaching that the bread and the wine in the Lord's Supper are literally transmuted into the body and blood of Jesus. According to Lindbeck, such a doctrine does not actually represent a truth proposition, but is rather set of rules about "sacramental thought and practice."[12] In other words, according Lindbeck, the doctrine of transubstantiation does not actually tell Roman Catholics what they are supposed to believe about the Lord's Supper. Rather, it tells them how they should speak and act in relationship to the practice of the Lord's Supper.

In endorsing this approach, Lindbeck commends this model as particularly helpful for ecumenism, because by reducing doctrine to cultural-linguistic rules it means that doctrines "can in other circumstances be harmonized by appropriate specifications of their respective domains, uses, and priorities."[13] In a sense, then, much like a German and a Mexican can respect and appreciate each other's cultures by accepting the mores of each in their respective contexts, so can Christians ecumenically accept each

---

8. Ibid., 33.
9. Ibid., 34.
10. Ibid., 17. See Loughlin, *Telling God's Story*, 46–51.
11. Lindbeck, *The Nature of Doctrine*, 18.
12. Ibid., 18.
13. Ibid., 18.

others' doctrinal claims as cultural-linguistic rules of speech valid in a particular ecclesiastical context.

Therefore, in order to achieve this lofty goal of ecumenical unity, every doctrine must be reduced to a level of a cultural-linguistic rule, so as to eliminate any potentially conflicting truth claims among varying Christian traditions.[14] According to Lindbeck, even the Nicene Creed really "does not make first-order truth claims."[15] It is only a set of rules about how Christians should speak about God and Christ; it makes no actual claims about the nature of the divine being. In terms of interreligious dialogue, the linguistic systems of Christianity and other religions do not overlap, and therefore a Christian cannot say anything is propositionally true or false about Buddhism.[16] This opens the possibility that "the missionary task of Christians may at times be to encourage Marxists to become better Marxists, Jews and Muslims to become better Jews and Muslims, and Buddhists to become better Buddhists."[17]

Ultimately, then, all doctrine truly does is regulate how communal discourse and practice operate; it does not make claims about what is really objectively true and what is not. This being said, the rules of thought and practice established by church doctrine allow one to come to truth propositions, or what Lindbeck refers to as "first-order truth claims." Nevertheless, one must first accept a particular idiom of thought and practice to achieve this.[18] Thus, propositional truth claims are only thinkable within an already accepted matrix of communal linguistic practice.

Strengths and Weaknesses of Lindbeck's Model

Lindbeck's model of doctrine is helpful, insofar as it clarifies the variety of different perspectives undergirding Christian theologies. This being said, Lindbeck's own advocacy of the linguistic-cultural model and his characterizations of some of the other models have drawn significant criticism

---

14. Carl Braaten has rightly characterized Lindbeck's concept of doctrine to be a form of "neopragmatism." This can be seen particularly in regard to ecumenical relations. See Braaten, *No Other Gospel*, 19. Also see Pecknold, *Transforming Postliberal Theology*..

15. Lindbeck, *The Nature of Doctrine*, 19.

16. Ibid., 61.

17. Ibid., 54.

18. Ibid., 63–69. See discussion in Loughlin, *Telling God's Story*, 38–42, 156–61.

from various theologians. Below, I will draw upon these, and also offer many of my own critiques.

The first point that should be recognized is that Christian doctrine necessarily possesses a propositional dimension. There is no escaping this fact, since it is clear that both the experiential and cultural-linguistic models of doctrine contain a latent propositional dimension. For example, if one believes that doctrine is merely a description of religious experience, there is necessarily a "something" which is being experienced. Even if this "something" is described in somewhat-hazy terms as "ineffable," this nevertheless remains a propositional claim about the "something" being described. Even the assertion that it is ineffable is a propositional truth claim.

A similar point might be made about the cultural-linguistic model. Lindbeck is absolutely correct that doctrine possesses the ability to, and in fact inevitably does, regulate communal linguistic practice. In other words, since we believe certain truths about God (such as that he is a Triune), we must insist that he be named "Father, Son, and Holy Spirit" in our speech about him (whether in academic debate or prayer). Nonetheless, one must ultimately ask, why would people allow their communal discourse to be regulated by certain rules of speech if they did not believe that these rules corresponded to certain propositional truths? For example, why follow the linguistic rule set down by the Nicene-Constantinopolitan Fathers that "God must be spoken of as one substance with three persons" if one does not think that this is actually the case? This is one of the reasons that Lindbeck's claim that the Nicene-Constantinopolitan Creed "does not make first-order truth claims" is so incredibly odd, insofar as it presupposes that the Nicene-Constantinopolitan Fathers set down rules for speaking about divine being without really intending to say anything about it. Moreover, it will not do (as Lindbeck is wont to argue) that Christians are only able to make propositional first-order truth claims within the linguistic rules set down by church.[19] Adopting such linguistic rules without actually believing in the propositions they presuppose is flatly absurd. For example, why would I agree to always speak about Jesus as God, if, in fact, I did not already accept the propositional truth that "Jesus is God"?

Since Lindbeck cannot explain why people would adopt a set of linguistic rules of governing their communal discourse to begin with, he also has the related difficulty explaining the origins of Christian doctrine. If doctrines are mere linguistic rules, which stand independent of

---

19. Lindbeck, *The Nature of Doctrine*, 19.

propositional truth or extra-linguistic events, where did they come from? In Lindbeck's model, it would appear that people in various religious communities (in particular, the Christian church) simply started to regulate their discourse in particular ways for no discernible reason. As Alister McGrath notes, Lindbeck effectively relegates Christian doctrine to "little more than a grammar of an ahistorical language, a language which—like Melchizedek—has no origins." In other words, Lindbeck simply seems to "assume that it [a system of linguistics] is simply there."[20] In all fairness, Lindbeck "makes the point that languages originate from the outside, thus raising the obvious question concerning the origins of the Christian tradition of speaking about God." Ultimately, then, how "does the Christian idiom come into being?"[21] McGrath also observes that, without a connection to an extra-linguistic reality, there is little room for reforming and criticizing of doctrine, a particular concern for those within the Reformation tradition.[22]

Moreover, since the linguistic rules of Christian doctrine must originate from outside of the church in extra-linguistic objective realities, the rules of speech proposed by Christian doctrine can be falsified or validated by reference to objective standards of truth. The Apostle remarked that, "if Christ has not been raised, then our preaching is in vain and your faith is in vain" (1 Cor 15:14). Early Christians could make up all sorts of rules about communal discourse, but if Christ had not been raised, the linguistic rules mandating that they speak of him as risen would become pointless.

Another example might be gleaned from non-Christian religious history. In the late nineteenth century, the so-called Ghost Dance religion spread among Native Americans. Originating with the Paiute prophet Wovoka, the Ghost Dance religion taught that, through the performance of Ghost Dance rituals, the Creator would bring about the apocalyptic destruction of white settlers and the return of the bison.[23] Though the religion was very popular among Native Americans in the western United States from 1889 to the end of 1890, it eventually became discredited after the Wounded Knee Creek massacre.[24] Wovoka taught his followers, that if they wore Ghost Shirts painted with magical symbols, they would be protected

---

20. McGrath, *The Genesis of Doctrine*, 28.
21. Ibid., 34.
22. Ibid., 7–8.
23. See discussion in Brown, *Bury My Heart*, 431–32.
24. Ibid., 439–45.

from any harm.²⁵ This claim was proven false when the United States army executed twenty-five individuals, loyal to the Lakota chief Big Foot, who were wearing Ghost Dance shirts.²⁶ The death of Big Foot proved that the communal rule of designating the Ghost Dance shirts as bulletproof was false and misguided, in that it did not, in fact, stop bullets.²⁷

Because doctrine is based on extra-linguistic realities and can be either validated or falsified, a propositional understanding of Christian doctrine is ultimately more flexible than Lindbeck allows. Christian theologians (particularly those standing in the Reformation tradition) have always recognized that no doctrine of the visible Christian church should be automatically accepted. All doctrines must be first tested against the word of God for their validation. Moreover, since doctrine ultimately refers to extra-linguistic reality, and said realities can be described using a variety of formulas, doctrines need not be stated in absolutely identical terms from one era to another. For example, some of the Ante-Nicene Fathers (Ignatius of Antioch, Melito of Sardis, and Irenaeus, to name a few) can be shown to have, in many respects, anticipated the Trinitarian confession of the first councils of Nicaea and Constantinople, although they lacked the precise terminology and the "grammar" (as one might call it) of the faith that the later fathers helpfully developed through their conflict with the fourth-century Arian heretics.

The possibility of the revision of Christian doctrinal formulas makes good sense in light of historic Christian orthodoxy's claims about the divine/human relationship. In the main, Christian theologians have recognized that, because of both human fallenness and finitude, doctrinal statements (though they may be true and certain) are never absolutely exhaustive and complete in their expression of the divine being. Simply because one believes that truth is propositional, one need not believe that human beings have always had the ability to apprehend it in a perfect or exhaustive manner. In response to the inflexibility that Lindbeck attributes to the propositional model, McGrath notes that, even in periods like the Middle Ages, when the propositional character of truth was most strongly

---

25. Ibid., 434.

26. Ibid., 439–45.

27. See George Hunsinger, "Truth as Self-Involving," 47–48. As Hunsinger notes, Lindbeck wrongly assumes that the truth of doctrine is only tied up in performance. Truth as a proposition transcends the ability of people to live in accordance with that truth. For this reason, Hunsinger notes that propositional truth has the power to falsify performance.

emphasized, "Most theologians . . . understood dogma as a dynamic concept, a 'perception of divine truth, tending towards this truth' [that is, the truth of doctrine], (*perceptio divinae veritatis tendens in ipsam*)."[28]

Similarly, Protestant Scholasticism of the sixteenth and seventeenth centuries recognized the same reality in its distinction (originating with Francis Junius) between archetypal theology and ectypal theology.[29] According to the Lutheran scholastic David Hollaz, "Archetypal Theology is the knowledge which God has of Himself."[30] Because of the distance between the human and divine (both because of sin and natural human limitations), God now communicates an incomplete theology (ectypal theology) through the mediums of nature and Scripture to humans on earth. In the future, he will communicate with humans more fully (though still incompletely) in heaven by way of direct and unmediated vision of himself. Concerning this theology, Quenstedt writes, "the Ectypal Theology of depraved men is either that of the Way, i.e., of this life, viz., of mortals, or that of the Home, i.e., of the other and happy life, viz., of the finally saved."[31] Such remarks mirror the Apostle Paul's own description of the knowledge of God possessed by the church-militant: "For we know in part and we prophesy in part, but when the perfect comes, the partial will pass away . . . For now we see in a mirror dimly, but then face to face. Now I know in part; then I shall know fully, even as I have been fully known" (1 Cor 13:9–10, 12). Hence our doctrinal statements may be adequate for representing God in part on earth, but they do not give us a full and direct revelation of the divine essence. Even in heaven, Christians will certainly not know God exhaustively (since God is infinite), even though they will see him "face to face." For this reason, Christian doctrine must be constantly tested and corrected by Scripture, until we finally behold God in his glory in heaven. Consequently, McGrath correctly states that: "Lindbeck attributes an unmerited inflexibility to cognitive approaches to doctrine through playing down the notion of 'relative adequacy' of doctrinal statements, where 'adequacy' can be assessed both in terms of the historical context of the doctrinal formulation and whatever referent it is alleged to represent."[32]

---

28. McGrath, *The Genesis of Doctrine*, 16.

29. See Junius, *A Treatise on Truth Theology*. Also see discussion in Muller, *Prolegomena to Theology*, 222–38.

30. Schmid, *Doctrinal Theology*, 16.

31. Ibid., 17.

32. McGrath, *The Genesis of Doctrine*, 16.

Moving on to an evaluation of the "experiential-expressive" model, Lindbeck's critique becomes much stronger. Supporters of this model claim that the theologian could somehow have access to raw human experience apart from any cultural and historical coloring. However, this is highly questionable. This, of course, does not mean that doctrine is totally unrelated to religious experience. Obviously, the truth claims made by Christian doctrine are a response to specific religious experiences (i.e., of the Resurrection). Nevertheless, the experience of the Resurrection and the doctrines they gave rise to are not symbolic expressions of interior experiences of something ineffable and abstract. Rather, they are propositional claims about real and accessible historical events directly experienced by the Apostles. Moreover, as I will discuss at some length below, the interpretation of these events was always colored by the linguistic-cultural heritage of Israel in the form of the Old Testament (Ps 110, Isa 53, Daniel 2, 7, 12, etc.).

Hence, Lindbeck is absolutely correct to assert that pre-linguistic or pre-cultural experiences do not really exist (though such a thing may exist in infants, or the rare so-called "feral" child) and they therefore cannot actually serve as the basis of our doctrinal claims. Human beings (for the most part) exist within a cultural-linguistic matrix. One may, of course, test the adequacy of his cultural paradigms and linguistic rules (as in the case of the Scientific Revolution or the Reformation), but one cannot operate without said paradigms. One paradigm is simply modified or replaced by another paradigm, not a neutral, disembodied vision of reality.

Lastly, in turning to the "linguistic-cultural" model, it is important to recognize several problems beyond the few I have already identified in my discussion of the propositional model. Chief among these is the fact that Lindbeck seems to operate with a rather narrow understanding of how language functions. The first aspect of this is that language is only one medium through which human beings receive information and interact with the external world. Of course, it is correct to assert (as I have previously observed) that it is impossible for human beings to interact with extra-linguistic realities apart from the mediums of language and culture. Nevertheless, because human beings are not limited to language as a way of interacting with reality, they are not limited to the datum of language. Hence, in describing the act of knowing, there is a complex interplay between the datum of sensory experience (which can often buck at linguistic rules and cultural expectations) and internalized cultural and linguistic paradigms that color that experience. For this reason, linguistic rules not only shape our perception of external reality, but extra-linguistic reality shapes linguistic rules through sensory perception.

For example, the Jews of the Second Temple period operated under the assumption that there would be a general resurrection at the end of time, and therefore did not understand that the Messiah would die and be resurrected ahead of the rest of the human race.[33] Hence, their cultural community established the linguistic rule that, when the resurrected is spoken of, it should be spoken of as something that happened at the end of time. This seems to be part of the reason why the Gospels tell us that the disciples were utterly unable to understand Jesus when he predicted his passion and resurrection. The passion predictions radically stood outside of their cultural-linguistic "grid" for interpreting reality, that the disciples assumed that Jesus could not possibly have meant what he said.

The actual events of the crucifixion and resurrection obviously changed expectations, due to the sensible and tangible reality of the empty tomb, as well as Jesus' physical presence with the disciples eating, drinking, and teaching. Such a reality stood in conflict with both their cultural expectations and with the linguistic rules of their community. As the New Testament tells us, it therefore caused them to significantly modify the linguistic rules of their community. Nevertheless, it must also be bourne in mind that their perception of the event as the beginning of the fulfillment of God's final purposes in the midst of history (i.e., Rom 5, 1 Cor 15, etc.) was colored by the Jewish understandings of the resurrection (rooted in the Old Testament and Second Temple Jewish tradition) as an event connected with the end times (Dan 12, etc.). As N. T. Wright has observed, an educated Roman citizen (operating with a different cultural-linguistic narrative framework than that of the Hebrew Scriptures) who might have heard about the resurrection would doubtless have thought of the risen Jesus as something like the myth of Nero Redivivus. According to this myth, the recently deceased Emperor Nero had not really died, but was waiting to reclaim his throne by gathering his army in the east.[34] In this sense, although their linguistic and cultural rules for organizing reality colored their perception of the resurrection, the event itself determined a radical reformulation of the disciples communal rules pertaining to speech and cultural expectations.

33. Wright, *Christian Origins*, 1:320–34.
34. Ibid., 3:720.

Because linguistic rules can be modified in this manner, language is necessarily a more flexible phenomenon that Lindbeck allows. New phenomenon can cause old linguistic rules to bend, flex, and even break. This is partially because humans possess common experiences of reality, as culturally and linguistically colored as it may be. As a result, humans can modify old rules of speech, and also recognize an analogical resemblance between different cultural-linguistic practices and perceptions of reality. We can see this in the phenomenon of the translatability of language. Hans-Georg Gadamer and Jürgen Habermas criticized Ludwig Wittgenstein's theory of language[35] (upon which Lindbeck largely draws from[36]) on precisely this basis.[37] Wittgenstein described language as representing a language game, whose rules (much like football or baseball) were heterogeneous and non-translatable. According to this theory, words do not correspond to objects in the world, but rather derive their meaning from the rules that govern them in a given context. One cannot translate one series of rules into another series of rules (i.e., cultural-linguistic usage) any more than one can translate football into cricket![38] As both Gadamer and Habermas point out, this ignores the reality that translation is possible across cultures. Anyone who has studied language recognizes that words between differing languages never actually directly correspond with one another. Nevertheless, there is a sort of "analogical similitude" between words and thought forms which allows for their translation into different idioms.[39]

This exposes one of the chief weaknesses with Lindbeck's model. Lindbeck seems to presuppose that linguistic systems (and hence systems of doctrine and belief) are completely self-contained. This is the primary reason why Lindbeck believes that, when properly understood, differing Christian theological traditions (and even various world religions) do not ultimately conflict with one another. For example, if the designation "savior of the world" is simply a linguistic rule governing how Mahayana Buddhists talk about Buddha and Christians talk about Christ in their

---

35. See the following works that deal with Wittgenstein's theory of language in its mature form: Wittgenstein, *The Blue and Brown Books*; Wittgenstein, *Philosophical Investigations*.

36. Pecknold, *Transforming Postliberal Theology*, 34–36.

37. See summary of Habermas and Gadamer's criticisms of Wittgenstein in Simpson, *Critical Social Theory*, 80–87.

38. See brief description in Addis, *Wittgenstein*, 68–72.

39. See similar criticism of Lindbeck and the cultural-linguistic approach in Vanhoozer, *The Drama of Doctrine*, 171–75.

respective contexts, then their doctrinal claims do not actually conflict. The problem, though, is that Mahayana Buddhists and Christians inhabit a common human world, wherein their communal linguistic rules are actually dependent on extra-linguistic realities. For this reason, the claims of both traditions can be translated into each other's idioms of thought through the analogical resonance (rooted in a commonly shared world) of what it means to be a "savior" in both traditions. Because the respective claims of salvation are translatable, the Christian's translation of his claim about Christ into the Mahayana Buddhist idiom will necessarily reveal the conflict between two traditions. The Christian cannot accept that Buddha is the savior, or even the validity of linguistic rules designating him as such within the Buddhist context. This is because the Christian knows and inhabits a common world with the Buddhist. Since this is the case, by designating Jesus as Lord, the Christian necessarily does so to the exclusion of the Buddha.

This analogical resonance and participation in the common reality of the created order makes many of Lindbeck's claims regarding the relativity and self-contained nature of differing doctrinal systems seem extremely odd at times. Probably the most unusual example of this is his insistence that it might be the imperative of Christian missionaries to encourage Marxists to be "better Marxists." Since orthodox Marxists consider all religion to be oppressive ("the opium of the people"[40]), and that Communist governments have tended to either suppress or even murder Christians, such a Christian missionary would be either deranged or suicidal. Obviously, the two communities assign the different linguistic rules governing the word "Christian." Nevertheless, for those Christians who have suffered persecution under Marxist regimes, it is hardly meaningful to say that because Marxists have different linguistic rules, they are not encouraging the persecution of any actual Christians.

Turning to ecumenical debates themselves, Evangelical Protestants and Roman Catholics have different linguistic rules governing speech about the Lord's Supper. Both sides agree that they are talking about the same sacramental practice within their separate ecclesiastical contexts. Ecumenical divisions are therefore not at all similar (to use Lindbeck's own analogy) to the division between countries that mandate driving on the right and those that mandate driving on the left. Rather, since both groups participate in the common historical reality of Christianity and

---

40. Marx, *Critique of Hegel's Philosophy*, 131.

base themselves on the same texts within the New Testament canon, both groups are seeking (to extend the analogy further) to drive on the same thoroughfare of truth. In fact, if they were not, there would be little point in seeking the visible, ecumenical unity that Lindbeck himself so strongly desires. Consequently, both sides cannot help but come into conflict with one another. If two groups cannot agree on their basic truth claims, but still insist on visible unity, they will be like persons from America trying to follow their own traffic laws in Britain. Just as traffic laws govern real and deadly vehicles, so communal speech rules govern real propositional truths. As a result, both sides will inevitably end up (metaphorically speaking) in a car accident or worse.

Having now reviewed the threefold taxonomy of doctrine, we can observe that each dimension of doctrine described by Lindbeck explicates a unique aspect of how God reveals himself to human beings and their reception of this revelation. I have shown that Lindbeck's own proposal is wanting because it reduces Christian doctrine to a single dimension (i.e., linguistic-cultural). This being said, it is important to assert that doctrine, at its root, must be understood as propositional statements about God and his objective reality. God's objective reality is communicated to human beings in time, and therefore produces knowledge of the divine being through the events recorded in the inerrant Scriptures. These experiences of history lead the community of the visible church to establish linguistic rules for regulating communal discourse.

Because God is Triune, these various dimensions of doctrine necessarily take on a Trinitarian shape. Much as God the Father is font of divinity and the source of the Son and the Spirit, so the objective reality of God in himself and his self-knowledge (archetypal theology) is the basis of all doctrinal claims. Nevertheless, such truths are manifested in time through the works of God culminating in the incarnation of the Son. God manifests himself in time, and therefore the propositional dimension of doctrine becomes knowable through the discrete historical experiences of Israel and the early church (ectypal theology). This experiential dimension of doctrine corresponds to the Son, who is begotten by and therefore perfectly manifests the Father (Matt 11:27; John 14:9), just as the experience of God's truth proceeds from and is a reflection on God's objectively revealed reality. Lastly, just as the Spirit proceeds from the Father and the Son and regulates their relationship in love, so too the linguistic-cultural dimension of doctrine proceeds from the church's experience of the Father's revelation of propositional truth through the manifestation of the Son. Based on their experiences, and the propositional knowledge of God that these experiences produced, the Apostles formulated linguistic rules for the regulation of the church's communal discourse under the inspiration of the Holy Spirit (2 Tim 3:21; 2 Pet 1:21).

Therefore, just as the Spirit proceeds from the Father and Son, thereby revealing the truth already present in them (John 16:13), so too the linguistic rules of doctrine established over time by the visible Christian church must be regulated by the original revelation of Christ deposited in the New Testament by the Apostles and their immediate followers under inspiration of the Holy Spirit (Luke 10:16; John 14:16–8). Because of human sin (1 Cor 2:14–5) and the many false teachers who continuously infect the church (Matt 7:15), the New Testament authors insisted that their readers must test the teaching of leaders of the visible church over against the word of Scripture (Acts 17:10–15; 1 Thess 5:21; 1 John 4:1–6). For this reason, in describing doctrine, it is important to also give an account of how Christian doctrine may be criticized, and also the relationship between Scripture and tradition. This is especially necessary in light of the fact that my purpose in this work is to critique how a particular Christian doctrine (i.e., the work of Christ) has been interpreted by a certain class of theologians.

Thomas Kuhn's Paradigms and Heiko Oberman's "Tradition I"

How, then, does one establish a proper basis for the formulation and criticism of Christian doctrine? As I noted earlier, one of the greatest difficulties with Lindbeck's position is that it simply assumes that doctrine lacks any reference to extra-linguistic realities or origins. He thereby greatly undermines any objective basis for formulating or criticizing Christian doctrine. On the other hand, Lindbeck correctly identified the fact that human beings must process reality from within a cultural-linguistic grid or lens. One need not say that these grids or lenses are necessarily wrong in their representation of reality, but we must nevertheless acknowledge their existence. Therefore, with these two truths in mind, this section will develop a critically realistic account of Christian doctrine, drawing upon the Thomas Kuhn's concept of paradigms, and the Dutch church historian Heiko Oberman's concept of "Tradition I."

In philosopher of science Thomas Kuhn's work entitled *The Structure of Scientific Revolutions*, he begins by defining the nature of "paradigms" within scientific history. Contrary to how scientists have often perceived themselves (that is, investigating scientific truth in a completely neutral and objective fashion), Kuhn recognizes that all scientists operate with a communally shared matrix of presuppositions.[41] Moreover, these presuppositions do not just exist on the periphery of the scientific enterprise, but are foundational to it. They cannot simply be jettisoned willy-nilly when scientists begin to find them cumbersome. Rather, these presuppositions make science possible as a practice. Such assumptions, or what might be more correctly designated "communally shared pictures of reality," Kuhn calls "Paradigms": "These [Paradigms] are traditions which the historian describes under such rubrics as 'Ptolemaic astronomy' (or 'Copernican'), 'Aristotelian dynamics' (or 'Newtonian'), 'corpuscular optics' (or 'wave optics'), and so on."[42]

In order to operate within any of the sciences, Scientists must be acculturated into the particular paradigm "with which he will later practice."[43] In other words, for the science to merely be practiced, scientists must accept a communally shared conception of the structure of reality within which facts are to be interpreted and processed. Such paradigms could, in a sense, be described as a tradition of interpretation:

> Because he [the scientist] there [in the given paradigm] joins men who learned the bases of their field from the same concrete models, his subsequent practice will seldom evoke overt disagreement over fundamentals. Men whose research is based on shared paradigms are committed to the same rules and standards of scientific practice. That commitment and the apparent consensus it produces are prerequisites for normal science, i.e., for the genesis and continuation of a particular research tradition.[44]

If this is the case, it suggests that the sciences are a set of communal traditions much like any other thought-tradition. Their validity ultimately rests on a particular scientific community's "belief" in the overall picture of reality as represented by the paradigm. Nevertheless, these pictures of reality are not divorced from the concrete and empirical datum of reality.

---

41. Kuhn, *The Structure of Scientific Revolutions*, 10–11.
42. Ibid., 10.
43. Ibid., 10.
44. Ibid., 11.

The entire point of having a picture of reality is to study the raw data of experience and to discover whether or not the community's picture of reality is true.[45]

The goal of the paradigm is therefore to lay out the theoretical framework within which the datum of reality can be interpreted, experiments may be performed, and the paradigm may be verified or falsified. For this reason, the validity of these models of reality are continuously tested. Such testing will either reinforce the validity of such models or uncover "anomalies."[46] Anomalies represent pieces of data that contradict the overall paradigm. Although paradigms survive small anomalies, major ones can disrupt to the community's faith in the validity of its picture of reality. Therefore, although reality is always interpreted through these communally shared lenses, anomalies can occur because new data is always coming into contact with the paradigm.

In this regard, anomalies are not purely negative phenomena, but rather make room for positive self-criticism and new discovery: "Discovery commences with the awareness of anomaly, i.e., with the recognition that nature has somehow violated the paradigm-induced expectations that govern normal science."[47] The appearance of an anomaly may lead the community of scientists to recognize that their model of reality needs to be modified. If, through the course of normal experimentation, the scientific community becomes aware of a massive amount of data that fundamentally contradicts the paradigm, the community and its picture of reality will enter into a state of "crisis."[48] A new paradigm will inevitably emerge from a crisis, and data is again able to be interpreted and configured in a coherent manner. Kuhn calls this a "paradigm shift."[49] He illustrates that the phenomenon uses the Copernican revolution of the early modern period, among others.[50]

How, then, does Kuhn's concept of the paradigm relate to the multidimensional phenomenon of Christian doctrine as outlined in the first section? To begin with, Kuhn's paradigm model encompasses all three dimensions of doctrine described in Lindbeck's taxonomy. First, the

45. Ibid., 11.
46. Ibid., 52.
47. Ibid., 52–53.
48. Ibid., 66–76.
49. Ibid., 111.
50. Ibid., 77–91.

paradigm functions as a picture of the world, and arranges actual facts about reality. Although at times Kuhn seems to imply that paradigms are merely functional in their representation of reality, the analogy between scientific paradigms and doctrinal ones (which are clearly meant to be realistic, rather than merely functional) remain valid insofar as both intend to portray reality in some sense. Therefore, paradigms possess (or at least point towards) the propositional and cognitive dimensions of Christian doctrine. Secondly, paradigms are connected to human experience. They are the results of human experiences of reality, and they are also always open to being tested and revised by new data. Lastly, paradigms regulate how the datum of reality is interpreted, how people are to speak about reality, and what methods are used to pursue inquiry. For this reason, the paradigm also encompasses the cultural-linguistic dimension of doctrine.

Not only is the concept of the paradigm able to encompass the threefold nature of doctrine, but it also provides a sound basis for the criticism of doctrine as well. With Lindbeck, Kuhn agrees that experience itself is never purely pre-cultural or pre-linguistic. Therefore, as we have previously noted, the datum of reality will always read in relation to a particular paradigm. Nevertheless, unlike Lindbeck, Kuhn recognizes that communally shared grids for processing reality may be criticized, modified, or even completely eliminated. Paradigms can come and go, based on whether they stand the test of reality.

Therefore, a similar conceptual scheme might be applied to the question of religious claims. I have already observed a number of applications of this model throughout the history of religion. The Ghost Dance religion ceased to function when one of its central tenets was disproven. The fact of Jesus' resurrection, while certainly interpreted within the framework of Second Temple Jewish eschatological expectations, nevertheless greatly modified these expectations. So much so, in fact, that it resulted in the formation of the Christian church as something distinct from mainstream Judaism.

Beyond these examples, Christians coming out of Reformation traditions might also add Luther's rediscovery of the gospel. In setting about to reform the church, Luther strongly supported the great ecumenical councils,[51] and did not actually disavow his earlier training in philosophi-

---

51. Two major examples of Luther's attempts at maintaining continuity with the earlier tradition come in "Concerning Rebaptism," LW 40:225–62; WA 26:144–74. Luther makes a somewhat unconvincing argument that, because the Christian church would cease to exist if it had been doing baptism wrong for the last fifteen centuries (i.e., infant baptism), then infant baptism must clearly be an acceptable practice. Although Luther

cal Nominalism.⁵² Therefore, it would be appropriate to say that these earlier traditions served as a lens through which he interpreted Scripture. Nevertheless, when Luther discovered that the Scriptures (as studied in their original languages) were in conflict with certain aspects of the earlier traditions, the Reformer greatly modified the theology he had received. This can be observed particularly in regard to the central discovery of the Reformation. Luther recognized that, in light of the biblical authority, divine grace could not be conceptualized (as it had been in much of the medieval tradition) as something that made humanity acceptable to God by changing its moral capacities. Rather, it had to be understood as divine favor that imputed Christ's righteousness to humans through faith. Luther did not come to these conclusions arbitrarily, but rather from the discovery (as mediated to him through the Humanistic tradition) that the Greek New Testament used the words "justification," "righteousness," and "repentance"⁵³ in a very different manner than did Jerome's Vulgate and its subsequent medieval interpreters.⁵⁴

For this reason, the Reformer's writings reveal a dual respect for the interpretative and creedal tradition of the visible historic church, along with the recognition that all things must be tested against the ultimate authority of Scripture. Church historian Heiko Oberman refers to this particular outlook displayed by Luther and other members of what is frequently referred to as the "Magisterial Reformation," as "Tradition I." In his essay "*Quo Vadis Petre*? Tradition from Irenaeus to *Humani Generis*,"⁵⁵ Oberman

---

may not make a good argument, the point stands that he considered it impossible that the church had lost its existence and continuity over time. If the church had ceased to exist, then God's faithfulness to his work in, under, and with word and sacrament would have been compromised. Also see his "On the Councils and the Church," *LW* 41:3–178; *WA* 50:509–653. Here, the Reformer makes his endorsement of the four great ecumenical councils. Nevertheless, he asserts that councils do not automatically make the Christian faith, and that we should measure all things against the bar of Scripture. Hence, Luther endorses a dialectical continuity with the earlier tradition.

52. See discussion of Luther and his relationship to *via moderna* in: McGrath, *Iustia Dei*, 188–97; McGrath, *Intellectual Origins*, 109–13; McGrath, *Reformation Thought*, 67–69; Oberman, *The Two Reformations*, 21–43; Ozment, *The Age of Reform*, 244.

53. McGrath, *Iustia Dei*, 1–16.

54. See description of Luther's own account of the so-called "Reformation Breakthrough" in the following: *LW* 34:323–38; *WA* 54:179–87. See discussions of it in the following select bibliography: Bayer, "Die Reformatorische Wende," 115–50; Green, *How Melanchthon Helped Luther*, 183–252; Yeago, "The Catholic Luther," 37–41.

55. Oberman, "*Quo Vadis Petre?*", 269–98

identifies three main interpretations of the relationship between Scripture and tradition throughout church history. The first, Tradition I, Oberman attributes to the early church fathers and the Reformers. It is the belief that, although Scripture is the supreme authority within the church, subsequent church tradition is good insofar as it correctly explains and confesses scriptural teaching within a variety of historical contexts.

A good example of this during the Reformation period might be found in Martin Chemnitz's treatment of churchly tradition in his famous *Examination of the Council of Trent* (1565–1573).[56] In the first volume, when discussing the Tridentine decree on Scripture and tradition (Session IV),[57] Chemnitz outlines eight different meanings of the word "tradition" (*traditio*).[58] He then delineates seven different forms of tradition that can serve as legitimate authorities within the church. These seven represent either the biblical materials themselves, or the exposition and application of them in the life of the church. He identifies only the eighth (which he defines as late, unwritten, and invented tradition[59]) as problematic, and therefore rejects it. This approach can also be seen in the early seventeenth century with Johann Gerhard's *Confessio Catholica*. In this work, Gerhard demonstrates the ancient (and even medieval) church's witness to divine truth as it was confessed by the Lutheran Reformers.[60]

For both Chemnitz and Gerhard, valid church tradition is the exposition of scriptural teaching in the history of the church. This valid tradition gives Christians a resource to guard against heresies and a means to see how the principles of Scripture can be applied in different contexts. As is easy to observe, Tradition I correlates well with Kuhn's concept of the paradigm, in that churchly tradition forms a lens through which Scripture is interpreted. This lens is not imposed on Scripture, but grows out of the universal church's collective activity of reading and interpreting the Scriptures under the influence of the Holy Spirit. Moreover, the lens of church tradition is not infallible and can be modified and even reconstructed if they fail to properly represent the teachings of the Bible.

Oberman defines the "Tradition II" idea of tradition as something that supplements Scripture with additional doctrinal content (according

---

56. Chemnitz, *Examination of the Council of Trent*.
57. Schroeder, *Canons and Decrees*, 17–20.
58. Chemnitz, *Examination of the Council of Trent*, 1:223–71.
59. Ibid., 1:272–313.
60. Gerhard, *Confessio Catholica*.

to him, something taught both by the Council of Trent and the medieval canon lawyers). One of the major difficulties with this way of describing the relationship between Scripture and tradition is that it undermines doctrinal criticism. From the perspective of Tradition II, the tradition of the visible church (in various ways) is to be directly identified with divine revelation. Therefore, church tradition ceases to be subordinate to the written word of God. Unwritten traditions (supposedly handed down from the Apostles) become authoritative on the basis of institutional church's own testimony as the custodian of said traditions. Therefore, what the institutional church officially teaches is, by and large, authoritative. This not only illegitimately adds extra revelations onto God's revelation in Scripture, but it also greatly limits the ability of Christians to criticize church doctrine. Criticism of the institutional church becomes an attack on revelation itself, and consequently is automatically illegitimate.

Other problems with this theory are also manifestly clear. Unwritten tradition is extremely easy to manipulate, and can hardly serve as a critical principle of the institutional church. Those who seek the truth of God are bidden to look within their own memories, or perhaps the memory of the magisterial authorities. One does not ultimately look outside himself to the external word of God.[61] Therefore, such a position inevitably encourages enthusiasm, which, as Luther famously argues, is the oldest sin.[62] Ultimately, then, the acceptance of unwritten tradition as a basis of the authority of the institutional church destroys the ability of the word of God to stand independently over against the visible church and call it to repentance.

In modern Roman Catholic thought, the already existing weaknesses of Tradition II are exacerbated by what Oberman refers to as "Tradition III." According to this model, doctrinal development itself (and not merely the visible church's unwritten traditions) is identified with the voice of the Holy Spirit. Here, the marginally regulative role of Scripture still present in Tradition II is almost completely destroyed. Scripture is now demoted almost to the level of insignificance, and therefore possesses little ability to check the unending development of official church teaching. Scripture becomes merely a single moment in the larger history of the Holy Spirit's continuous revelation to magisterium of the institutional church. If Tradition II encouraged a somewhat adulterated enthusiasm, Tradition III represents enthusiasm in a very nearly pure form.

---

61. See Barth's similar remarks in *CD* 1.1:104–11.
62. SA, III:8; *CT*, 495–96.

Returning to Tradition I and its appropriation by the Reformers, the ultimate point of this scheme is not that church tradition is bad, but merely that it should be subordinated to, and derived from, Scripture. Ultimately, Tradition I represents a rejection of Tradition II and III's supplementation of Scripture through other authorities. Tradition I is what the Reformers understood by the principle of *Sola Scriptura*. The principle of *Sola Scriptura* means that Scripture is the only infallible and final source of authority in the matters of faith. This does not mean that there cannot be subordinate and derivative authorities in the form of liturgy, commentary, creeds, and confessions.

Similarly, Tradition I represents a rejection of the model of *solo Scriptura,* or what a number of authors have called "Tradition O."[63] This model originates with the Anabaptist movement, and has been the popular understanding of the *Sola Scriptura* (as historically and conceptually inaccurate as this may be) among Anglo-American evangelicals. It posits that adherence to the Scripture principle of the Reformation means a total rejection of all church tradition, even if this tradition is merely intended as an application or confession of what Scriptures teaches (Nicaea, Augsburg Confession, etc.).

The difficulty with *solo Scriptura*, or Tradition O, is that it is an illusion. All ideas have a history, just as all readings of the Bible do. The Bible is the word of God, and therefore checks all attempts on the part of subsequent church tradition to invent new dogmas. Nevertheless, it must at the same time be recognized that every explication of what the Bible teaches is part of a historic theological tradition. These traditions may or may not be accurate representations of what the Bible teaches, but they are traditions nonetheless. *Solo Scriptura* is therefore problematic, because it lacks the self-awareness to distinguish between the Bible and a given church community's historically formed understanding of the Bible. For this reason, Tradition O inevitably drifts into a covert form of Tradition II. Without a self-conscious recognition of the hermeneutical presuppositions with which the ecclesial community approaches the Bible and their historical origins, certain non-biblical traditions (for example, the insistence on the metaphorical nature of the words of institution, the sinner's prayer, and the ban on alcohol) are treated as if they are self-evidently scriptural.

---

63. McGrath, *Reformation Thought*, 107–8; Mathison, *The Shape of Sola Scriptura*, 152–53.

Returning to the scientific analogy, Tradition O's understanding of scriptural authority is not unlike the pre-Copernican scientific worldview, in which people simply identified geocentricism with reality, with little reflection of where such a belief came from, or whether such a belief correlated to reality itself. Hence, the ironic result is that this supposedly radical commitment to Scripture actually undermines its authority through the introduction of unacknowledged, non-biblical traditions into the canons of authority. In contrast to this, advocates of Tradition I put a distance between their present community's confession and the Bible. This makes it possible to engage in appropriate doctrinal criticism when necessary, since the church recognizes where its historic confession of faith originated from and the reasons behind it. When a given theological tradition's presuppositions are acknowledge and made explicit, they can be subordinated to and tested against the word of God.

Ultimately then, if the Scriptures are going to be applied, interpreted, and confessed in contexts other than their original ones, the visible church will necessarily draw up confessions of faith, creeds, and bodies of interpretation. Churchly tradition always contains within itself a kernel of truth. Even in circumstances when much of the truth of the gospel is obscured, God the Holy Spirit nevertheless preserves the church in every age through word and sacrament (Matt 16:18). Since a remnant of the faithful is present in every era of church history, there also remains a valid interpretative tradition, even if it is often difficult to detect. The faithful Christian should therefore read the Scriptures with the Church catholic, while at the same time recognizing that, since members of the church are not infallible, everything must be tested against the bar of God's original revelation.

The Confessional Lutheran Paradigm

Tradition I and the concept of the Paradigm provide a clear basis for doctrinal criticism that will be applied in the coming chapters. As is clear from the previous discussion, doctrine can be criticized in roughly two ways. First, the content of Scripture and/or aspects of a previous doctrinal tradition may either validate or negate a particular doctrinal paradigm. That is to say, a theologian may be judged on the basis of his faithfulness to the datum of revelation. I have already mentioned something similar to this approach in Luther's criticism of late medieval Christianity. Alternatively, one can also invoke the coherence of a particular set of doctrinal proposals in relation to an already-shared common paradigm. For example, one could validly criticize a Roman Catholic who accepted birth control and abortion for holding beliefs that are inconsistent with the Catholic paradigm. This could be done even if one did not accept the presuppositions of the Catholic worldview.

For this reason, in using the method outlined above, I will make my criticism in this book from the perspective of what will be termed the "Confessional Lutheran Paradigm." This means evaluating different nominally Lutheran theologians on the basis of their theology's overall coherence with core Lutheran claims as they are expressed within the biblical and confessional authorities. Beginning with Scripture, much like the other theological traditions that emerged from the Reformation, Lutherans accept the principle of *sola Scriptura*. For orthodox Lutherans, the Bible is the inerrant word of God and therefore serves as the *norma normans*, the "norming norm" of all Christian doctrinal claims. The Formula of Concord begins by stating that "we receive and embrace with our whole heart the Prophetic and Apostolic Scripture of the Old and New Testaments as the pure, clear fountain of Israel which is the only standard which all teachers and doctrines are to be judged."[64]

Nevertheless, Lutherans have also used the documents of the *Book of Concord* as a confession of the content of Scripture.[65] Although not everyone claiming the name "Lutheran" has agreed with this normativity, this study presupposes that there is an inner agreement between the teachings of Scripture, the main points of Luther's theology, and the confessional documents of the *Book of Concord*. Therefore, the creeds and confessions of the *Book of Concord* will also serve as a norm, but one that is itself normed (*norma normata*), namely by the authority of Scripture. In this regard, the authors of the Formula of Concord go on to state that the secondary authority and framework through which they understand the Scriptures are "the three Ecumenical creeds, namely, the Apostles, the Nicene, and

---

64. FC, SD, Norm and Rule, par 1; *CT*, 851. I specifically have chosen to use the *Concordia Triglotta* over newer editions of the *Book of Concord*. For justification of this practice, see the following article: Ziegler, "New English Translation," 145–65.

65. The documents included in the *Book of Concord* are as follows: The Apostles' Creed, The Nicene Creed, The Athanasian Creed, The Unaltered Augsburg Confession, The Apology to the Augsburg Confession, The Schmalkald Articles, The Large Catechism, The Small Catechism, The Treatise on the Power and Primacy of the Pope, The Formula of Concord.

Athanasian,"[66] as well as the previous confessions of the Evangelical Lutheran Church[67] and Luther's Catechisms.[68]

In this, the *Book of Concord* has a peculiar status in the Evangelical Lutheran Church. Whereas the Reformed confessions are typically of local significance and view themselves as being of temporary value, the Lutheran symbolic writings view themselves as summaries of evangelical and catholic teaching on the level of Nicaea or Chalcedon.[69] They therefore possess a universal and permanent value as statements of fundamental Christian dogma.

Finally, with the Concordists, Lutherans have historically appealed to the secondary authority of Luther's writings: "to his [Luther's] doctrinal and polemical writings we wish to appeal."[70] The authors of the Formula of Concord recognized Luther as a figure who God had raised up by his providential care to teach the pure gospel to the church in the last days. Although Luther was thought of as a private theologian, and not everything he wrote is authoritative (a point strongly emphasized by Luther himself[71]), his writings nevertheless rank as an important secondary authority below that of the ecumenical creeds and the other confessions of the church. Beyond his special status for the confessional authors, he will (as I will show) also be important in later chapters. Many of the authors discussed (particularly Gerhard Forde) constantly appeal to Reformer's authority.

Having established the basis for understanding Christian doctrine and the criterion upon which to evaluate the various theologians (chief among them Forde), in the next chapter I turn to the history of the Lutheran doctrine of atonement. This investigation begins with a study of Luther's own theology of atonement.

---

66. FC, SD, Norm and Rule, para 2; *CT*, 851.

67. Ibid., para 3; Ibid., 851.

68. Ibid., para 6; Ibid., 853.

69. See Karl Barth's insightful description in *The Theology of the Reformed Confessions*, 1–8. In support of Barth's characterization of Lutheranism, it should be noted that the Formula of Concord describes the Unaltered Augsburg Confession as "our symbol for this time" and compares its formulation with the Nicene Creed (FC, SD, Comprehensive Summary; *CT*, 851, 853). Similarly, in characterizing its own teaching, the Formula claims that it is a "comprehensive summary of our religion and faith [which is] simple, immutable, permanent truth" (FC, SD Comprehensive Summary; *CT*, 859).

70. FC, SD, Norm and Rule, para 6; *CT*, 853.

71. See *LW* 50:172–73; *WA* Br 8:99–100.

2

Martin Luther's View of Atonement

Introduction

In studying the question of Martin Luther's view of atonement, one immediately encounters the problem of the sheer volume of the material. As of 2017, there have been one hundred and twenty volumes of the Weimar edition of Luther's works published.[1] Beyond this bulk of material, researchers must also contend with the difficulty of the various stages of the Reformer's thought. This naturally gives rise to the question of which writings should be chosen as being most representative.

Despite these difficulties being acknowledged, it will be my contention in this chapter that Luther's teaching on the doctrine of atonement was relatively consistent throughout his career. In order to demonstrate this point, I will take a diachronic approach to the Reformer's writings. This means that I will take into account highly representative writings from the entirety of his career. In my preliminary discussion in each section, I will explain why each is representative of Luther's thought at a given stage. The texts that I will examine are as follows: *Psalms Lectures* (1513–1515), *The Freedom of a Christian* (1520), and lastly the *Great Galatians Commentary* (transcribed in 1531, published in 1535).

Beyond these academic writings, I will also add a discussion of both the Large and Small Catechisms (1529). If the first three texts give examples of what Luther taught in classroom settings, the catechisms will help us discover what the Reformer thought most important to teach laypersons.

1. Luther, *D. Martin Luthers Werke.*

Similarly, along with *The Bondage of the Will* (1525), Luther considered the catechisms to be his most important works.[2] Therefore, in examining what Luther believed about atonement, the Catechisms represent extremely important sources.

The History of Scholarship on Luther's View of Atonement

As scholarly debates go, the question of the nature of Luther's doctrine of atonement is relatively recent, dating back roughly to the mid-nineteenth century. Between that time and the mid-sixteenth century, it appears that most Lutheran theologians supported the doctrine of penal substitution and gave little thought to whether or not they stood in continuity with the Reformer.[3]

This consensus was eventually broken in the mid-nineteenth century by the theologian Johannes von Hofmann, who taught at the University of Erlangen. In brief, von Hofmann developed a highly experientially oriented theology wherein salvation history was understood to be the arena of the Triune God's self-actualization.[4] As a result of this perspective, von Hofmann radically reworked the doctrines of law and gospel in a manner that significantly deviated from the historic Lutheran tradition. These reinterpretations of the Lutheran law-gospel paradigm led to dissatisfaction with the doctrine of substitutionary atonement that he had received from the Lutheran scholastics. Because von Hofmann wished to remain within the Lutheran tradition, he therefore set out to prove that Luther had never actually taught substitutionary atonement. Von Hofmann primarily described atonement as God's conquest of demonic forces through Jesus.[5] For him, the chief demonic force was the human rejection of God and the ensuing existential alienation that it brought about. The conflict between God and humanity resolved itself when Christ donated himself on the cross

---

2. See *LW* 50:172–73; *WA* Br 8:99–100. Luther writes: "Regarding the plan to collect my writings in volumes, I am quite cool and not at all eager about it because, roused by a Saturnian hunger, I would rather see them all devoured. For I acknowledge none of them to be really a book of mine, except perhaps the *Bondage of the Will* and the Catechism."

3. See summary in Forde, *Law-Gospel Debate*, 3–12.

4. See discussion in ibid., 12–36; Green, *The Erlangen School of Theology*, 105–33. See the following on von Hofmann's theology and life work: Becker, *The Self-Giving God*.

5. Forde, *Law-Gospel Debate*, 63–64.

as unbounded love to sinners in order to overcome their resistance to his graciousness. Therefore, there is no need to posit a doctrine of penal substitution, because the conquering power of unbounded love overcomes all resistance and sin. Von Hofmann largely did not think of sin as a form of guilt, but rather as a state of alienation from God.[6] In his treatment of the earlier tradition, von Hofmann pointed to Luther's use of the imagery of cosmic conquest in his description of Christ's work. He thereby argued that the Reformer's emphasis had been similar to his own.[7] Over the last century, this reading of Luther has been reproduced in various modified forms by several theologians and historians of dogma including Gustaf Aulén, Lennart Pinomaa, Philip Watson, and Gerhard Forde.[8]

Needless to say, von Hofmann's proposal was met with significant resistance, particularly from the Lutheran theologians Gottfried Thomasius and Friedrich Philippi.[9] Nonetheless, the contributions of these two authors to the debate were mainly theological rather than historical. Theodosius Harnack (a colleague of von Hofmann at Erlangen) engaged the historical question of Luther's position. The fruit of Harnack's study appeared in the form of a massive two-volume interpretation on Luther's theology. In this work, (written over a period of roughly twenty-years), Harnack highlighted the problem that von Hofmann's reading of Luther could not solve: if Luther rejected penal substitution, why does he so often speak of the satisfaction of the law by Christ? Harnack admitted that Luther had indeed used the imagery of cosmic warfare against demonic forces to describe the event of atonement. Nevertheless, despite the use of such imagery, Luther had strongly upheld a doctrine of penal substitution.[10] The law was an eternal and objective standard that needed to be fulfilled by sinful humanity.[11] The demonic forces that held humanity in their sway (law, death, and the devil) were not masters who had assumed their offices arbitrarily. Rather, these forces dominated the world because of human sin, and were manifestations

---

6. In a similar manner to Schleiermacher, von Hofmann saw Jesus' obedience as being his faithfulness to his calling under extreme opposition. See von Hofmann, *Encyclopädie der Theologie*, 85.

7. Forde, *Law-Gospel Debate*, 63–64.

8. Aulén, *Christus Victor*, 107–8; Forde, "The Work of Christ," 2:47–65; Pinomaa, *Faith Victorious*, 46–57; Watson, *Let God Be God!*, 116–25.

9. See summary of this debate in Forde, *Law-Gospel Debate*, 49–68; Green, *The Erlangen School*, 125.

10. Harnack, *Luthers Theologie*, 2:242.

11. Ibid., 1:364–67.

of God's wrath.[12] Since humanity was subject to these powers because of sin, then such powers could only be overcome by the satisfaction of the law. The value in this reading was that Harnack could explain Luther's use of both the conquest motif and the language of satisfaction. In later generations, both Paul Althaus and Werner Elert would continue to follow Harnack's reading of Luther. More contemporary Luther scholars such as Bernhard Lohse, Ian D. Kingston Siggins, and Heinrich Bornkamm have similarly acknowledged either Luther's acceptance of the doctrine of penal satisfaction, or at least his appropriation of significant elements of it.[13]

In this chapter, I will largely work from the tradition of Harnack. Put succinctly, Harnack's interpretation of Luther is superior to that of von Hofmann's because it possesses the ability to account for all the data found in the Reformer's writings. As will be observed below, there are passages in Luther's work that both describe Christ's satisfaction of the law and his conquest of demonic forces. Beyond this, Luther is consistently clear that there is connection between human disobedience to the law and their domination by the dark powers of the old creation. Focusing on one aspect of Luther's description of the work of Christ and explaining away the other passages in an ad hoc manner will simply not do.

Previous Atonement Theologies

It is important to recognize that Luther did not form his views of atonement in a vacuum, but was influenced by the teachings of previous theologians. For this reason, I will briefly review the three main motifs of atonement as they have been schematized by the Swedish Lutheran theologian Gustaf Aulén in his book *Christus Victor*.[14] These three main motifs are the conquest motif, the substitution motif, and the revelational/moral influence motif.[15] By "motif," Aulén does not mean a complete, precisely delineated doctrinal concept that is universally agreed upon by a group of theologians.

12. Ibid.,1:253–68.

13. See the following: Althaus, *The Theology of Martin Luther*, 201–23; Bornkamm, *Luther's World of Thought*, 156–75; Elert, *The Structure of Lutheranism*, 106–26; Lohse, *Martin Luther's Theology*, 223–28; Siggins, *Martin Luther's Doctrine of Christ*, 108–43.

14. See the aforementioned Aulén, *Christus Victor*. Though Aulén's model is not satisfactory in every respect, it remains a helpful shorthand for broad similarities between different Christian thinkers.

15. Some of this material also appears summarized/paraphrased in a somewhat-different form in my earlier publication: Kilcrease, *The Self-Donation of God*, 201–6.

Rather, for Aulén, a "motif" describes an image or general orientation of a class of thinkers regarding how they answer a central doctrinal question.

The first atonement motif is the conquest motif. Aulén describes it as the classical motif because of its predominance in the early church. Within this motif, Aulén groups together a number of theologians who are surprisingly diverse. For example, within this category, Aulén places Irenaeus of Lyons, who emphasized the Pauline concept of Christ as the second Adam and recapitulator of creation (Rom 5, 1 Cor 15, etc.).[16] As a second Adam, Christ freed humanity by overcoming the destructive elements of the old creation. He fulfilled this task by entering into the stages of creation's development and persevering where humanity had previously failed.[17] Within the same motif, Aulén also places Origen of Alexandria, who taught that Christ served as a divine ransom.[18] On the cross, Jesus was given over to the devil in exchange for the human race. Because he was ignorant of the fact that Jesus was God, Satan accepted the ransom and released humanity from his dark power. After three days under Satan's dominion, Christ overcame the devil by his divine power and rose from the dead as a victorious conqueror.[19] Although there is a wide divergence between these two descriptions of the work of Christ, they share the central thrust of the conquest motif: Jesus is the divine savior, who enters into creation in order to rescue it from the power of demonic forces (sin, death, the devil, etc.).

The conquest motif was the chief model of redemption in the early church, and was used by most of the Greek patristic theologians. Over time, it became more and more elaborate. Athanasius's theology of atonement is an appropriate example of this. In his short work *On the Incarnation of the Word*, he argues that the incarnation occurred in order to overcome the fetters that had held humanity back from its own movement towards participation in the divine life.[20] In the Eastern Orthodox Church, this idea of participation in divinity is referred as "*theosis*" or deification. In order to accomplish this transformation, the divine Son entered the human

---

16. Aulén, *Christus Victor*, 16–35. Also see Osborn, "Irenaeus of Lyons," 121–26; Wingren, *Man and the Incarnation*.

17. For a relatively short and very easy-to-read summary of Irenaeus' position see Irenaeus of Lyons, *On Apostolic Preaching*.

18. Aulén, *Christus Victor*, 38, 49, 51.

19. See a full account of Origen's system in Origen, *On First Principles*.

20. See Athanasius, "On the Incarnation of the Word," section 4, 58.

story, deified his assumed humanity, and defeated death and the devil.[21] The form the Messiah's death had taken was necessary because "the devil, the enemy of our race, having fallen from heaven, wanders about in the lower atmosphere." Therefore "it was quite fitting that the Lord suffered this death . . . being lifted up he cleared the air of the malignity both of the devil and of demons of all kinds . . . and made a new opening of the way up into heaven."[22]

For Athanasius, this was not the only reason for Christ's work on the cross. In Jesus' death, the curse of death was exhausted: "all being held to have died in him, the law involving the ruin of men might be undone (insofar as its power was fully spent in the Lord's body, and had no longer holding ground against men, his peer)." Beyond this, Athanasius also understood Jesus' death as a sacrifice of sin: "by offering unto death he himself had taken as an offering and sacrifice free from stain, straightway he put away death from all his peers by offering an equivalent."[23] Therefore, contrary to the claims of many, the motif of conquest does not exclude the idea that Jesus died in order to pay for the sin of humanity. Nevertheless, for Athanasius the substitution motif is a subplot in a larger drama of God's conquest of death and the devil.

Elaborations on these same themes continued in the later Greek patristic theologies of Maximus the Confessor and John of Damascus.[24] In the theology of Saint Maximus, it was Adam's task not only to reach deification, but also to resolve various dualities within creation (the divergence between male and female, heaven and earth, etc.) that had been left unresolved by God after his initial creation. Having fallen into sin and under the dominion of Satan, Adam was unable to perform this task.[25] Through his redemptive work, Christ was not only victorious over the demonic forces of the old creation, but was also about to reconcile the dualities that Adam failed to reconcile.[26]

According to John of Damascus, even prior to the fall, it was humanity's vocation to ascend toward the divine life, and by so doing, to bring the

21. Ibid., section 13, 67–68.
22. Ibid., section 25, 80.
23. Ibid., section 9, 63.
24. Meyendorf, *Christ in Eastern Christian Thought*, 137–40.
25. Ibid., 137.
26. Ibid., 137–39.

whole creation into union with God's being.[27] To do this, it was necessary for Adam to strive for deification: "And so it was necessary first for man to be tested, since one who is untried and untested deserves no credit. Then when trial had made him perfect through his keeping of the commandment he should thus win incorruptibility." Satan interfered by tempting Adam with offer of divine knowledge too early in the process of deification: "[the Devil] tempted that wretched man with the very hope of divinity."[28] In spite of his emphasis on Christ's conquest of the devil, the Damascene specifically rejects Origen's interpretation of a ransom paid to the devil: "God forbid that the Lord's blood should be offered to the tyrant!"[29] Like Athanasius, he emphasized that Jesus overcame the devil by absorbing the curse suffered by humans under sin: "He appropriated our curse and dereliction and such things as are not according to nature, not because He was or had been such, but because He took on our appearance and was reckoned as one of us. And such is the sense of the words, 'being made a curse for us.'"[30] Jesus is the savior of the human race in that he completed human destiny by overcoming the demonic forces of the old creation and ascended into a heavenly existence.[31]

In contrast to the elaborate development of the conquest motif in the Eastern Church, Latin Christianity came to emphasize Christ's role as a substitute for sin. Starting with the North African Father Tertullian in the third century, Latin theologians began to emphasize the idea of Christ's death as a form of meritorious substitution, while still holding onto elements of the conquest motif.[32] The predominance of this doctrinal motif developed along with the Latin system of penance and merit, drawing heavily on the concept of "supererogatoria."[33] According to this concept, an individual could make himself worthy of higher merits before God through following the divine law more rigorously than was actually necessary. This could take the form of preserving virginity, the intentional seeking of martyrdom, or fasting. Tertullian himself was a strong proponent of such a view, as well as the idea that Christ's death had been a substitution for

27. Louth, *St. John Damascene*, 117–43.
28. John of Damascus, *John of Damascus*, 265–66.
29. Ibid., 332.
30. Ibid., 330–31.
31. Louth, *St. John Damascene*, 144–78.
32. Aulén, *Christus Victor*, 82.
33. See Tertullian, *Tertullian*, 16–17.

sin. Although Tertullian appears to have never believed that merit from the acts of the faithful could be transferred from one person to another, his student Cyprian came to hold such an opinion, and promoted it among his contemporaries.[34]

By the eleventh century, Latin Christianity had developed an elaborate system of merit and penance under the influence of the aforementioned theories, as well as certain concepts borrowed from Germanic law. Due to this fact, it is easy to see why Latin Christianity finally began to move away from the conquest motif. This was largely because in the minds of Latin theologians, slavery to Satan now took a back seat to the problem of the debt of sin. Anselm of Canterbury represents the first theologian in the west to develop a concept of atonement that consciously dethrones the primary function of atonement as the destruction of demonic forces.[35] In some of the early passages of what is probably his best-known work, *Cur Deus homo?,* he vigorously attacked the idea that Satan exercised any kind of rights over the human race: "As for saying that he [Jesus] came to conquer the Devil for you, in what sense do you dare assert that? Does not the omnipotence of God reign everywhere? How then did God need to come down from heaven to defeat the Devil?"[36] Instead, drawing on the old Latin North African idea of merit and its transferability, Anselm argued that, by dying on the cross, Christ had performed an act of unprecedented supererogation: "No man besides him ever gave to God, by dying, what he was not necessarily going to lose at some time, or paid what he did not owe. But this man freely offered to the Father what he would never have lost by any necessity, and paid for sinners what he did not owe himself."[37]

Because humanity had fallen into sin, it could not, by its own efforts, merit salvation. By human disobedience, God was robbed of honor. Following the logic of medieval feudalism, Anselm posited that, to make up for this dishonor, something greater had to be given back for the sake of compensation. This was impossible, however. Since all rational creatures owe God absolute allegiance, Anselm explained, any act of obedience performed by creatures would be only giving what was already owed. Consequently, acts of obedience could by no means make up for past acts of

---

34. Aulén, *Christus Victor*, 82.

35. Ibid., 84–92; Deme, *Christology of Anselm*, 175–208; Evans, "Anselm of Canterbury," 94–101.

36. Anselm of Canterbury, "Cur Deus homo?", 107.

37. Ibid., 177.

disobedience: "Every inclination of the rational creature ought to be subject to God... This is the debt angels and humans owe to God. No one who pays it sins."[38]

In order to bring about salvation, someone who was not already a debtor would have to pay the debt. Because Jesus was God, he did not owe the debt. Furthermore, Jesus could pay the debt incurred by fallen humans because he himself was greater than the whole of creation: "If he is to give something of his own to God, which surpasses everything that is beneath God, it is also necessary for him to be greater than everything that is not God."[39] On the other hand, being true man, he was capable of paying the debt owed by other humans. Living a perfect life, Jesus was not obligated to die in the manner of other fallen humans.[40] Therefore, by dying when it was unnecessary for him to do so, Jesus gained an infinite treasury of merit from God that he could, in turn, donate to the human race.

Anselm's theology does not exhaust the description of the substitution motif. In contrast to Anselm's description of Christ's vicarious death as meritorious, the Reformers and Protestant scholastics described Christ's work both as meritorious action and as a punishment for sin.[41] The early Lutheran theologian Matthias Flacius developed the categories of "active" and "passive" righteousness as a means of describing Christ's act of substitution in these dual aspects.[42] Later, I will discuss and explore the implications of understanding atonement in this manner. At this point though, it should be observed that, although the Reformers and Protestant scholastics deviated from Anselm in many details, important continuities remain between their two respective positions.

The last motif is the revelational or moral influence theory of atonement.[43] This motif was first developed by Abelard in the twelfth century.[44] According to Abelard, killing the Son of God would not result in the expia-

---

38. Ibid., 119. See also ibid., 139: "Therefore, you do not make satisfaction unless you repay something greater than that for the sake of which you were obliged not to commit the sin."

39. Ibid., 150.

40. Ibid., 179.

41. See Schmid, *Doctrinal Theology*, 342–70 and Heppe, *Reformed Dogmatics*, 448–81.

42. Schmid, *Doctrinal Theology*, 354.

43. Aulén, *Christus Victor*, 133–42.

44. See Abelard, "Exposition of the Epistle," 276–87. Also see the summary in the following: Aulén, *Christus Victor*, 95–98; Bromiley, *Historical Theology*, 185–88.

tion of sin, but would instead be an even greater sin than that of Adam. God in Christ, therefore, did not die in order to atone for sin, but rather to demonstrate his love for humanity. This communication of love would lead to reciprocal love on the part of the human race. A form of this motif was promoted in the early modern period by the Socinians, a group of early Unitarians.[45] In the Socninian version, Jesus mainly serves as an exemplar of moral virtue by his death. Such an example was meant to influence the human race to engage in virtuous behavior. Various versions of the revelational/moral influence motif have also been promoted by modern liberal theologians, notably Friedrich Schleiermacher and Albrecht Ritschl.[46] In essence, this motif posits that God in Christ communicates his truth to humanity in an effective way, and thereby morally transforms them by it.

What should we make of these three motifs in relationship to Luther? Following the tradition of Theodosius Harnack, I will argue that Luther draws elements of the first two motifs (i.e., conquest and substitution). This is particularly evident in his teachings in the Catechisms and the *Great Galatians Commentary*. The major difference that can be discerned between the previous tradition and Luther's treatment of these motifs is the Reformer's focus on the paradigm of law and gospel. Because of this focus, Luther sees redemption as primarily the ultimate outworking of Christ's self-giving promise standing juxtaposed to God's "alien work" (Latin *opus alienum*) of wrath and law. Because he has promised redemption to the human race, God must personally enter into the condemnation of the law and the tyranny of demonic forces in order to overcome them. This involves an unprecedented act of self-surrender. By experiencing the vicissitudes of human existence under the law and ultimately suffering damnation, Christ redeems humanity by the power of his cross and resurrection. Through faith, an exchange of realities occurs between Christ and believers: Christ receives sin and death, whereas sinners receive righteousness and life.

Luther's Early Psalms Commentaries (1513–1515)

The Psalms commentaries emerged from the context of Luther's early career as a professor of Bible at Wittenberg. The theological background of these

---

45. Socinus, *The Racovian Catechism*, 297–320.

46. Ritschl, *Christliche Lehre*, 3:364–455; Schleiermacher, *The Christian Faith*, 425–75.

texts was the young Luther's spiritual crisis and his subsequent relationship with Johannes von Staupitz, his superior in the Augustinian order.

The young Luther studied at the University of Erfurt, which on the eve of the Reformation was a stronghold of a theology referred to as the *via moderna* (or the "modern way").[47] This theology was different than what is often referred to as the *via antiqua*, or the "old way," which was embodied by theologians like Thomas Aquinas. In particular, at this stage of his career, Luther was heavily influenced by the theology of Gabriel Biel, an adherent of many of the aspects of William of Occam's theology and philosophy. Luther studied Biel so closely that, according to Melanchthon, he was able to quote long passages by heart, even later in life.[48]

Generally speaking, scholars have more often than not suggested that the Reformer's early struggle to establish his own righteousness in the monastery was largely colored by the Occamist theology of sin and grace as it was transmitted to him through various sources, including Biel.[49] Put succinctly, the *via moderna* taught that sinners must "do what was within them" (in Latin, *facere quod in se est*), and, as a result, God in his mercy would impute such an effort as meritorious enough (though in actuality it possessed no intrinsic value) for him to bestow upon them the first grace.[50] As should be clear, taken literally the demand to "do what is within" would necessarily lead to a cycle of penitential hyperactivity followed by periods of massive despair and self-recrimination. As one might expect, this pattern both explicitly and implicitly matches Luther's own autobiographical fragments regarding his life prior to the so-called "Reformation breakthrough."[51]

Beyond the influence of the Occamism, David Steinmetz has pointed to the influence of contemporary penitential theories present in popular piety. Such theories emphasized the need for the penitent to have a nearly perfect disposition in order to cause the sacrament of penance function

---

47. See discussion of Luther and his relationship to *via moderna* in: Lohse, *Martin Luther's Theology*, 21–22; McGrath, *Intellectual Origins*, 109–13; McGrath, *Reformation Thought*, 67–69; Oberman, *Two Reformations*, 21–43; McSorley, *Luther*, 191–223.

48. Oberman, *Luther*, 138.

49. Lohse, *Martin Luther's Theology*, 33. See Luther's description in 1545: *LW* 34:323–38; *WA* 54:179–87.

50. See a number of examples: Kolb, *Martin Luther*, 32–34; Lohse, *Martin Luther's Theology*, 32–34; McGrath, *Iustia Dei*, 83–91.

51. *LW* 34:323–38; *WA* 54:179–87.

correctly.[52] All things considered, the accent of late-medieval religious practice and theology (at least as Luther had imbibed and perceived it) was on human effort, rather than on God's grace and promise.

The initial cure for Luther's psychological and spiritual torment was the pastoral care of his superior in the Augustinian order, Johannes von Staupitz. To simplify an extremely complex relationship, Staupitz counseled Luther to draw his focus away from his own penitential efforts and to focus on the crucified Christ. Following from this, both Heiko Oberman and David Steinmetz have argued that Staupitz's thought contains the kernels of several later themes in Luther's theology. One theme that Staupitz was particularly fond of emphasizing was that there was a kind of exchange of sin and righteousness that occurred between the believer and Christ. Christ's relationship to the believer consisted of a "happy exchange" between the sin and death in the believer and righteousness and life in Christ.[53] Steinmetz has noted the presence of this theme in the earlier theology of Augustine, who was a major influence on both Luther and Staupitz.[54] One could also point to the presence of the idea in the writings of other church fathers.[55] Of course, it is impossible to directly discern Luther's inner thoughts through reading the contents of his first Psalm commentaries. Nevertheless, it might be speculated that certain aspects of Staupitz's pastoral care seep into and thereby find expression in the young Reformer's exegetical choices. Several aspects of Luther's treatment of the Psalms suggest this.

First, Luther's exegetical techniques stood both in continuity and discontinuity with the previous thousand years of Christian commentary. Marc Liehard has highlighted the significance of Luther's decision to interpret the Psalms as prayers of Jesus.[56] In one respect, this method was nothing more than the repetition of a tradition of interpretation stretching back to Augustine. In other respects, however, Luther broke with the tradition by reading the penitential Psalms as the words of Christ. According to Lienhard, Augustine (and the later medieval tradition) had refused to do this out of the fear that such an action would impiously impute sin to the

---

52. David Steinmetz, *Luther in Context*, 2–5.

53. For the relationship between Luther and Staupitz, see the following: Oberman, *Luther*, 184; Steinmetz, *Luther and Staupitz*, 29–30; Steinmetz, *Misericordia Dei*, 90–91.

54. See Steinmetz, *Luther and Staupitz*, 29–30.

55. For example see Irenaeus, *Adversus Haereses*, 3.10.2; *ANF*, 1:424.

56. Lienhard, *Luther*, 25; Wicks, *Man Yearning for Grace*, 42–43.

sinless Christ.[57] Nevertheless, in light of the motif of the exchange of realities between Christ and the believer taken from Staupitz, such an exegetical decision made a great deal of sense.

Turning to these lectures themselves, Luther emphasizes the strength of Christ's solidarity with the human race's sufferings and sin. In his discussion of Psalm 69, Luther writes that the Psalm is about Jesus on the cross: "This general word gives expression to all misery. Therefore He [Jesus] seeks to be set free from all of them." Again, he states:

> He would have no punishments if it were not for our sins and our punishments. Thus the Psalm is speaking about Him and about us at the same time, and it must be read with the most devoted love for Christ. Let us, I say, understand our sins and His punishment at the same time, expressed in the same words.[58]

Luther therefore makes clear that Christ has entered into and suffered the vicissitudes of humanity's plight under sin and death. Because he gave himself over to unrighteous humanity completely, he suffered what they suffer and is threatened by what threatens them.

This theme appears in an even more intensified form in Luther's statement regarding Psalm 8:4: "Whoever heard of strength being destroyed by weakness? But this is what Christ did. In lowliness, weakness and shame He stripped the whole world of its strength, honor, and glory, and altogether annihilated it and transferred it to himself."[59] Christ assumes the weakness and distress of the human race. In effect, Luther states that, by doing so, Christ was able to annihilate the controlling power of the dark forces of the old creation. Later, Luther explains that this could happen because, not only did Jesus suffer for our sins, he also identified with the human situation completely: "Therefore Christ was stuck in our mud, namely, in the lust of our flesh, which leads Him into the deep and abyss."[60]

The Psalm lectures show that Luther took a step in a new theological direction. Jesus was seen as exchanging the human reality of sin and death with his own. For Luther, Jesus had completely identified with the sin of the human race so that, by suffering God's wrath and judgment on the cross, he overcame God's judgment as embodied in the powers of death

---

57. Lienhard, *Luther: Witness to Jesus Christ*, 25.
58. *LW* 10:354; *WA* 3:418.
59. *LW* 10:89; *WA* 3:82.
60. *LW* 10:355; *WA* 3:419.

and destruction. As can be observed, this theology of atonement stands in continuity with both earlier theological traditions of the Middle Ages and the patristic era. However, in some respects, Luther stands in discontinuity with the earlier tradition. Unlike the church fathers and medieval theologians, Luther radicalized the motif of exchange by making it extend even to the imputation of Christ with human sin.

The Freedom of a Christian (1520)[61]

The short treatise *Freedom of a Christian* (1520) is central to understanding Luther's theological development in the wake of the indulgence controversy.[62] As any worthy historian is aware, influence is one of the most difficult things to demonstrate. Nevertheless, it is not inappropriate to suggest some possible influences on Luther's thinking as he wrote the treatise.

Luther emphasizes the bridal-mystical relationship between Christ and the believer throughout the treatise. Though there are a number of sources of this motif (going back to the Scriptures themselves), it is possible that Luther drew on aspects of Bernard of Clairvaux's use of the motif in his sermons on the Song of Songs. Indeed, numerous scholarly investigations have shown that Luther was very familiar with Bernard's writings.[63] In particular, Luther was familiar with Bernard's sermons on the Song of Songs.[64] In recent scholarship, Franz Posset has forcefully argued that Bernard was a major influence on Luther. In support of this thesis, he points to Melanchthon's later claim that an elderly monk's use of a quotation from Bernard had first impelled Luther toward his great reformational insight.[65] Though these are interesting suggestions, it should also be emphasized that Luther was also acquainted with the teachings of a number of mystical and spiritual writers who had ideas similar to those of Bernard.[66] In

---

61. Much of the material in this section has appeared in a similar, though not identical, form in my article "The Bridal-Mystical Motif," 263–79.

62. *LW* 31:327–78; *WA* 7:12–38.

63. For example, see: Bell, *Divus Bemhardus*; Posset, *Pater Bernhardus*; Posset, *The Real Luther*.

64. Posset, *Pater Berhardus*, 4.

65. Posset, *The Real Luther*, 85–129, 149–70.

66. For a discussion of Luther and his relationship to mysticism, see the following selected sources: Hamm, "Wie mystisch war der," 237–87; Hoffman, *Luther and the Mystics*.

fact, it seems that, early on, Luther read a variety of mystical writings. The Reformer's early fascination with the mystical text *The German Theology* has been especially well-documented.[67]

The historical and political context also influenced Luther's writing. Luther's treatise was written in the wake of several significant events, including the Leipzig debate,[68] his excommunication by Pope Leo X,[69] and very probably the so-called "Reformation breakthrough."[70] Whatever other pastoral or political purposes Luther had in mind, his main theological goal was to explain his new understanding of the justification of the sinner before God. During this same period, the Reformer also wrote two other major works. The first was *The Babylonian Captivity of the Church*, which was written largely to explain how his sacramental views had shifted due to his new understanding of justification.[71] During this period, Luther also wrote a letter *To the Christian Nobility of the German Nation*, which dealt with general issues of civil and ecclesiastical reform.[72]

Luther begins the treatise by telling his readers that the Christian is a "perfectly free lord of all, subject to none [and] . . . a perfectly dutiful servant of all, subject to all."[73] Luther explicates the first part of this description ("perfectly free lord of all, subject to none") by noting that the proposition concerns the reality of the inner person of the believer before the eyes of God. The inner person is first humbled and made ready for the reception of passive righteousness by the proclamation of the law: "[through the proclamation of] the commandments [the believer comes] to recognize his helplessness."[74] Recognizing this makes the sinner "truly humble and reduced to nothing."[75] Being empty, the inner person is now able to be filled with God's own unilateral self-donation in Christ.

Luther's emphasis on humility goes back to the 1510s and was part of the larger mystical theme of "self-hatred" (in Latin, *odium sui*), which

---

67. See Luther's preface in *WA* 1:375–79.
68. *LW* 31:307-26; *WA* 2:158–61.
69. See Luther's response in *WA* 6:576–629.
70. Luther's description in 1545 suggests this. See *LW* 34:323–38; *WA* 54:179–87.
71. *LW* 36:301–26; *WA* 6:484–573.
72. *LW* 44:115–219; *WA* 6:381–469.
73. *LW* 31:344; *WA* 7:21.
74. *LW* 31:348; *WA* 7:23.
75. *LW* 31:348; *WA* 7:23.

figured prominently in his theology during this period.[76] Early in Luther's career, this theme was integrated into a mystical theology focused on the love and desire of God. In this framework, the human subject hates himself as an earthly object in competition with God. In this treatise, though, the theme of humility appears to be transformed into the biblical call to repentance and receptivity toward divine favor.

Being made passive, humble, and aware of the impossibility of self-justification, the human being now receives God's proper work through the proclamation of the gospel. God works saving faith through the proclamation of the gospel. By faith, the believer receives the fullness of Christ's righteousness through the word. In the word of promise, Christ utterly surrenders himself to the believing person. Just as there is an exchange of goods when a man and woman are married, so too there is an exchange of realities between Christ and the believer:

> Accordingly the believing soul can boast of and glory in whatever Christ has as though it were its own, and whatever the soul has Christ claims as his own. Let us compare these and we shall see inestimable benefits. Christ is full of grace, life and salvation. The soul is full of sins, death, and damnation. Now let faith come between them and sins, death, and damnation will be Christ's, while grace, life, and salvation will be the soul's; for if Christ is a bridegroom, he must take upon himself the things which are the bride's and bestow upon her the things that are his.[77]

It should be noted again that not only the bridal motif, but also Luther's accompanying image of exchange, has a long history—as I observed earlier—going back to Augustine,[78] and probably farther. Beyond this, within the Reformer's immediate environment, the exchange motif was also used by German mystical authors and in the theology of von Staupitz.[79] Nevertheless, these earlier authors very strongly emphasize the soul being transformed and conformed to Christ, and not vice versa.

By contrast, for Luther, Christ not only lends his personal righteousness to the believer, but the believer lends his reality to Christ. The believer's

---

76. This theme is present throughout the Romans commentary of 1515–1516 and as late as the Ninety-Five Theses. In thesis 4, Luther writes of "self-hatred" as being the content of true repentance, which continues throughout earthly life (*WA* 1:233).

77. *LW* 31:351; *WA* 7:25–26.

78. See Congar, "Regards et Réflexions," 3:488–89; Iserloh, "Luther und die Mystik," 71–75; Steinmetz, *Luther and Staupitz*, 29.

79. Ibid., 29–30; Steinmetz, *Misericordia Dei*, 90–91.

"gift" is not a positive contribution to the relationship, but rather the unpleasant baggage of sin and death. As bridegroom of the soul, Christ takes the full ugliness of sin and death upon himself. Therefore, in describing the redemptive relationship between Christ and the soul, Luther makes Christ active and the soul passive. Neither is this reception of the bride's goods merely fictive. In the aforementioned passage, Luther insists that the believer's sin really personally belongs to Christ. This is quite consistent with, and in many respects a continuation of, the theology found in Luther's earlier commentaries on the Psalms.

In short, Luther's treatment of the bridal relationship deviates from the previous tradition in some significant ways. Unlike the spiritual authors, and others of the preceding generations, Luther held that Christ really took the condemnation of sin upon his own person as the bridegroom of the soul. Neither does the bride become attractive by way of her moral virtues for Luther. As Steven Ozment observes, these differences with the earlier tradition were not lost on Luther's contemporaries. He quotes the Dominican inquisitor Jacob Hochstraten, who writes:

> [Luther] *lists no preconditions* for the spiritual marriage of the soul with Christ except only that we believe Christ . . . and trust that he will bestow all [that he promises]. Not a single word is said about the *mutual love by which the soul loves Christ* . . . nor do we hear anything about the *other divine commandments*, to which the keeper of which eternal life is *both promised and owed.*
>
> What else do those who boast of such a base spectacle do than make of the soul . . . a prostitute and an adulteress, who knowingly and wittingly connives to deceive her husband [Christ] and, daily committing fornication upon fornication and adultery upon adultery, makes the most chaste of men a pimp? *As if Christ does not take the trouble . . . to choose . . . a pure and honorable lover!* As if Christ requires of her only belief and trust and has no interest in her righteousness and the other virtues! As if a certain mingling of righteousness with iniquity and Christ with Belial were possible![80]

In other words, according to Hochstraten, for the mystical marriage to work, the believer must possess virtues enticing enough to attract Christ. Christ could never be attracted to the soul that was not first made attractive to him. Moreover, for Hochstraten there appears to be no real exchange of

---

80. Cited from Ozment, *A Mighty Fortress*, 84 (emphasis added). Ozment cites Hochstraten, "Iacobi Hoochstrati Disputationes," 609–10.

realities between Christ and believer. The Christ does not take upon himself the real imputation of his bride's sin.

Again, Luther construes the work of atonement and justification as an exchange of realities. Christ redeems humanity by fully entering into its place. This allows him to donate his reality to the sinner through faith in the word of God. Moreover, as can be observed, this description of redemption stands in continuity with the older appropriations of the motif of exchange in the patristic and medieval traditions. Nevertheless, at the same time, Luther reframes the bridal-image in light of his discovery of the biblical teaching of justification as the unilateral love of God made manifest in the cross and empty tomb.

Luther's Small and Large Catechisms (1529)

The Catechisms reveal what Luther believed were the most important aspects of the Christian faith to communicate to laypersons. Contextually, Luther wrote the Catechisms in the wake of the Saxon visitations. After these events, it was recognized that both laypeople and clergy were banefully ignorant of even the most rudimentary teachings of Christianity (i.e., the Creed and the Ten Commandments).[81]

Beginning with the Small Catechism, Luther gives relatively brief and compact explanations of the work of Christ. The Reformer writes:

> I believe that Jesus Christ, true God, begotten of the Father from eternity, and also true man, born of the Virgin Mary, is my Lord, who has redeemed me, a lost and condemned creature, purchased and won me from all my sins, from death, and from the power of the devil, not with gold or silver, but with His holy, precious blood and with His innocent suffering and death.[82]

There are several significant aspects of Luther's account. First, for Luther, atonement involves both Christ's divinity and humanity. In other words, it is Christ's divine nature active in and through his human nature that destroys the power of the dark forces of the old creation. Secondly, in this particular text, Luther places a very heavy accent on the conquest motif. That is to say, the emphasis is clearly on Christ as a redeemer from Satan's

---

81. Bente, *Historical Introductions*, 62–92; Gritsch, *A History of Lutheranism*, 37–46.
82. SC II:2; *CT*, 545.

power.[83] This is not the whole story, though, since Luther also employs the substitution motif. He clearly states that Jesus "purchases sinners" using his "holy, precious blood" and his "innocent sufferings and death." It should be noticed that the use of the words "holy" and "innocent" suggest a contrast with the guilt and debt of sin.[84]

Luther's combination of the two motifs becomes even more pronounced and explicit in his more-detailed account of the Large Catechism. First, the Large Catechism clarifies how bondage to the devil and the wrath and law of God are connected.

> For when we had been created by God the Father, and had received from Him all manner of good, the devil came and led us into disobedience, sin, death, and all evil, so that we fell under His [God's] wrath and displeasure and were doomed to eternal damnation, as we had merited and deserved.[85]

In other words, the demonic forces of the world gained their power over human beings as a result of sin. The devil led human beings into sin, thereby making them slaves to "sin, death and all evil." The violation of God's law incurred his wrath, which allowed humans to be held by these powers of darkness. These forces serve as a mask of God's infinite wrath against sin.

In spite of this, Jesus Christ has purchased the human race by his satisfaction of the law's righteous demands. He accomplished this through his life of obedience and death on the cross. Having blotted out the guilt of sin and removed the blight of evil from creation, he renewed the world by the power of his resurrection. He did this by surrendering his very person to humanity in a supreme act of self-donation:

> [What do we learn from the second article?] . . . namely, how He has completely poured forth Himself and withheld nothing from us that he has not given us. . . . He became man, conceived and born without [any stain of] sin, of the Holy Ghost and of the Virgin Mary, that He might overcome sin; moreover, that He suffered, died and was buried, that He might make satisfaction for me and pay what I owe, not with silver nor gold, but with His own precious

---

83. Arand, "Luther and the Creed," 154–55; Peters, *Commentary on Luther's Catechisms*, 156–59.

84. Peters, *Creed*, 159–63.

85. LC II:2; *CT*, 685.

blood. . . . And after that He rose again from the dead, swallowed up and devoured death and finally ascended into heaven.[86]

Christ's redemptive power means that he has "poured" (*effuderit*) himself out and given himself completely to humanity. As Luther also argued in the Psalm lectures and *On the Freedom of a Christian*, Christ's act of total self-giving entails entering into the realities that threaten humanity as well. In order to maintain his love and promise of redemption, he had to overcome these powers by his fulfillment of the law in order to pacify divine wrath expressed through the demonic forces.[87]

Great Galatians Commentary (1531, 1535)

Luther's *Great Galatians Commentary* (transcribed by his students from lectures delivered in 1531 and published in 1535) represents an extremely rich exposition of the Reformer's mature understanding of the work of Christ. Beyond these virtues, the commentary possesses a quasi-confessional status since the Formula of Concord both recommended and endorses it as a full and correct exposition of the doctrine of justification.[88] This judgment appears to follow from Luther's own understanding of the work. The Reformer did not conceive of it as merely his private teaching or a series of personal opinions. Rather, he understood it as a response (paralleling the Apology to the Augsburg Confession) to the Papal Confutation.[89]

In his explanation of justification and the work of Christ, Luther's starting point is the plight of humanity under sin, death, and wrath. God, as hidden in majesty and wrath, stands in conflict with human sin. God in Christ changes his relationship to the world by donating himself to humanity in order to do battle with divine judgment: "Thus the curse, which is divine wrath against the whole world, has the same conflict with the blessing, that is, with eternal grace and mercy of God in Christ. Therefore the curse clashes with the blessing and wants to damn it and annihilate it. But it cannot."[90] This paradoxical conflict takes place because, whereas God as active and incarnate in Christ donates himself in unbounded love to hu-

---

86. LC II:2; *CT*, 685, 687. Emphasis added.
87. Peters, *Creed*, 159–63.
88. FC, SD III; *CT*, 937.
89. Vainio, *Justification and Participation*, 19–20.
90. *LW* 26:281; *WA* 40.I:440.

manity, God as hidden in his majesty persists in his wrath. God's law and judgment are manifested in his wrathful activities through the "masks" of his creatures.[91]

As the embodiment of the promise of God's unconditional grace, Christ bound himself totally to humanity, and has become its "Slave."[92] Christ must therefore bear all burdens and take upon himself the condemnation of the law.[93] Again, we see the theme of the exchange of realities present in both the early Psalms commentaries and *On the Freedom of a Christian*. As Erich Seeberg rightly observes, Christ anticipates the fact that the believer is "at the same time saint and sinner," in that he unites in himself both blessedness and the curse, sin and death with life and righteousness.[94] In fact, I will go further than Seeberg and suggest that, for Luther in the Galatians commentary, Christ truly is "at the same time saint and sinner." Nevertheless, Christ is both saint and sinner in the opposite way that the believer is: righteous in himself, yet imputed as sinful.[95]

In entering into the life of sinners, Christ had to take humanity's sin upon himself and suffer the wrath of God. Luther writes: "all the prophets saw this, that Christ was to become the greatest thief, murder, adulterer, robber, desecrator, blasphemer, etc., there has ever been anywhere in the world. . . He is a sinner."[96] But if Christ was sinless in himself, how then could this take place? Luther explains that it was possible because of God's imputation:

> Thus a magistrate regards someone as a criminal and punishes him if he catches him among thieves, even though the man has never committed anything evil or worthy of death. Christ was not found among sinners; but of His own free will and by the will of the Father He wanted to be an associate of sinners and thieves and those who were immersed in all sorts of sin. Therefore, when the Law found Him among thieves, it condemned and executed Him as a thief.[97]

---

91. *LW* 26: 95; *WA* 40.I:173. Luther writes: "the whole creation is a face or mask of God."
92. *LW* 26:288; *WA* 40.I:448.
93. Lienhard, *Luther*, 281.
94. Seeberg, *Luthers Theologie*, 8.
95. Lienhard, *Luther*, 283–85; Vainio, *Justification and Participation*, 22–23.
96. *LW* 26:277; *WA* 40.I:434.
97. *LW* 26:277–78; *WA* 40.I:434.

The Finnish Luther scholar Tuomo Mannermaa notes that, for Luther, Christ becomes three things through identifying with humanity and its sin: he is the "greatest person," "the greatest sinner," and the "only sinner."[98] As Luther writes: "because in the same Person, who is the highest, the greatest, and the only sinner, there is also eternal and invincible righteousness, therefore two converge: the highest, greatest and only sin; and the highest, the greatest, and the only righteousness."[99] Therefore, Mannermaa correctly concludes that, according "to Luther . . . the Logos [the divine Son] did not take upon himself merely human nature, in a 'neutral' form, but precisely the concrete and actual human nature. This means that Christ really has and bears the sins of all human beings in the human nature he has assumed."[100]

For God to judge human sin, it was necessary that Christ be imputed as a sinner: "He has and bears all sins of all men in His body—not in the sense that He has committed them but in the sense that He took these sins, committed by us, upon His body, in order to make satisfaction for them with His own blood."[101] Christ objectively took the sins of the whole human race upon himself and rendered satisfaction for them: "He [God the Father] sent His Son into the world . . . and said to Him . . . be the person of all men, the one who committed the sins of all men. And see to it that You pay and make satisfaction for them."[102] By describing Christ as the righteous one imputed with humanity's sin, Luther appears to anticipate Flacius' later designation of Christ's "active" and "passive" righteousness.[103]

Much like Anselm, Luther considers redemption contingent on the payment of an infinite satisfaction for sin. Through his obedience to the Father, and his willing reception of the imputation of sin, Christ rendered an infinite satisfaction on behalf of sinners:

> In addition, it follows that our sins are so great, so infinite and invincible, that the whole world could not make satisfaction for even one of them. Certainly the greatness of the ransom—namely, the blood of the Son of God—makes it sufficiently clear that we

---

98. Mannrmaa, *Christ Present in Faith*, 13–19; Vainio, *Justification and Participation*, 22–23.

99. *LW* 26:281; *WA* 40.I:438.

100. Mannermaa, *Christ Present in Faith*, 13.

101. *LW* 26:277; *WA* 40.I:434.

102. *LW* 26: 280; *WA* 40.I:437. Emphasis added.

103. Schmid, *Doctrinal Theology*, 342–70. See brief comment in Vainio, *Justification and Participation*, 25.

> can neither make satisfaction for our sin nor prevail over it . . . But we should note here the infinite greatness of the price paid for it. Then it will be evident that its power is so great that it could not be removed by any means except that the Son of God be given for it. Anyone who considers this carefully will understand the one word "sin" includes the eternal wrath of God and the entire kingdom of Satan, and that sin is no trifle.[104]

Luther here emphasizes the fact that satisfaction is rendered by Christ's total divine-human person. This emphasis is consistent with Luther's understanding of the exchange of properties between the divine and human natures developed elsewhere.[105] For Luther, all activities of either nature are attributable to the total divine-human person ("God has suffered, the Man has created heaven and earth . . . the Servant [Christ] . . . is the Creator of all things"[106]). In fact, this teaching would also form the basis of the Formula of Concord and Lutheran scholasticism's concept of atonement.

By rendering infinite satisfaction and neutralizing the threat of the law, Christ is also victorious over the demonic forces of the old creation. All these forces are masks of God's wrath, in that "the whole creation is a face or mask of God."[107] The powers of darkness enslave and define persons living apart from the grace of God. When the law is satisfied, the proclamation of the word of God first kills and then breathes new life into the person of faith:

> "I am crucified with Christ." Paul adds this word because he wants to explain how the Law is devoured by the Law. . . When by this faith I am crucified and die to the Law, then the Law loses all its jurisdiction over me, as it lost it over Christ. Thus, just as Christ Himself was crucified to the Law, sin, death, and the Devil, so that they have no further jurisdiction over Him, so through faith I, having been crucified with Christ in spirit, am crucified and die to the Law, sin, etc., so that they have no further jurisdiction over me but are now crucified and dead to me.[108]

---

104. *LW* 26:33; *WA* 40.I:84.

105. Vainio, *Justification and Participation*, 22–23, 25–56.

106. Lohse, *Martin Luther's Theology*, 229. cited from *WA* 39.II: 280. Roy Harrisville's translation.

107. *LW* 26:95; *WA* 40.I:173.

108. *LW* 26: 165; *WA* 40.I:280.

Through being united to Christ, the believer is victorious over the dark powers of the old creation. The old man is killed and resurrected in Christ. Therefore, the believer ceases to be subjected to the powers of the old order through the imputation of righteousness.[109] Robert Bertram comments:

> Christ bears our sins in his body, not only because they are thereby destroyed, but because they are ours. There is no question in Luther's mind that Christ could have vanquished the tyrants without submitting to the cross, by an outright exercise of his divine sovereignty. But such an alternative overlooks how intimately the victory was to be ours and how it was therefore to be achieved in "our sinful person."[110]

By entering into humanity's life under sin, death, the devil, and the law, Christ was able to destroy their power by bearing their attacks and thereby overcoming them.[111] He is therefore capable of sharing his victory with believers.

Faith is united with the new resurrected life through the gospel. Therefore, faith receives God's self-donation by unity with Christ's person.[112] Just as Jesus once gave himself over to the imputation of sin, he now gives himself over to sinners through the imputation of righteousness as mediated by word and sacrament. The promise of Christ's total self-giving affects the mystical union between Christ and the believer:

> But faith must be taught correctly, namely, that by it you are so cemented to Christ that He and you are as one person, which cannot be separated but remains attached to Him forever and declares "I am as Christ." And Christ in turn says "I am as that sinner who is attached to Me, and I to him. For by faith we are joined together into one flesh and one bone."[113]

Therefore, by faith the believer receives all that is Christ's: "The one who has faith is a completely divine man, a son of God, the inheritor of the universe. He is victor over the world, sin, death, and the devil."[114]

---

109. Vainio, *Justification and Participation*, 30–31.

110. Bertram, "How Our Sins Were Christ's," 9.

111. Lienhard, *Luther*, 285; Vainio, *Justification and Participation*, 24–25.

112. Lienhard, *Luther*, 287–88; Mannermaa, *Christ Present in Faith*, 39–42; Vainio, *Justification and Participation*, 38–42.

113. *LW* 26:168; *WA* 40.I:285.

114. *LW* 26:247; *WA* 40.I:390.

Although the word, and the saving faith which it creates, sanctifies the inner person, this does not exclude a person from remaining a sinner until temporal death. For this reason, "acceptance or imputation is extremely necessary, first because we are not yet purely righteous, but sin is still clinging to our flesh during this life."[115] Believers, considered in themselves apart from the imputation of Christ's righteousness, remain worthy of judgment. Sin is "so great, so infinite and invincible, that the whole world could not make satisfaction for even one of them."[116]

This simultaneity ("at the same time saint and sinner") of Christian existence is evident in God's address in the form of law and gospel. Law always addresses the believer as a sinner. Conversely, the gospel continuously addresses the believer as justified. The knowledge of one's self as a sinner to whom Christ's righteousness is given kills the old man and kindles faith, leading to good works: "truly good works, which flow from this faith and joy conceived in the heart because we have the forgiveness of sins freely through Christ."[117]

Conclusion

In conclusion, Luther's teachings regarding atonement exhibits a fair amount of consistency over his life span. Christ, having entered human existence, identifies and exchanges his reality with that of humanity under the power of sin, death, and the devil. By fulfilling the law and rendering satisfaction, Christ neutralizes the wrath of God and disarms the dark powers of the old creation. This victory, which is manifested in his resurrection, is shared by believers through the imputation of righteousness received by faith, and subsequently through mystical union.

---

115. *LW* 26:132–33; *WA* 40.I:233.
116. *LW* 26:33; *WA* 40.I:84.
117. *LW* 26:133; *WA* 40.I:234.

3

Atonement in the Lutheran Confessions and Scholasticism

Introduction

ALONG WITH LUTHER'S OWN theology of atonement, the Lutheran theology of the sixteenth and seventeenth centuries represent an important resource for the delineation of the Lutheran paradigm. This is the period within which the Lutheran Reformation was consolidated through the establishment of the confessional documents of the *Book of Concord*. It is also the period in which the dogmatic claims of the *Book of Concord* were interpreted and applied to a variety of new theological problems in a generally faithful manner by the theologians of the Age of Orthodoxy. Examining the confessional documents and the great theologians of early Lutheranism provides a fuller outline of the Lutheran doctrine of atonement. Although Luther set the basic tone for the tradition, others (Chemnitz, Flacius, Gerhard, etc.) gave fuller systematic expression to the Reformer's ideas and addressed problems that he did not encounter.

The Lutheran Confessors and Scholastics: Philipp Melanchthon

Philipp Melanchthon (1497–1560) is likely, second to Luther, the most important figure in the early history of the Wittenberg reformation. Melanchthon stands out as the author of the Augsburg Confession, The Apology, and The Treatise on the Power and Primacy of the Pope. As an academic theologian, he may be credited with the development of the first Lutheran systematic theologies in the various editions of his *Loci communes theologici*.

Because of the brevity of our discussion here, I cannot do justice to the scope of Melanchthon's achievement in the development of Protestant systematic theology. As Richard Muller demonstrates, Melanchthon's *Loci communes* served as a new model for systematic theology in early Protestantism. Both Reformed and Lutheran scholastics of the sixteenth and seventeenth centuries more or less followed Melanchthon's method of delineating specific "theological common places" (in Latin, *Loci communes theologici*) or doctrine topics (sin, grace, creation, providence, etc.) and carefully establishing said doctrines by the gathering together of the grammatically clear passages that pertained to the given topic. These biblical passages were referred to as "seats of doctrine" (in Latin, *sedes doctrinae*). Each passage was allowed to mutually interpret the others and therefore checked the tendency of interpreters of reading their own ideas into the text. This way of doing theology was referred to as the "loci method."[1]

Turning to *Loci communes 1521* (the first edition of the work was written when Melanchthon was only twenty-four), one discovers only a few references to the work of Christ. Melanchthon begins the work by stating that he will confine himself mainly to the topics of sin and grace. In this initial attempt at systematic theology, Melanchthon opines that he finds even a detailed discussion of the doctrine of the Trinity far too speculative.[2] There are, of course, frequently references to the person and work of Christ: "Christ, whom he [God the Father] gave as an Intercessor, Sacrifice, and Satisfaction for us, deserved his goodwill."[3] In spite of such references, there are nonetheless no extended discussions of the specific nature of atonement.

As each successive version of *Loci communes* was published through the mid-sixteenth century, Melanchthon both clarified his thought and increasingly occupied himself with a larger number of traditional theological loci. This is likely due to Melanchthon's greater intellectual maturity, as well as to the recognition that, in order to advance the Wittenberg reformation, he needed to engage the same theological methods and questions as other theologians of the era. The later editions of his dogmatic compendium therefore remain focused on the doctrines of sin and grace, but also

---

1. See Muller, *Prolegomena to Theology*, 96–102, 177–79.
2. Pauck, *Melanchthon*, 21.
3. Ibid., 104.

increasingly possess robust discussions of topics such as the Trinity, creation, and personal ethics.

In his penultimate edition of the *Loci communes 1555*, Melanchthon provides one of the most detailed descriptions of his doctrine of atonement. This was largely prompted by his conflict with both Andreas Osiander and Francisco Stancarus over the doctrine of justification and its relationship to the work of Christ. The issues surrounding the Osianderian controversy will be dealt with later. Here we will primarily concern ourselves with Melanchthon's response to Stancarus.

Francisco Stancarus was a somewhat eccentric Italian theologian operating in Germany during the 1550s. Although Stancarus supported the Reformation, he continued to be enamored with the theology of the older Scholastics (those of the "old way," or in Latin, *via antiqua*) rather than the Reformers themselves.[4] As a result, he was more inclined to follow the older medieval tradition (Lombard, Aquinas, etc.) in its claim that Christ was mediator according to his humanity alone.[5]

In *Loci communes 1555*, Melanchthon's main goal was to refute Stancarus by showing the importance of both Christ's divinity and humanity in the work of redemption. Melanchthon claims that what Stancarus failed to take into account that that Christ needed not only to atone for sin (which was accomplished through his humanity), but also to defeat death and the devil (primarily the work of his divine nature).[6] Therefore, in treating atonement, Melanchthon develops this argument by first noting the greatness of the incarnation and the atonement: "This is a wondrous counsel which determined that the union with the human nature should be made, that the Son should humble and take upon himself human nature, and that the Son of God and man should become a sacrifice!" The great mystery of divine redemption consists in the unity of God's wrath and love, righteousness and mercy: "And so both mercy and righteousness are present in this deed. Out of great love and mercy for mankind the Son prays . . . Nevertheless, so that righteousness may be upheld, the punishment, or an equally great payment, is laid upon the Son."[7] Integrating a series of atonement motifs

---

4. Vainio, *Justification and Participation*, 107n57.

5. Bente, *Historical Introductions*, 159; Ritschl, *Dogmengeschichte des Protestantismus*, 2:325, 475, 482; Seeberg, *Text-Book*, 2:374; Vainio, *Justification and Participation*, 107–9.

6. Ibid., 108.

7. Melanchthon, *Melanchthon on Christian Doctrine*, 33.

(in a fashion similar to Luther), the elderly Melanchthon draws up six main reasons why the incarnation and sacrifice of the cross were necessary:

> First, note that inasmuch as mankind fell into sin, the one to be punished and to pay the penalty had to be a man, but one without sin. Secondly, in order for the payment to be equal and even better, the one who pays is not simply a man or an angel, but is a divine person. Thirdly, no angel and no man could have borne the great burden of divine wrath against our sin. For that reason, the Son of God, who is omnipotent, out of immeasurable love and mercy toward men, laid upon himself this great wrath. Fourthly, no angel and no man is able to walk in the mysterious counsel of the divine Majesty. The Mediator prays for all men and especially for every petitioner, and the divine Majesty hear their desires, and then acts accordingly. All this pertains to an omnipotent person. In the Letter to the Hebrews, when only the High Priest enters into the *Sanctum sanctorum* (Holy of Holies), when only the High Priest, and no one else, is allowed to go into the secret altar in the temple, it means that only the Redeemer is to be in the secret counsel of divine Majesty, and wholly see and know the heart of the Father. Fifthly, no angel and no man might have conquered death and taken life again, for this belongs only to an omnipotent person. Sixthly, the Redeemer is to be a power [*kräftig*] within us; he bears and sustains our weak nature, beholds the hearts of all men, hears all sighs, prays for all, is and lives in the faithful, and creates in them new obedience, righteousness, and eternal life. All this pertains only to an omnipotent person; Immanuel, i.e. God *with* us and *in* us.[8]

Though Melanchthon's description of atonement is, in some ways, more systematic than Luther's, there is a large amount of overlap between their two positions. Both emphasize the substitutionary nature of the work of Christ in accordance with the forensic nature of justification. At the same time, they do not give short shrift to the conquest motif. The main difference would appear to be that Melanchthon develops the notion of the communion of Christ's actions within his divine-human person less clearly than does Luther. This has the rather unfortunate effect of dividing up Christ's human and divine actions in redemption, a problem present in many of Melanchthon's writing on Christology.[9] Later, Martin Chemnitz overcame

---

8. Ibid., 33–34.
9. See discussion in Haga, *Was there a Lutheran Metaphysics?*, 91–114.

these difficulties by reasserting the central aspects of Luther's Christology in his treatment of the doctrine of the incarnation and atonement.

Finally, Melanchthon's contributions to the Lutheran symbolic writings paint much the same picture as his private writings. In the Augsburg Confession, under the third article, we read: "Christ, true God and true man, who was born of the Virgin Mary, truly suffered, was crucified, dead, and buried, that He might reconcile the Father unto us, and be a sacrifice, not only for original guilt, but also for all actual sins of men."[10] In the fourth article on justification by faith, Melanchthon states again that: "sins are forgiven for Christ's sake, who by His death, has made satisfaction for our sins."[11] The *Apology of the Augsburg Confession* does not add anything to the question of atonement, but merely reiterates what Melanchthon had previously said in his private writings and the earlier confession. He does, however, add a few references to Christ's defeat of the demonic powers: "Christ was given to us to remove both these sins (actual and original) and these punishments, and to destroy the kingdom of the devil, sin and death."[12]

It is therefore clear that, throughout his career, Melanchthon accepted and taught the doctrine of penal substitution. His writings contain no hesitation or ambiguity about the purpose of Christ's death. Melanchthon is very clear that Christ died as an atoning sacrifice for sin. Melanchthon's theology of atonement supports the previous chapter's claim that Luther must be seen as an advocate of penal substitution. It would be strange if two theologians working in such great cooperation would not have noticed that they did not understand the death of Christ in the same way. Moreover, if they did disagree about the work of Christ, then Luther's praise of the Augsburg Confession[13] (which clearly teaches penal substitution) would have been highly disingenuous.

Martin Chemnitz and the Formula of Concord

Next to Luther and Melanchthon, Martin Chemnitz (1522-1586)[14] is likely the theologian who had the greatest impact on the theological

10. CA, III; *CT*, 45.
11. CA IV; *CT*, 45.
12. Ap II; *CT*, 119.
13. See description in Bente, *Historical Introductions*, 20-21.
14. Much of the same material in this section is covered in a different form in my

development of the early Lutheran Church. In particular, Chemnitz's contributions lie in his systematization and clarification of Melanchthon and Luther's theological proposals. On the level of church politics, Chemnitz's co-authorship of the Formula of Concord was instrumental in the resolution of many of the controversies that plagued the nascent Lutheran Church during its second generation.

In *The Two Natures in Christ*, Chemnitz sets out to systematize a slightly modified version of Luther's Christology. The systematization of the distinctions regarding the person of Christ do not represent a merely abstract intellectual exercise, but are rather driven by a desire to clarify the theological truth of Christ and his benefits. Olli-Pekka Vainio comments: "[f]or Chemnitz, *communicatio idiomatum* [the communication of attributes within the divine-human person of Christ] is first and foremost a soteriological concept."[15] In other words, the person of Christ is inexorably tied up with the work of Christ, and also therefore the practical question of salvation for the individual Christian. Beyond this, a discussion of the communication of attributes within Christ's divine-human person was necessary in light of Lutheran controversies with the Reformed over the Lord's Supper and its relationship to the Christology.[16] To explain Luther's position, Chemnitz divides and systematizes biblical statements about the communication of attributes between the two natures into three genera.

Chemnitz terms the first genus the *genus idiomaticum*.[17] Most post-Chalcedonian Christians could very likely agree with the content of this genus. According to the *genus idiomaticum*, the properties of both natures are to be attributed to the total divine-human person of Christ when considered in the concrete. "Concrete" refers to the actual lived unity of the incarnation, wherein Christ in his person unites two natures. Therefore, here

---

article, "Thomas Aquinas and Martin Chemnitz," 1–32.

15. Vainio, *Justification and Participation*, 136.

16. Hägglund, *History of Theology*, 272, 278.

17. FC, SD VIII; CT, 1027. "[F]irst, since in Christ two distinct natures exist and remain unchanged and unconfused in their natural essence and properties, and yet of both natures there is only one person, hence, that which is, indeed, an attribute of only one nature is ascribed not to that nature alone, as separate, but to the entire person, which is at the same time God and man (whether it is called God or man). But in *hoc genere*, that is, in this mode of speaking, it does not follow that what is ascribed to the person is at the same time a property of both natures, but it is distinctively explained what nature it is according to which anything is ascribed to the person. Thus *the Son of God was born of the seed of David according to the flesh*, Rom 1:3. Also: *Christ was put to death according to the flesh, and hath suffered for us in, or according to, the flesh*, 1 Pet 3:18; 4:1."

Chemnitz posits that, because Christ unites within his person a divine and human nature (within which, there is no division), the qualities of both are attributable to Christ's total person when considered in its concrete unity.[18] For this reason, it is possible to validly say "Christ is fleshly" and "Christ is omnipotent" without specifying which nature "fleshliness" or "omnipotence" belongs to. Within the lived unity of the two natures, all divine and human qualities belong to the totality of Christ's person.

The second category, the *genus apotelesmaticum*,[19] represents the communication of activities within the person of Christ. Due to the concrete unity of the person of Christ, it is possible to say that when the man Jesus died, the eternal Son died. Of course, when considered in the abstract (that is, simply by itself alone), the divine nature can neither suffer nor die.[20] Nevertheless, because of the unity of the person of Christ in the concrete, it is possible to say that things done or suffered by either nature are attributable to the person of Christ. In keeping with this, it is conversely possible to point to the man Jesus and say that he created the universe.[21] Again, although the human nature was not present at the creation of the world, in the concrete reality of the incarnation, Christ's humanity must properly be considered from the perspective of its subsistence within eternal Son, who did create the universe.

Moreover, beyond the mere recognition of the unity of Christ's agency, the *genus apotelesmaticum* also has significant implications for the doctrine of atonement. The unified agency of both natures within the unity of Christ's person means that each nature participates in the act of

18. Chemnitz, *The Two Natures*, 173–74.

19. FC, SD VIII; *CT*, 1031. "Secondly, as to the execution of the office of Christ, the person does not act and work in, with, through, or according to only one nature, but in, according to, with, and through both natures, or, as the Council of Chalcedon expresses it, one nature operates in communion with the other what is a property of each. Therefore Christ is our Mediator, Redeemer, King, High Priest, Head, Shepherd, etc., not according to one nature only, whether it be the divine or the human, but according to both natures, as this doctrine has been treated more fully in other places."

20. Chemnitz, *The Two Natures*, 215–30.

21. This is consistent with Luther's rejection of Zwingli's Christology. Luther writes in *LW* 41:103–4; *WA* 50:590: "Consequently Christ is God and man in one person because whatever is said of him as man must also be said of him as God, namely, Christ has died, and Christ is God; therefore God died—not the separated God, but God united with humanity . . . [similarly,] whatever is said of God must also be said of man, namely, God created the world and is almighty; the man Christ is God, therefore the man Christ created the world and is almighty. The reason for this is that since God and man have become one person, it follows that this person bears the *idiomata* of both natures."

redemption. In this regard, Chemnitz states that the work of redemption "pertains to the person of Christ not according to either the divine or the human nature alone but to both. And the person, in carrying out these works, possesses activities or operations in both natures and not only in one."[22] Therefore, atonement is described as an event in which each nature plays its own particular role in concert with the other. Hence, the divine nature "does not turn away from the suffering but permits the human nature to suffer and die, yet strengthens and sustains it so that it can endure the immeasurable burden of the sins of the world and the total wrath of God, thus making those sufferings precious before God and saving the world."[23] Moreover, without its unity with an infinite, divine person, the human nature in and of itself would not represent a sufficient payment for the sins of the world. Chemnitz writes that "there would not have been an adequate ransom . . . for sin and God's wrath, which are boundless evils. For this reason, therefore, the price is so great and the merit of the suffering and death of Christ [so great] that it is the propitiation for the sins of the whole world." Indeed, "the creature [Christ's human nature] by itself could not have borne the enormous burden of the wrath of God which was owed for the sins of the entire world."[24] At this point, it can be observed that Chemnitz echoes both Anselm and Luther.

The last and most controversial category is the *genus majestaticum*.[25] According to this genus, the humanity of Jesus possesses the fullness of

---

22. Chemnitz, *The Two Natures*, 217.
23. Ibid., 216.
24. Ibid., 148.
25. FC, SD VIII; CT, 1041: "We, therefore, hold and teach, in conformity with the ancient Orthodox Church, as it has explained this doctrine from the Scriptures, that the human nature in Christ has received this majesty according to the manner of the personal union, namely, because the entire fullness of the divinity dwells in Christ, not as in other holy men or angels, but bodily, as in its own body, so that it shines forth with all its majesty, power, glory, and efficacy in the assumed human nature, voluntarily when and as He [Christ] wills, and in, with, and through the same manifests, exercises, and executes His divine power, glory, and efficacy, as the soul does in the body and fire in glowing iron (for by means of these illustrations, as was also mentioned above, the entire ancient church has explained this doctrine). This was concealed and withheld [for the greater part] at the time of the humiliation; but now, after the form of a servant [or exinanition] has been laid aside, it is fully, powerfully, and publicly exercised before all saints, in heaven and on earth; and in the life to come we shall also behold this His glory face to face, John 17:24."

divine attributes when considered in the abstract.[26] Again, by "abstract," Chemnitz means the human nature considered simply by itself. He writes:

> [For] when we speak of these matters in the schools we can be correct not only in calling Christ a man or saying that the Son of Man makes alive, but also we can then rightly speak in the abstract or in abstract language of the assumed nature as being united with the Logos [the eternal Son]. We can say that the flesh of Christ, which is united with the Logos, makes alive and that the blood of Christ cleanses from sin."[27]

The possession of such attributes is not essential to Christ's humanity (against the teaching of the early Christian heretic Eutychus), but rather is communicated through the unity of the human nature with the person of the eternal Son. In order to explain this, Chemnitz invokes a simile involving heated metal that was used in certain quarters of the early church: "fire communicates itself totally, with all its attributes, to heated iron."[28] Of course, fire does not in some sense transmute the metal into fire. Heated metal retains all its essential properties as metal. Nonetheless, considered in itself, the glow and the heat become real qualities of the metal when united with the fire. Similarly, the human nature participates in divine attributes of the person of the eternal Son while not abrogating its essential human qualities.

Again, it should be reiterated that the communication of glory is also real when considered in the abstract, not merely in the concrete. It is proper to say this because, even when considered in itself alone, Christ's humanity possesses no reality apart from its identity as a human nature that subsists in the person of the eternal Son. Scripture bears witness to this when it describes the man Christ in and of himself as being capable of forgiving sins through his blood: "Moreover, the Scripture teaches in concrete terms that Christ cleanses and that the Son of Man forgives sins; and also in abstract terms, as they say in the schools, with terms which indicate the assumed nature in union with the Logos, that the blood of Christ cleanses."[29] Ultimately, then, the implication of this genus for atonement is that the divine nature is present and active in the humanity of Christ in the act of

---

26. Chemnitz, *The Two Natures*, 241–47.
27. Ibid., 32.
28. Ibid., 309.
29. Ibid., 334.

redemption. Redemption would not be possible without this communication of glory, because God alone can redeem from sin and resurrect from death.

Turning to the teachings of the Formula of Concord, one finds that Chemnitz and the other Concordists' understanding of Christ's person and its relationship to atonement does not substantially differ from the presentation in *The Two Natures in Christ*. In the Formula's Christological teaching, all three genera described above are present in abridged form, although Chemnitz's titles are not used. The treatment of the work of Christ assumes the validity of substitutionary atonement. Moreover, the heresies of both Osiander and Stancarus are condemned in the article on justification. The Concordists reject these theologians' errors, and predicate the unity of Christ's mediatorship on the basis of the unity of his divine-human person: "Christ is called our Righteousness in the affair of justification, namely, that our righteousness rests not upon one or the other nature, but upon the entire person of Christ, who as God and man is our Righteousness in His only, entire, and complete obedience." It is further explained that "the human nature alone, without the divine, could neither by obedience nor suffering render satisfaction to eternal almighty God for the sins of all the world; however, the divinity alone without the humanity could not mediate between God and us." Therefore, "it is a complete satisfaction and expiation for the human race, by which the eternal and immutable righteousness of God, revealed in the Law, has been satisfied, and is thus our righteousness."[30]

The Lutheran Scholastics: Two Developments

Having overcome many of the disputes of the second generation, the Lutheran church entered into what is often called the Age of Orthodoxy (ca. 1580–1725). The Lutheran scholastic authors of this era continued Melanchthon and Chemnitz's process of systematizing Luther's theology. The Lutheran scholastics essentially functioned in the same trajectory as these earlier figures, while formulating the faith in conceptually original ways. Rather than investigating their theology by examining their writings author-by-author, I will instead focus on two significant developments found throughout a number of important figures. These two developments are the threefold office of Christ and the distinction between active and passive righteousness.

30. FC, SD, VIII; *CT*, 1027, 1031, 1033.

Within the Lutheran scholastic tradition, Johann Gerhard was the first to treat the doctrine of the threefold office of Christ.[31] The doctrine did not originate within Lutheranism itself, since Gerhard seems to have taken it over from John Calvin.[32] By contrast, Lutheran theologians of the first and second generation typically only spoke of Christ as priest and king.[33] Gerhard himself notes that it is not entirely necessary to call Christ a prophet, since it was also the vocation of the levitical priests to teach the people, which thereby also fulfilled the prophetic role.[34] Nevertheless, the threefold office ultimately proved conceptually satisfying for the Lutheran scholastics, and therefore became widespread. As nineteenth-century Lutheran theologian and historian of dogma Heinrich Schmid correctly notes, this description of the work of Christ presupposed an understanding on the part of the Lutheran scholastic theologians that the work of Christ stood in direct continuity with Old Testament Israel's laws and public vocations.[35] This was in keeping with the Lutheran claim that Christ had fulfilled the law in the place of sinners.

According to Gerhard (as well as the other Lutheran scholastics), Christ's work of reconciliation expressed itself in multiple ways, and therefore took the shape of the threefold office. Gerhard describes the offices' function and benefits as follows:

> The office of Christ is ordinarily stated as threefold, that of a prophet, a priest, and a king ... Christ atones before God for the guilt of our sins ... which is a work peculiar to a priest. Christ

---

31. Schmid, *The Doctrinal Theology*, 337–38. See Gerhard, *On the Person and Office*, 318–31. Also see *ICR*, 2.15.1–6 in Calvin, *The Institutes of the Christian Religion*, 1:494–503. Also see brief remarks in Hägglund, *History of Theology*, 313. The medieval scholastic and patristic traditions do not appear to have used this schema for the work of Christ. The only precedent for Calvin's use of the schema (beyond its presence in the Scriptures themselves) is a remark found in Eusebius. See Eusebius, *Church History*, 1.3 in *The Church History*, 28. As Eusebius writes, "all [three] [the prophets, priests and kings of the Old Testament] refer to the true Christ, the divine Word, who is the only High Priest of the universe, the only King of all creation, and the only Archprophet of the Father."

32. Hägglund, *History of Theology*, 313.

33. See Luther's treatment in his commentary on Psalm 110 in *LW* 13:225–338; *WA* 41:79–269, and Hütter, *Compendium Locorum Theologicorum*, 2:933–35. Also, regarding Luther's treatment of the offices of Christ, see Siggins, *Martin Luther's Doctrine of Christ*, 48–64.

34. Gerhard, *On the Person and Office*, 318.

35. Schmid, *Doctrinal Theology*, 338.

publishes to us God's counsel concerning our redemption and salvation, which is the work of a prophet. Christ efficaciously applies to us the benefit of redemption and salvation, and rules us by the scepter of His Word and Holy Ghost, which is the work of a king.[36]

Christ's work is therefore tied up with his whole time-bound existence from the manger to the cross. The fullness of Christ's human life both rendered the work of satisfaction and communicated it.

The second major development of Lutheran scholasticism was the doctrine of the active and passive righteousness of Christ.[37] Although this distinction was originally explicated in the second generation of the Wittenberg reformation by the Croatian theologian Matthias Flacius Illyricus, it gained wider use and became standard teaching in the seventeenth century, due to its inclusion in the Formula of Concord.[38]

Specifically, Flacius articulated the doctrine in order to counteract the teaching of Andreas Osiander.[39] Historically, Osiander has been remembered for propagating the opposite heresy of that proposed by Stancarus.[40] That is to say, whereas Stancarus claimed that Christ was the mediator of redemption according to his human nature alone, Osiander claimed that Christ saved through the infusion of his divine nature and righteousness into believers. In this sense, the divine nature became the mediator of salvation, apart from the work of the human nature. The authors of the later Formula of Concord remembered Osiander (although they did not directly mention him by name) mainly for his rejection of a purely forensic doctrine of justification. Instead of basing all righteousness on Christ's work, claimed the authors, Osiander had taught that humanity could become acceptable to God through sanctification.[41]

In recent years this interpretation has been rejected by a number of scholars. For example, Olli-Pekka Vainio has suggested an alternative

36. Ibid., 339.

37. See a similar discussion and theological critique present in this section in my earlier book: Kilcrease, *The Self-Donation of God*, 171–73.

38. Schmid, *Doctrinal Theology*, 354.

39. See the following sources on Osiander and his controversy: Bente, *Historical Introductions*, 152–59; Hamann, "The Righteousness of Faith," 137–62; Lawrenz, "On Justification," 149–74; Vainio, *Justification and Participation*, 95–118; Wengert, *Defending Faith*.

40. Bente, *Historical Introductions*, 152–59; Hirsch, *Die Theologie*, 172–202; Kolb, "Historical Background," 149–74.

41. FC, SD III; *CT*, 917–37.

interpretation to the traditional reading of Osiander. Vainio states that, although Osiander's position seems extremely different than that of Stancarus on the surface, a closer reading of Osiander suggests that the two may be less far apart than they initially appear. Unlike Chemnitz and Melanchthon's interpretation of Osiander, Vainio claims that it is unclear whether or not Osiander believed that the works produced by the indwelling of Christ affected one's relationship with God.[42] Stephen Strehle has pointed out that even Joachim Mörlin (one of bitterest critics of Osiander) thought that Melanchthon's accusations of works righteousness were essentially baseless.[43] After studying Osiander's writings themselves, Vainio states that there is some ambiguity regarding the role of works.[44] In certain passages, Osiander appears to suggest that they ultimately do not affect one's relationship to God. Vainio writes: "When Osiander speaks about God acting wrongly if he reckons as righteous someone who is not righteous *in re* [in themselves], he does not refer to human properties but to God, who is the justifying righteousness through faith."[45]

Secondly, according to Vainio, Osiander's rejection of forensic justification was mainly the result of his rejection of communication of attributes in a manner harmonious with the larger Lutheran tradition. Osiander believed that the divine nature was not communicable, and therefore he utterly disavowed Luther's (and Chemnitz's) understanding of the communication of activities (*genus apotelesmaticum*) within the divine-human person of Christ. As a result, he taught that Christ had died only according to his human nature, and that this was sufficient for the forgiveness of sins.[46] Although forgiveness was a positive condition for the release of divine grace, it was not sufficient to reconcile humanity with God.[47] Forgiveness does not mean that we can stand as positively righteous before God. Christ's death and obedience to God was merely human righteousness, which was always based on the performance of the law.[48] The sort of righteousness that would ultimately avail before God was divine righteousness, a predicate

---

42. Vainio, *Justification and Participation*, 105–6. Also see Strehle, *Catholic Roots*, 73–75.

43. Strehle, *Catholic Roots*, 74.

44. Vainio, *Justification and Participation*, 101–2.

45. Ibid., 102.

46. Stehle, *Catholic Roots*, 76–78; Vainio, *Justification and Participation*, 99.

47. Vainio, *Justification and Participation*, 100.

48. Ibid., 102.

of God's personal reality alone.[49] God could only impute humans as righteous by looking at his own eternal and immutable righteousness dwelling in them.[50] Hence, justification consisted not only of the imputation of the forgiveness of sins won by the death of Christ's human nature, but also of the indwelling of his infinite and eternal divine righteousness.[51] According to Vainio, the Christological implications of this position are clear: "What Christ does is therefore separated from who Christ is."[52]

Flacius did not explicitly develop the theme of the communication of attributes in the manner that Chemnitz did. Nevertheless, it could be argued that he did so implicitly.[53] He writes in his *Concerning Righteousness vs. Osiander* (1552):

> The justice of God, as revealed in the Law, demands of us, poor, unrighteous, disobedient men, two items of righteousness. The first is, that we render to God complete satisfaction for the transgression and sin already committed; the second, that we thenceforth be heartily and perfectly obedient to His Law if we wish to enter life. If we do not thus accomplish this, it threatens us with eternal damnation. And therefore the essential justice of God includes us under sin and the wrath of God . . . Therefore the righteousness of the obedience of Christ, which He rendered to the Law for us, consists in these two features, viz., in His suffering and in perfect obedience to the commands of God.[54]

Osiander had earlier taught that our righteousness before God was divided between Christ's human nature (forgiveness) and his divine nature (positive righteousness). Flacius asserts the fact that humanity is justified both positively and negatively before God through Christ's activity as a single divine-human person. Therefore, what Christ did cannot be divided from what he is. Christ's divine person works positive righteousness in and through his human nature's obedience. The divine person dies through the man Jesus in order to satisfy the infinite judgment of the law.[55]

49. Strehle, *Catholic Roots*, 75–78; Vainio, *Justification and Participation*, 102.
50. Ibid., 99.
51. Ibid., 98–99.
52. Ibid., 99.
53. Ibid., 116n96. Also see Haikola, *Gesetz und Evangelium*, 172–76.
54. Schmid, *Doctrinal Theology*, 354. Also see discussion in Haikola, *Gesetz und Evangelium*, 318–23; Ritschl, *Critical History*, 219–21, 226–29.
55. Some of this material also appears summarized/paraphrased in a somewhat-different form in my earlier publication: Kilcrease, *The Self-Donation of God*.

As I showed in the last chapter's discussion of the work of Christ in Luther's Galatians commentary, Flacius' interpretation of Christ's work as a unified action of his total person is clearly in keeping with Luther's assertions that it was necessary for Christ to render an infinite satisfaction through his humanity. Moreover, the concepts of "active" and "passive" righteousness are in keeping with Luther's statement that Christ is the "only sin" and the "only righteousness" in the same commentary.

Conclusion

From Luther to the theologians of the Age of Orthodoxy, there is a remarkable consistency in their description of the work of Christ. All theologians discussed above held to the doctrine of penal substitution as a corollary of the proper articulation of the doctrine of justification. Although the doctrine of atonement obviously developed over time beyond Luther's formulations, these developments took place under the assumption of principles originally put forth by the Reformer.

Recognizing this continuity is particularly important. As I will show in the coming chapters, many modern Lutheran theologians claim a break between Luther and the later theologians of the confessional writings and the Age of Orthodoxy. However, as can be seen from the previous two chapters' direct engagement with primary texts, this interpretation can by no means be sustained. Although modern theologians are certainly free to criticize the doctrine of substitutionary atonement as articulated by the Lutheran confessions and the theologians of the Age of Orthodoxy, in light of the historical facts discussed above, they cannot call upon Luther in support of their criticisms.

4

Modern Rethinking of the Lutheran Doctrine of Atonement

Moderate Revisionists

Introduction

As I HAVE SHOWN, the Lutheran doctrine of atonement as presented by the theologians of the sixteenth and seventeenth centuries not only remained relatively consistent over time, but stood in complete coherence with the chief article of justification. Moreover, it was the conviction of these theologians that these doctrines were not merely coherent, but that that they were the supreme expression of the infallible teaching of Scripture itself. But if this is the case, why have modern "Lutheran" theologians come to disagree with doctrine of substititionary atonement? In order to understand this, I will examine and offer a short critique of a number of modern Lutheran theological reinterpretations of the work of Christ. It should, of course, also be mentioned in passing that not all modern Lutheran theologians believed that revision was necessary. Theologians such as Francis Pieper, John Schaller, and Adolf Hoenecke all followed the basic structure of the doctrine of atonement established in the *Book of Concord* and upheld by the theologians of the Age of Orthodoxy.[1]

I will first examine a group of moderate revisionists, represented by Werner Elert, Gustaf Aulén, and Gustaf Wingren. In the next chapter, I will

---

1. Hoenecke, *Evangelical Lutheran Dogmatics*, 3:179–217; Pieper, *Christian Dogmatics*, 2:342–82; Schaller, *Biblical Christology*, 135–87.

then discuss a group of radical revisionists represented by Wolfhart Pannenberg, Robert Jenson, and Eberhard Jüngel. Classifying these thinkers as either "moderate" or "radical" has less to do with the content of their theologies than what might characterized as their driving concerns. Whereas the first group of theologians wished to revise the tradition in order to fulfill what they rightly or wrongly believed was the real trajectory of the Lutheran Reformation, the second group mainly wishes to revise the Lutheran theology in light of contemporary secular political and philosophical concerns. Whereas the first group of theologians are still primarily concerned with the question of sin and grace, the second group are far more concerned to justify Christian belief to modern secular audiences.

Werner Elert

Werner Elert (1885–1954) was a theologian and scholar of Luther at the University of Erlangen. In order to examine Elert's theology of atonement, I will focus on one of his shorter works, entitled *Law and Gospel*. Among the theologians examined, Elert tends to be by far the least willing to revise the position of the Lutheran confessors and scholastics. Distinct from many of his contemporaries (as will be shown in the next section, Aulén being foremost among them), Elert had a relatively positive assessment of the sixteenth- and seventeenth-century Lutheran theology of atonement, as evidenced by his magnum opus, *The Structure of Lutheranism*.[2]

In this shorter work on law and gospel, Elert attacks the early twentieth-century Reformed theologian Karl Barth and the theology of the Barmen Declaration for reducing all of God's words to a single word of grace.[3] Indeed, Barth contended that the fact that God even speaks to us is grace. But Elert argues that this position destroys the integrity of the biblical message: "[The] statement of the Decalogue about God visiting the iniquities of the fathers upon the children has some significance. 'God threatens to punish' is the way Luther interprets this, and without a doubt he is correct."[4] This does not mean that these words of judgment are intended to be ends in themselves. Law is always ordered towards promise, insofar as the second

---

2. Elert, *The Structure of Lutheranism*, 106–17.

3. Elert, *Law and Gospel*, 4–5. (This is a translation of Zwischen Gnade und Ungnade). Elert is responding to the following work by Barth: "Gospel and Law," 71–100.

4. Elert, *Law and Gospel*, 6.

use of the law is the chief one. Nonetheless, law is not grace and grace is not law.

Elert moves on to discuss the distinction between law and gospel, something he sees very clearly rooted in the ministry of Jesus. In the Gospels, Christ came to both fulfill and intensify the law.[5] Nevertheless, though Christ performed this work of the law, his proper office is one of reconciliation. Christ's use of the law is ultimately in the service of the gospel.[6] Christ used the law in order to uncover unrighteousness, thereby demonstrating to his contemporaries that not one of them was righteous. Those who claimed to be righteous were able to play at being sinless before Jesus revealed true righteousness through the proper preaching of the law.[7] By contrast, Christ crossed many social and cultural boundaries in order to show grace and mercy to the weak and sinners. To many, this made Christ appear as if he was in fact a sinner, when he was not.[8]

The ministry of Jesus therefore had three consequences. First, sinners who encountered Jesus came to recognize that he was not a sinner. Purity, truth, and innocence cannot therefore be conveyed to us by abstract dogmas or commandments, but rather must ultimately come through a person; that is, the person of Christ: "They are the criteria of human personhood, and there is no other person in whom they assume visual form for us than the person of Christ." The second consequence is that an absolute difference between Christ and those with whom he associates himself becomes evident. Humanity comes to recognize that they are wholly sinful in relation to Christ: "It is a total difference, the difference between the whole Christ and the whole man—as a sinner." The third consequence is that, as a result of the first two revelations, humans who are united with Christ through faith come to recognize themselves as sinners "in truth."[9] In other words, a person is something "in truth" according to Elert, when he ceases to engage in the hypocritical attempt to be something that he is not, and finally admits his true status as a sinner. Hence, a mere encounter with the person of Christ may fulfill the convicting function of the law.

In light of these implications and distinctions, Elert moves on to discuss how we should understand the death of Christ. Humanity is caught

   5. Ibid., 18–19.
   6. Ibid., 19.
   7. Ibid., 20–21.
   8. Ibid., 21–25.
   9. Ibid., 23.

up in what he refers to as "nomological" existence. Nomological existence means that humanity exists under the law and its ethos of retribution and self-justification. Christ's ministry transcended the law by reaching out to sinners without consideration of their guilt. Those who adhered to the ethos of the law and sought their own self-justification through it, administered the death of Jesus. They killed Christ in order to "help the law against the promise." Nonetheless, Christ's death was also an act of God's retributive wrath, since the law without the gospel not only consigns humanity to a cycle of self-justification, but works God's wrath against sin.[10]

The cross both exposes and judges humanity's nomological existence: "[The] death of Christ is judgment. God is here administering justice according to the law of retribution. Here the nomological being of mankind is not only exposed in its falsehood, but, because expiation must occur right here, it is mortally wounded."[11] The law is undone by being fulfilled once and for all. Since the law works divine wrath through retribution (this is true of civil and divine justice), its fulfillment necessitated a final and definitive act of retribution on God's part.

In this sense, the death of Jesus can function as both law and gospel. It is a fulfillment of the promise of God to redeem from the power of law as foreshadowed in the suffering servant songs.[12] Considered in itself alone, it is only law in that it represents God's absolute judgment of sin through the cross. Only through the resurrection does God vindicate Jesus' enactment of a new order of forgiveness. In this new order of grace, the voice of the law is utterly abolished. In fact, "the law no longer has any voice whatsoever."[13] By this, Elert does not mean that Christians are no longer to be obedient to God's commands in the kingdom of the world (a point upon which he is quite clear in *The Christian Ethos*[14]). Rather, Elert is merely claiming that, in relationship to the question of salvation, God's law no longer condemns the Christians.

---

10. Ibid., 28.
11. Ibid., 29.
12. Ibid., 29–30.
13. Ibid., 30.
14. See discussion in Elert, *The Christian Ethos*, 49–135.

Evaluation

Although Elert's position appears to be similar to Luther, the Lutheran confessors, and the seventeenth-century scholastics, there are some notable differences. For Elert, there is more of an emphasis on Jesus' earthly ministry than in the aforementioned theologians. Also, in contrast—particularly to Chemnitz—there is little reflection on the relationship between the unity of divinity and humanity in Christ and the execution of his redemptive work. Otherwise, Elert largely upholds the traditional Lutheran doctrine of atonement, albeit in an incomplete manner.

Gustaf Aulén

Much like Werner Elert, the Swedish Lutheran bishop Gustaf Aulén (1879–1977) possessed throughout most of the twentieth century a good reputation within both Lutheran and ecumenical circles as a theologian and historian of dogma. His best-known work, *Christus Victor*, represents something of a hybrid between theological reflection on the nature of atonement and the history of the doctrine from Christian antiquity to the present.[15] Since the second chapter addressed much of his thesis and historical conclusions regarding atonement, here the focus will be on his dogmatic treatment of the nature of atonement as described in his systematic theology, *The Faith of the Christian Church*.

At the end of *Christus Victor*, Aulén expresses his strong dislike of both the "Latin" or "Penal" theory of atonement and the moral influence theory, due to what he considers to be their rationalistic underpinnings.[16] Both theories, claims Aulén, take metaphysical speculation about the abstract nature of God as their starting point. Both theories try to establish some sort of rational mechanism as the basis of reconciliation between God and human beings. According to Aulén, a proper Christian understanding of atonement needs an image and not a rationalistic theory, something that (according to him) was recognized by both Luther and the church fathers.[17]

Nevertheless, Aulén believes contemporary dogmatics should not rely too much on the past. He asserts that one cannot simply use the old images

---

15. Aulén, *Christus Victor*.
16. Ibid., 154–59.
17. Ibid., 158–59.

for the victory of Christ from the church fathers.[18] The image of Christ as a ransom or snare to Satan is not suitable for modern people. It will not express to them (as perhaps it did to the original audience faced by the church fathers) the victory of Christ over the dark forces that ensnare them in the contemporary world. The victory motif is capable of being expressed through a number of different images. One cannot dictate what forms will be used to express the victory of Christ in the future. Nevertheless, the basic truth of the conquest motif (namely, that Christ entered creation in order to overcome demonic forces) remains valid for the contemporary church.[19]

Aulén attempts to do something very much like this proposed updating of the victory motif in his later systematic theology, *The Faith of the Christian Church*. First, according to Aulén, in describing the incarnation, the accent must lie very heavily on the fact that it was God himself who was the subject of the incarnation. Therefore, God must ultimately be seen as the one acting in the work of reconciliation: "Reconciliation between the two hostile parties is based entirely on the activity of one party, the God of love." The God of love does not simply wave a magical wand and create a new relationship with his creation—rather, he must enter the heat of conflict for its redemption: "If we are to investigate how Christian faith understands the meaning of the work of Christ finished on the cross, we must first of all note the motif of struggle and victory revealed here. The divine will carry out its purpose through bitter struggle with hostile forces."[20] In this regard, Aulén observes the ubiquitous theme of Jesus' conflict with demonic forces throughout the New Testament. The conflict motif describes Christ as entering into a *mirabile duellum*, that is, "a wonderful struggle."[21] The object of Christ's struggle is evil itself. Evil is, when properly understood, merely the antithesis of the divine will of love: "Since the divine will is radically antagonistic to evil and since God cannot therefore be reconciled to evil, this reconciliation entails the destruction of the power of evil and its dominion."[22]

Much like Luther, Aulén argues that God works through the dark powers of the old creation as his masks (in Latin, *larva Dei*). However, "hostile power cannot serve the divine will except in so far as the divine will overcomes it and turns it into good." Recognizing our subjection to

---

18. Ibid., 158–59.
19. Ibid., 159.
20. Aulén, *The Faith of the Christian Church*, 199.
21. Ibid., 200. This is Luther's phrase.
22. Ibid., 201.

demonic forces, we come to understand ourselves as standing under the threat of divine judgment. This prepares us for divine love and grace: "The religious point of view hidden behind the drastic figures is that the loving will of God prepares a way for itself through judgment."[23]

Aulén now delineates the main point of his theory of atonement: that divine love overcomes divine wrath and law. For when "the law and wrath are included among the destructive powers, the concept of reconciliation becomes even more profound."[24] Unlike the theory of penal substitution, where the legal and rational order simply persists in a new form,[25] divine love becomes manifest in a new way: "Under these circumstances the 'victory over the law' means that divine love in Christ breaks through the legal order of justice and establishes a new order in the relationship between God and man."[26] Aulén feels that this is the best explanation of atonement that we can give; namely that, in Christ, divine love simply persists and overcomes divine wrath:

> The overcoming of wrath means, in this analysis, that the inmost nature of God, the divine love, "the blessing," makes a way for itself through wrath, "the curse." This occurs when Christ submits to wrath and bears the burden it imposes, or, in other words, through the self-giving sacrifice of love. Divine wrath is thus "reconciled"; it is, so to speak, fused with love. But this act of atonement through which wrath is reconciled is at the same time a divine act, the act of divine love itself. It is hardly possible to penetrate deeper into the mystery of the atonement. The act of reconciliation appears with crystal clarity as the victory of divine love itself. But it remains nevertheless a mystery, the mystery of divine love.[27]

Overall, Aulén holds that this idea gives real depth to the idea of the atonement, rather than rendering it "superficial"[28] as in the penal theory. For Aulén, the mystery of redemption remains a mystery. The image of victory therefore provides a narrative of the triumph of divine love, rather than a rational theory.

23. Ibid., 202.
24. Ibid., 202.
25. Ibid., 210.
26. Ibid., 203.
27. Ibid., 204.
28. Ibid., 204.

Evaluation

Although it is certainly admirable that Aulén attempted to resist the unfortunate rationalistic tendencies of many theologians, his theology of atonement ultimately fails. First of all, the need for the law to be fulfilled and the irreconcilability of the holiness of God and sin are not rationalistic abstractions to Aulén. Rather, they are the underlying assumptions of all the biblical authors. Indeed, it is the presupposition of all accounts of redemption in the Old and New Testament is that the law must be fulfilled in order that redemption might be achieved. For example, Paul's argument in the first few chapters of Romans would make very little sense if it was unnecessary to fulfill the law. Hence, simply saying that God's wrath and grace have striven with one another, and, for whatever reason, grace has triumphed, does not remotely do justice to the biblical material. The biblical authors give a clear witness to the fact that the Law has been overcome by the gospel means of Christ's fulfillment of the Law on the cross (see Isa 53, Rom 3:25, 2 Cor 5:21, and 1 Pet 2:24, to name only a few verses).

Secondly, Aulén's account undermines the assurance that the gospel brings. If, for no apparent reason, God's love has simply overcame his wrath at some point in human history, what is there to guarantee the sinner that God's wrath will simply not at some future point overcome his love? Ironically, Aulén makes God's wrath and love into abstractions. For Aulén, love and wrath are abstract forces that mysteriously strove with one another. In the Bible, though, God's wrath and love are embodied in the two words of law and gospel. Both words possess clearly articulated promises to which God must be faithful in the concrete history of redemption if he is indeed truthful. If God abandoned his promise to punish sinners (Deut 32:35, Rom 12:19) by fiat, then there would be no reason to suppose that he might not again capriciously change his mind and abandon the gospel of love as well?

Ultimately, then, for the love of the gospel to be real, sinners must be assured that God acted out of love, in a way that permanently neutralized his wrath. If one posits that the gospel has left the law unfulfilled, then there would always be a possibility that the law might return again and destroy the gospel's promise. For this reason, Aulén fails to articulate an appropriate doctrine of atonement.

The Doctrine of Atonement

Gustaf Wingren

I will last turn to the theology of the Swedish Lutheran theologian Gustaf Wingren (1910–2000). While Wingren's main interests centered on the doctrine of creation, he nevertheless had many valuable things to say regarding the work of Christ and its relationship to the article of creation. One of Wingren's consummate concerns was the denigration of the doctrine of creation within twentieth-century continental Protestant theology. In his classic work *Creation and Law*, Wingren blames Karl Barth and dialectical theology in general for the persistence of this trend.[29] Within the articles of the creed and narrative presented to us in Sacred Scripture, creation comes before redemption. Therefore, if it is the task of Christian theology to properly describe God and his works on the basis of biblical revelation, then God is known first as creator, and only secondly as redeemer. By contrast, on an existential level, humanity receives knowledge of God as redeemer through the preaching of the gospel, and then only subsequently knows God as creator. The irony of Barth's theology and the other dialectical theologians is that, by placing the second article first in their exposition of dogma, they continue the tradition of theological Liberalism by making the human subject's experience of redemption primary: "Man and his knowledge determine the Creed, and not God and His works." Ultimately, then, in Barth and the works of theologians like him, "the anthropocentric character [of their theology] is unbroken."[30]

This nevertheless provokes the following question: how does placing the article of creation first position the work of redemption in its proper light? Much like Luther, Wingren believes the law functions through the medium of the created order. God works via his creaturely masks (*larva Dei*) in accordance with his will of law. The reality of the law present in these masks has the positive role of preserving creation through the created orders (family, state, and church).[31] Nevertheless there is also a negative side to God's activity in these means: humanity's inexorable and unrelenting experience of divine judgment. When a person is forced by the authorities to perform certain acts in accordance with God's law, his conscience is necessarily accused. When egocentric humans are deprived of that which they most desire, they feel the accusation of the law. Indeed, a person's everyday conduct "reveals that his heart is godless. We might say that man's

---

29. Wingren, *Creation and Law*, 12–14.
30. Ibid., 12.
31. Ibid., 149–73. Also see Wingren, *Luther on Vocation*.

conscience has a continual foretaste of the Last Judgment."[32] In this sense, also, the emphasis of Barth and the dialectical theologians upon the unknowability of God apart from revelation is meaningless. The real issue is not the knowledge of God, but rather whether or not saving knowledge of God is attainable.

In spite of the fact that the world has become a realm of unrelenting judgment, creation in and of itself remains good and is an object of God's redemptive love. Redemption is necessary because fallen humanity suffers the enslavement of sin, death, the devil, and the law. Ultimately, the human race must be freed by God's conquest of the demonic forces of the old creation. In his book *The Living Word*, which strikes a similar note to Aulén, Wingren frequently uses the motifs of conquest and new creation to discuss the work of Christ. Early in this work, Wingren argues that the "Bible's theme is the conflict of God and the Devil."[33] Some liberal scholars might object to this idea on the grounds that the devil is not directly mentioned in the earlier books of the Bible. Wingren insists that the absence of Satan has little to do with the lack of the demonic presences in the Old Testament and more to do with the limited horizon of national conflict and apostasy within which early Israel operated. Early Israel's experience of conflict and temptation by the idols of the pagan nations surrounding them was but a microcosm of the cosmic battle between God and the devil. With the advent of the universal horizon of Jewish apocalypticism, Israel (and the church after it) could finally fully understood that the saving work of God was directed against a single demonic force behind the masks of the idols. Hence, Jesus is seen throughout the New Testament as a second Adam and restorer of creation who has entered into conflict with the universal destroyer of creation, Satan.[34]

Therefore, Christ's task as the self-donating God is to free creation, thereby restoring and fulfilling God's original purpose: "Christ's task is to enter human life, destroy satanic might and free man." For Wingren, this is the true implication of the Lutheran understanding of the communication of attributes within the divine-human person of Christ. Christ's humanity does not simply echo God's pre-temporal decrees to us (contra Barth), but is itself the very presence of God entering into the fray of the battle for creation as our champion: "Christ's humanity is no limitation of the majesty of

---

32. Wingren, *Creation and Law*, 174.
33. Wingren, *The Living Word*, 42.
34. Ibid., 42–44.

God, as Barth argues. Christ's humanity is the conqueror's—*God's*—presence on the field of battle where Satan is to be laid low in the conqueror's death and resurrection and forced to let go his grip on men."[35]

Freedom from Satan and the wrath of God necessarily means the death and resurrection of the sinner. God's own presence is manifest not only in the flesh of Christ, but also in the word of judgment and grace that he has given the church to proclaim: "Even in the passage and even in preaching, the *communicatio idiomatum* [the communication of divine and humans attributes within the person of Christ] holds sway." The activity of the word is divine: "The Word of the Bible, carries within itself Christ's coming as its general aim, to which all tends . . . It is in the simple words, in what is human in the Bible, that God's power is hidden; divine and human must not be separated."[36] Therefore, the battle of Christ for creation is continued through God's two words of law and gospel. By God's effective word, old sinners are killed and resurrected as new beings of faith. This is because "'law and grace' is 'death and resurrection.'"[37]

Nevertheless, this explanation of the saving power and presence of God does not specifically describe the means through which redemption is accomplished. Wingren's answer to this question comes in his seminal work, *Gospel and Church*, in which he develops a doctrine of recapitulation. Wingren not only favors this idea because of his engagement with Irenaeus of Lyon (the fruit of which was his masterful study *Man and the Incarnation*[38]), but because of his earlier use of Luther's theme of the unity of law and creation. If the biblical word of law expresses the pattern of God's ordering, judging, and coercing activity in creation, then a redemptive fulfillment of the law on behalf of humanity must also logically mean the recapitulation and renewal of creation. Similarly, if the demonic forces that enslave creation are God's masks and instruments of his wrath against sin, then fulfillment of the law would logically conqueror the tyrants who hold creation in their sway.

Recapitulating Adam, Jesus enters into the place of sinful humanity: "*As man* Christ stands under the law. Under the law and under wrath Christ lives the life of Adam, i.e. our human life, which means that He is tempted." In his descent to human existence Christ did not merely assume

---

35. Ibid., 32.
36. Ibid., 208.
37. Ibid., 137.
38. See Wingren, *Man and the Incarnation*.

human nature, but also entered into all the terrors humans face under the tutelage of the hidden God: "In His temptation He is divested of His divinity in such a way that in the end it is His dread in the presence of God which binds Him to God." Indeed, he was tempted like Adam to seek divinity and not to take upon himself the form of the servant. Perpetually confronted by temptation, Christ's obedience to the Father grew ever deeper throughout his temporal life: "His temptations come to a climax in Gethsemane and on the cross." His obedience actualizes what Adam should have been as a creature, and as such breaks the power of wrath and the law: "In the life which He lived as a man Christ succeeded in rendering obedience, even though he had 'emptied Himself.' And this obedience broke the power of the law and did away with wrath." His victory is manifested in the resurrection: "The uncorrupted life is free from the law and therefore from death. But this life has been realized only in the resurrection of Christ. Humanity is to be found only in the one who rose on the third day, and if we would attain humanity we must seek it from Him."[39]

Christ's obedience is salvific precisely because he himself is the very presence of God. Wingren coordinates his description of Christ's human obedience with the Lutheran doctrine of the communication of attributes within the person of Christ. God acted from within Jesus' human ministry that: "The power of His divinity to destroy the dominion of the law is effective even in his humiliation, for His humiliation is obedience that puts an end to the law and to wrath."[40] Indeed, "God's freedom from the law and His power to create are not in effect apart from Christ's human conflict." Hence, God manifests his divinity in, under, and with Christ's humanity by redeeming, recapitulating, and recreating the world from within. For "[a]s *God* Christ is at work in begetting and creating in others the life which they themselves do not possess. Adam did not have the power to create even in his God-appointed state of purity."[41] He re-creates humanity by his effective word of forgiveness: "Since the dominion of death and the destruction of human life arose in man's disobedience and yielding to temptation, Christ brings His creative power to bear at the critical point when He forgives sins. His divinity was to be seen in his earthly life in His forgiving of men their sins." Therefore, Christ's divinity immanent in his humanity (*genus majestaticum*) broke the power of the law: "And it is manifest that His of-

39. Wingren, *Gospel and Church*, 95.
40. Ibid., 96–97.
41. Ibid., 97.

fer to forgive sins annuls the judgment which the law passes against man. But He began to break the power of the law even before His death, and in this we see His divine nature revealed." The power of his resurrection then enacts the freedom of the new creation. This freedom is freedom from the condemnation of the law: "His resurrection has an added factor which marks it off from the resuscitation of others who were dead, viz. the offer of forgiveness. This is the heart of His resurrection."[42]

Evaluation

From the perspective of the confessional Lutheran paradigm, it is very difficult to find much problematic in Wingren's account. Although the accent falls very heavily on Christ's conquest of demonic forces in his understanding of atonement, nevertheless there is an acknowledgement on the author's part that it was necessary for Christ to fulfill the law as a substitute for sinners. If one was to be critical of Wingren on this point, it should be observed that, much like Elert's account, there is unfortunately little use of the theme of Christ's unique ability to fulfill the infinite demand of the law based on his divine-human reality. As I argued earlier, this was an important theme in the work of Luther, Melanchthon, and Chemnitz. It also played a significant role in the orthodox Lutheran response to Osiander.

In light of these facts, Wingren's approach is merely revisionist insofar as it seeks to highlight the themes of recapitulation and conquest in ways that the later Lutheran confessional authors and scholastics tended not to. It should be said, though, that his use of these themes does not contradict their descriptions of atonement. Moreover, as I have shown, the conquest motif is present in Luther (particularly in his account of atonement in the Large and Small Catechisms); Wingren's account helpfully gives a greater emphasis to a particular confessional and biblical theme that was sometimes downplayed because of the necessities of certain polemical situations (i.e., the Osianderian controversy, etc.). Although Wingren's theology cannot be considered orthodox in every regard (for example, his indefensible rejection of the inerrancy of the Bible), there is much value in his thought for confessional Lutherans.

---

42. Ibid., 96.

5

Modern Rethinking of the Lutheran Doctrine of Atonement

Radical Revisionists

Introduction

WOLFHART PANNENBERG, ROBERT JENSON, and Eberhard Jüngel represent a radically revisionist Lutheran atonement theology. Their revisionism may be characterized as "radical" insofar as they consistently subordinate the traditional Lutheran theological concern for the question of salvation, to more secular and philosophical ones. For the most part, these thinkers are concerned with finding a theological criterion which will make Christianity more plausible to a modern secular audience.[1] In the process, the gospel tends to be either eclipsed or mutilated.

Wolfhart Pannenberg

Among the many modern "Lutheran" theologians who have sought major revisions to the Lutheran paradigm, the German theologian Wolfhart Pannenberg (1928–2014) holds a significant place. Starting with the publication of *Revelation as History*[2] in the early 1960s, Pannenberg has

---

1. Mark Mattes has made a similar argument regarding these theologians' doctrine of justification. See Mattes, *Role of Justification*.

2. Pannenberg et al., *Revelation as History*.

distinguished himself as a significant voice in twentieth-century German Protestant theology. One major reason for this is the uniqueness of his approach to the task of systematic theology. Notably, Pannenberg's theology is in large measure a reaction against both Liberal Protestantism and dialectical theology, both of which he believed failed to create an objective basis for dogmatics as a universal science.[3] In order to solve this difficulty, Pannenberg has sought to create a post-foundationalist dogmatics based on universal history and eschatology.[4] This move did not come about in a vacuum, but was heavily influenced by his context. Alister McGrath has noted that Pannenberg's theological project germinated within the soil of post-World War II West Germany. In this context, the political philosophy of Marxism, which placed eschatological hope within the sphere of historical development, provided an outlet for a profound sense of collective social alienation.[5] McGrath claims that Pannenberg sought to offer a Christian alternative to Marxism's secular eschatology.

As a result, Pannenberg's concept of the work of Christ, is bound up with his theology of history. His mature position is set down in his *Systematic Theology* of the early 1990s.[6] However, the position presented there is in actuality nothing but a further embellishment and development of his views in the now classic *Jesus: God and Man* (1964).[7]

Unlike Barth and other Protestant theologians of the twentieth century, Pannenberg lacks an aversion to natural theology. For Pannenberg, when understood properly, theology is a rational enterprise by its very nature. Not unlike for the theology of Thomas Aquinas,[8] Pannenberg believed that, for the dogmatic enterprise to be "rational," practitioners must recognize the unit of all truth. It therefore seeks its own coherence with other forms of human knowledge.[9] A general awareness of divinity is recognizable alongside other forms of knowledge present in the human community. Such awareness is universal, and has only in recent centuries

---

3. Grenz, *Reason for Hope*, 17–19.
4. See Shults, *Postfoundationalist Task of Theology*.
5. McGrath, *A Scientific Theology*, 300.
6. Pannenberg, *Systematic Theology*.
7. Pannenberg, *Jesus*.
8. Aquinas writes in the *Summa* that he proper definition of theology is: "All things are dwelt on by this science [theology], yet held in their relationship to God" (*ST* 1a, q. 1, art. 7; BF 1:27).
9. Pannenberg, *Systematic Theology*, 1:17–26.

been challenged. Hence, humanity as a matter of course (though obviously in differing degrees) is aware of God's existence: "By nature, i.e., from creation, God, the God of the apostolic gospel (Rom 1:19–20), is known to all people."[10]

This natural awareness of God does not take the theologian very far, though. In the end, knowledge of the mere existence of divinity does not sort out the question of which divinity is real and true. Therefore, the confirmation and falsification of competing religious claims is the most important task of theology with regard to the question of the true knowledge of God. Following from the rationality of the theological enterprise, religious claims are confirmable or falsifiable in themselves. In the Old Testament, a variety of religious claims were made (YHWH vs. Baal, for example), which could either be confirmed or falsified: "The question of the confirmation or nonconfirmation of belief in a deity, and therefore the truth or untruth of the deity itself, often stands under the competitive pressure of the truth claims of other deities which claim the same sphere of experience of the world as proof."[11] Israel's own history led to greater and greater degrees of confirmation within its historical relationship to YHWH: "In the process an awareness also necessarily developed that each confirmation of faith in God in a[sic] historical situation, each experience of new acts of God, not only sets all that precedes in a new light but also itself proves to be provisional." Nevertheless, due to this provisionality, the question of YHWH's ultimate self-demonstration became a significant problem. That is to say, within this situation the question ultimately arose as to when the God of Israel would definitively confirm his character and status as not only Israel's covenant Lord, but as the universal God of history and creation: "There thus arises the question of a future definitive self-demonstration of the deity of God, a question which arose in Israel especially in exilic prophecy and was later taken up by apocalyptic into expectation of end-time events."[12]

Noting its apocalyptic context, Pannenberg argues that the ministry of Jesus is the eschatological fulfillment of this history of verification: "The eternal deity of the Trinitarian God moves in history toward its final confirmation, and so, too, does the truth of his revelation." As observed earlier, there must be a final and universal revelation of God's deity at the end of history. The apocalyptic tradition of the prophets and of late Second

10. Ibid., 1:107.
11. Ibid., 1:168.
12. Ibid., 1:169.

Temple Judaism understood that this ultimate verification would be tied up with the resurrection of the dead. For this reason, Jesus demonstrates the universal lordship of God in his resurrection.[13] Because he reveals the goal of history in a completed form paradoxically actualized ahead of the end of time by his resurrection, he demonstrates the nature of God's being and his plan for creation: "Jesus Christ, then, is the Word of God as the quintessence of the divine plan for creation and history and of its end-time but already proleptic revelation."[14] This is indeed why Jesus is the *Logos*, that is, the pattern of creation. By demonstrating the universal deity of the God of Israel, he unveils ahead of time the goal and consummation of creation.[15]

Insofar as Jesus serves as God's ultimate self-revelation, he himself must be divine. That which reveals God in itself, must be identical with God. Consequently, the resurrection possesses a "retroactive force" with regard to Jesus' identity. It makes possible a full identification between the Second Person of the Trinity and the man Jesus throughout his earthly ministry. Since the resurrection is the means through which Jesus makes his ultimate revelation of God, without it the identification of Jesus as true God would be impossible.[16] Just as creation is constituted and defined by its goal, so too is the life of Jesus.

In light of this description of the nature of salvation history and the theological task, it is clear that the quest for religious knowledge represents the major overture of Pannenberg's thought. The questions of sin and grace are therefore relegated to a less prominent role, and ultimately do not function as the driving forces that they have typically done so in Lutheran theology. That being said, Pannenberg is still concerned about salvation, and therefore treats the question of atonement to a certain degree in his *Systematic Theology*.

Since, as has been previously noted, eschatology is one of the driving elements of Pannenberg's thought, it should be no surprise that the reconciling work of Christ is interpreted through this lens. Jesus suffered at the hands of the whole human race, represented in his Passion and trials by the Jewish and Roman authorities.[17] The Sanhedrin believed that Jesus' claims were arrogant because they implicitly made him equal with God. For this

---

13. Ibid., 1:332.
14. Ibid., 1:257.
15. Ibid., 1:256.
16. Ibid., 2:365.
17. Ibid., 2:425–26.

Modern Rethinking of Atonement: Radical Revisionists

reason, they handed him over to the Romans to be killed, thereby proving that they themselves were actually guilty of such a charge.[18] In sentencing Jesus to death, the Romans served as the representatives of the Gentiles. When dying on the cross, Jesus took upon himself the proper fate of those who killed him in an act of vicarious and representative suffering: "The man who was handed over as a blasphemer and executed as an agitator suffered death in the place of, and on behalf of, all those who as sinners live in arrogated equality with God and actual rebellion against him and who thus bring death upon themselves."[19]

To be united with Jesus' death, then, is also to participate in his resurrection as the one who opens up the eschatological future: "Representation and expiation do not mean that those who are represented do not have to die themselves." But rather: "those whom Jesus represents have the possibility in their death, by reason of its linking to the death of Jesus, of attaining to the hope of participation in the new resurrection life that has already become manifest in Jesus (Rom 6:5)."[20]

Moreover, Pannenberg claims that his use of the idea of representation does not mean that he relies exclusively on a version of the vicarious satisfaction motif. Rather, he sees Christ's ultimate significance as one who inaugurates a new creation. Indeed, following the description of the Apostle Paul, Christ is most properly to be understood as the "new Adam."[21] In Jesus, the old Adam who is enslaved to sin, separated from God, and barred from the eschatological future "dies in the death of Christ." This death and resurrection is affected by the "whole course of Christ's life." In this sense, like Wingren, Pannenberg finds the concept of recapitulation useful. Through entering into and actualizing the eschatological future, "Jesus Christ is the paradigm of all humanity in its relation to God."[22]

Evaluation

From a confessional Lutheran perspective, Pannenberg's theology is objectionable in a number of respects. First, he makes a series of highly questionable philosophical assumptions. Chief among them is that realities are not

---

18. Ibid., 2:425.
19. Ibid., 2:426–27.
20. Ibid., 2:427.
21. Ibid., 2:430.
22. Ibid., 2:430.

fully themselves apart from fulfilling a particular goal. As can be observed, in Pannenberg's theology this has the effect of making the knowledge of God in Israel only preliminary and uncertain. It also makes Jesus' personal divinity a reality only in an incomplete and provisional sense prior to his resurrection. Although space precludes further details, it suffices to say that both of these claims are foreign to the teaching of Scripture and are instead based primarily on extra-biblical philosophical traditions (the German philosophers Heidegger, Hegel, etc.).

Secondly, as previously noted, Pannenberg's theology is overwhelmingly driven not by a concern about salvation, but by an interest in the means by which rational knowledge of God can be achieved. Though the quest for the true knowledge of God is certainly tied up with question of salvation, Pannenberg's approach in many respects seems to consider the former apart from the latter. For this reason, the subject of theology ceases to be "the sinning human being and the justifying God" (Luther), but God who justifies himself before the rationality of humans.[23] In this sense, Luther's (and Scripture's—see John 20:31, 1 Cor 2:2, Rev 19:10) definition of true theology is reversed. This is not to say, of course, that there is no role for apologetics in theology. Nevertheless, the justification of the sinner and not the apologetic task must be conceptualized as the theologian's central enterprise.

In Pannenberg's rationalistic enterprise, the authority of Scripture and its true witness to the history of salvation cannot be trusted in an ultimate sense. Rather, all theological knowledge must conform to the canon of what Pannenberg views as universal human rationality. In this view, God must conform to the reason of humanity. As a result, not only are the claims of revelation mutilated before the arbitrary criterion of human rationality, but Christ's atoning work also becomes largely tacked on as an afterthought. This is true, even though much of what Pannenberg says about Christ's atoning work is in conformity with the teaching of Scripture. Nevertheless, Christ's primary office becomes a means to provide a genuinely rational knowledge of God, and only secondarily salvation from sin.

Robert Jenson

The American Lutheran theologian Robert Jenson (1928–2017) has a long list of publications amassed over many decades. Nevertheless, instead of

---

23. WA 40.II:328; *LW* 12:311. Cited from Bayer, *Martin Luther's Theology*, 37. Bayer offers similar criticisms of Pannenberg in this section.

describing each of his works in detail, I will primarily focus on the ultimate synthesis of his thinking in his *Systematic Theology* (1997–1999). Examining this work will suffice insofar as Jenson's thought has remained relatively consistent over the decades. Also, his treatment of the issue of atonement in *Systematic Theology* constitutes one of his longer discussions of the subject.

Much like Pannenberg, Jenson's theology is focused on a concept of divine self-actualization within the history of salvation. But in contrast to Pannenberg, Jenson emphasizes that theology is inherently an ecclesial task.[24] That is to say, Jenson wishes to use the foundational biblical narrative of redemption to find the internal, ecumenical coherence of the historical proclamation of the church. As the reader might recall, Pannenberg is primarily interested in the coherence of Christian truth claims with those of the wider human community within the context of universal history. For Jenson, Christian theology operates within the specific communal narrative of the people of God, founded in the biblical history of Israel and the church. By engaging in the theological task, the people of God are able to identify and explain the reality of the one God through their participation in his ongoing narrative. God's self-definition and identification through the exodus of Israel from Egypt and the resurrection of Jesus is foundational to the ongoing narrative.[25]

For Jenson, the structure of being itself is inherently narrative. Therefore, the fullness of God's reality and life only possess their proper character from within the total story of creation and salvation: "Since the Lord's self-identity is constituted in dramatic coherence, it is established not from the beginning but from the end." For this reason, "the biblical God is not eternally himself in that he persistently instantiates a beginning in which he already is all he ever will be; he is eternally himself in that he unrestrictedly anticipates an end in which he will be all he ever could be."[26] Oliver Crisp describes Jenson's concept of God thus: "It is rather as if God exists through time by projecting himself backward in time from his future to his past and present."[27] For this reason, knowledge of the Triune God is properly discerned from the biblical narrative itself. In this narrative, God actualized his being by projecting its reality backward from the fullness of its completed form in the future eschaton.

24. Jenson, *Systematic Theology*, 1:23–26.
25. Ibid., 1:60.
26. Ibid., 1:66.
27. Crisp, "Robert Jenson," 32.

In history, the biblical God identifies himself with Israel to the extent that he becomes an actor within its ongoing drama.[28] Israel's history under the old covenant already anticipated its eschatological fulfillment in Christ. Indeed, Christ was already present as the "narrative pattern in the history of Israel." God chooses to be the God that he is by eternally willing himself to be the man Jesus. Therefore, the pre-incarnate Son gains his identity by being caught up in an eternal movement towards the terminus of the earthly life of Jesus. This movement is determinative of the whole structure and coherence of the Triune being: "What in eternity precedes the Son's birth to Mary is not an unincarnate *state* of the Son, but a pattern of movement within the event of incarnation, the movement to incarnation, as itself a pattern of God's triune life."[29]

In light of the fact that the movement toward incarnation eternally defines the very being of the Son, it logically follows that the Son finds himself exhaustively defined in the narrative of Jesus' earthly life. In Jenson's theology, there is no room for an account of the divinity of the Son existing apart from unity with the man Christ. This is not merely the case for the incarnate Christ (something that confessional Lutherans can agree with Jenson on), but also for the reality of the pre-incarnate Son. Put bluntly, this places Jenson at odds with historic Christian orthodoxy. In keeping with his emphasis on the unity of the Son with the man Jesus (even, in a sense, from eternity), Jenson follows Luther and the Swabian Lutherans of the sixteenth and seventeenth centuries in ardently supporting the absolute omnipresence of Christ's humanity.[30] It nevertheless must be stressed that Jenson only affirms certain aspects of classical Lutheran Christology. In other areas, such as his aforementioned concept of Christ's pre-existence, he deviates from orthodox Lutheranism.

Viewed from the ecumenical intention of Jenson's theology,[31] his Christological proposals are somewhat ironic. Contrary to his intention, at least in respect to Christology, Jenson has reproduced the accent of his particular tradition in an even more pronounced and less ecumenically-friendly form than many of his co-religionists. Recognizing this problem,

---

28. Jenson, *Systematic Theology*, 1:75.
29. Ibid., 1:141.
30. Ibid., 1:203–5.
31. Ibid., 1:23–26.

his former student Colin Gunton has suggested that Jenson might want to consider drawing up a Christology along more ecumenical lines.[32]

This theological framework forms a necessary background for a proper understanding of the work of Christ within Jenson's system. The meaning of the work of Christ comes into focus in light of his history of divine self-actualization. Humanity's true destiny is integration into the life of the Trinity: "God will let the redeemed see him: the Father by the Spirit will make Christ's eyes their eyes. Under all rubrics, the redeemed will be appropriated to God's own being."[33] Therefore, Jenson casts the work of Christ not so much as atonement for sin or defeat of demonic forces, but rather as God's self-identification with sinful humans and his reconciliation with them through their integration with the divine being by way of mystical union. Sin is therefore not so much seen as debt resulting from law-breaking, but as a general state of alienation necessitating re-integration.

Jenson's Christology and theology of atonement conjures up specters of the German philosopher Hegel's "Speculative Good Friday."[34] Put succinctly, according to Hegel, at the beginning of creation God engaged in an act of self-alienation as a means of self-understanding and self-actualization. For Hegel, the crucifixion of Jesus symbolically represents the culmination of this history in which God integrates his opposite (namely, death and nothingness) into himself as a means of fulfilling his being and resolving the tensions of human historical development. From this perspective, the real dilemma of the divine-human relationship is the distance between two opposite metaphysical polarities (being and nothingness, infinitude and finitude, etc.) rather than the question of sin and grace. Hegel's position finds an echo in Jenson. Moreover, for Jenson (as for Hegel), God's activity in history is not really one of pure grace, but is actually a means self-development. Since God needs creation for self-development, Jenson's conception not only calls into question God's own absoluteness (i.e., his identity as God is in some measure dependent on creation), but it also makes God into a rather selfish being using his creatures as a means of finding personal development and fulfillment.[35]

32. Gunton, "Creation and Mediation," 80–94.

33. Jenson, *Systematic Theology*, 2:369.

34. Hegel, *Faith and Knowledge*, 190–91. Also see discussion in Anderson, *Hegel's Speculative Good Friday*.

35. See Hart, *Beauty of the Infinite*, 155–67. Hart defends the historic Christian doctrine of divine immutability by pointing out that much of modern theology makes God incapable of creating and redeeming the world in an act of pure gratuity. In this section,

The Doctrine of Atonement

Entering into a more general discussion of atonement, Jenson first rejects both Anselm's and other theories of substitutionary atonement. For Jenson, atonement must be about our reconciliation with God, rather than his reconciliation with us. Nowhere, claims Jenson, does the New Testament speak about God's reconciliation to us; rather, Jenson claims that it consistently speaks about our reconciliation to God.[36] Similarly, subjective theories of atonement (here Jenson mentions Schleiermacher) are problematic in that they make the communication of consciousness the real goal of redemption. Such conceptions of the work of Christ make no distinction between reconciliation as a subjective and objective event. For the tradition of Liberal Protestantism, Jesus died merely because his vocational duty was to communicate his religious consciousness. He refused to renounce such consciousness and therefore stayed loyal to his divine mission to the end. Nevertheless, he could very well have also communicated said consciousness if he had not died a brutal death. Ultimately, then, it is completely irrelevant whether he died on the cross or "in bed."[37]

Beyond these atonement motifs, Jenson also reviews Gustaf Aulén and his promotion of the conquest motif. Aulén's theological construction is doubtless appealing due to its richness. Among various atonement motifs, the conquest motif is most attractive to Jenson in that it makes the resurrection a true victory.[38] According to Jenson, this makes the conquest motif superior to Anselm's theory of atonement, which makes the resurrection irrelevant because all is already accomplished on the cross.[39] Nonetheless, Jenson believes that conquest motif as explicated by Aulén is deficient for at least two reasons. First, it constructs a theory from "bits of Biblical and Patristic language" while abandoning the actual narrative of Jesus' Passion as witnessed to by the Gospels. Instead, the conquest motif replaces the Gospel narrative with a newly invented story of Jesus' struggle against demonic forces. Secondly, this theory suffers from the weakness of being unable to give a coherent answer to the question of why God bothers to enter into the struggle of redemption in the first place. What sense does it make for Jesus to do battle with Satan, when "victory is easily attained." This

---

Jenson is mentioned as an object of criticism.

36. Jenson, *Systematic Theology*, 1:186.
37. Ibid., 1:187.
38. Ibid., 1:188.
39. Ibid., 1:186.

also creates the similar problem of how what Jesus "does for himself" (i.e., defeating the demonic forces) becomes "actual" for us.[40]

Over against these theories of atonement, Jenson proposes a modified version of Gerhard Forde's view, which is the topic of future chapters. Crucifixion is what it actually "costs" God to remain a loving and forgiving Father. Jesus reveals the Father to us and identifies with us in our sin and brokenness. He wishes for us to share in his relationship with this loving Father. We do not want to share this relationship because we "do not want there to be a Father." The ultimate result of this rejection is the crucifixion of Christ by sinful humanity. Humanity's sinful status is made manifest when Jesus was raised from the dead in the power of the Spirit. We are truly the wicked vineyard keepers of Jesus' parable. Nonetheless, the Son finds "his own identity in the *totus Christus*, in the Son identified with us."[41] This theme of the *totus Christus* (popularized by Augustine and originating with the Donatist Tyconius[42]) is extremely important to Jenson. Classically, the term refers to Christ and the church together as single body and subject, a theme that Jenson exploits in his ecclesiology. This concept has been especially important for the modern Roman Catholic ecclesiologies upon which Jenson often appears to be drawing.[43] Through suffering crucifixion, Jesus identifies to the end with the effects of human sin that are present in the members of his mystical body. He moves to identify with the very depths of human existence and thereby integrates sinful humanity into the life of God.

This brings Jenson to the nature of sacrifice. The idea that Christ's death was a sacrifice is an important idea in the Scriptures, and also in the history of the church. What therefore, asks Jenson, is the meaning and significance of this concept? According to him, we should not exclusively identify sacrifice with propitiation. Rather, we should look at sacrifice as a kind of prayer, one "spoken not only with language, but with words and gestures." Christ's death was a prayer in which he gave himself over to us

---

40. Ibid., 1:188.
41. Ibid., 1:191.
42. See discussion in Bavel, "Church," 170–71.
43. In particular, see Möhler, *Symbolism*; Adam, *The Spirit of Catholicism*. Both theologians exhibit Hegelian/German Idealist influences like Jenson. Incidentally, one can also find the influence of this idea in British converts to Roman Catholicism during the heyday of the Oxford movement. See Manning, *Why I Became a Catholic*, 50. Cardinal Manning writes: "The *Church* has always been conscious that it is the *prolongation* and perpetuity of the *Incarnation*."

in love and prayed for us to the Father. His one prayer incorporates many prayers of his body, the people of God. Jesus' resurrection represents not so much his acceptance, but rather of his body the church as it subsists in him as the *totus Christus*. In the power of his resurrection, Christ now becomes the true priest, able to baptize with the Spirit. The church is reconciled "only when we are actually brought together with him and his Father in one community; that is, in that their communal Spirit becomes that of a community in and by which we live."[44] The resurrection therefore structures the being and identity of the Son, by manifesting him as the true Logos of creation. Echoing Pannenberg, for Jenson, the resurrection confirms Jesus' status as the originator and goal of creation, thereby making him the true Logos of creation.

The demonic forces of the old creation are also defeated by the death of the Son. Although Jenson does not deny that Jesus performed exorcisms and strove with actual demons, he believes that it is more important that Jesus' victory was primarily over the unholy alliance of the high priest and the Roman procurator. This being said, Jenson is reticent about how exactly this victory is accomplished.[45] One may infer that Jenson believes that Jesus' resurrection overcame and defeated the sinful actions of these governing authorities, but he does not directly state this.

Ultimately, for Jenson, the sacrificial and conquest motifs are but minor and passing themes. Moreover, he radically reinterprets them to the point that they cease to have much resemblance to their classical forms. The main accent consistently falls on the Son's integration of humanity into the Trinitarian relationships. This can be observed in how Jenson deals with the resurrection and the overall concept of sacrifice. Reconciliation primarily consists of Christ's identification with humanity. Jesus draws humanity into the inner life of God by the power of his resurrection and giving of the Spirit. In the power of the Spirit, the visible church becomes the prolongation of the incarnation: "The Church is ontologically the risen Christ's human body."[46] Indeed, Jenson goes so far as to state, "the Church is the risen Christ's Ego."[47] In this, the bond of humanity established in the incarnation is universally communicated through the ministry of the church.

---

44. Jenson, *Systematic Theology*, 1:192.
45. Ibid., 1:192.
46. Ibid., 2:213.
47. Ibid., 2:215.

Evaluation

Jenson's account of atonement is probably the most arbitrary among those examined in this chapter. Moreover, Jenson's account is also conspicuous for its extremely tenuous connection to Scripture. Not only are many of Jenson's statements at odds with Scripture, but there is not even the slightest effort on his part to find biblical texts that will back up his doctrinal positions. Rather, Jenson simply states what he feels would be most fitting for the atonement to consist of, and asserts that it must be that way. It is rather like a physicist insisting that it would be "fitting" for the laws of nature to be a certain way and then claiming that this is proof that they are.

In fairness to Jenson, in light of his stated theological method, he would likely claim that he is not being arbitrary. Rather, his doctrine of atonement is simply the one most consistent with the history of the people of God as it is manifest in the continuing evolution of the *totus Christus*. Divine truth as expressed through the structure of the evolving *totus Christus* (and not Scripture in and of itself) is, for Jenson, the ultimate theological criterion. It appears that Scripture only functions as an authority insofar as it is a manifestation of, and cooperates in, the ongoing reality of the work of the Holy Spirit through the life of the Church catholic. That being said, it is unclear on what basis Jenson claims to be able to perceive this ongoing process and its true meaning. Since Jenson appeals to no direct revelation from God for the knowledge of this process or its meaning, it remains at the level of his own arbitrarily chosen way of reading the history of the people of God.

Secondly, although Jenson acknowledges the problem of sin, he does not view it from the perspective of the biblical and confessional authorities as an objective transgression against God's law[48] and an ensuing debt which must be paid for.[49] Rather, his tendency is to reduce sin to a form of alienation from God. Though sin certainly is a condition of alienation from God, the reality of this alienation does not exhaust the reality of sin as it is described by the biblical authority. As a result, Jenson's reductionistic treatment of the problem of sin, the solution to the condition of sin becomes a simple matter of reintegration of the alienated individual with the life of God. Hence, payment for sin as objective transgression becomes unnecessary.

---

48. See for example: John 2:10; 1 John 3:4.

49. See for example: Exod 21:24, 30:12–16; Lev 17:11; Matt 6:9–13; Luke 7:41–50; Rom 6:23; Col 2:14

In this, Jenson's claim that we, and not God, need reconciliation, is deeply problematic. First of all, this makes Jenson's theory of atonement precisely what he has criticized, namely, a Liberal Protestant moral influence theory. If the problem is not God's anger, but rather merely human alienation, then the drift of any system of theology will be toward a form of the moral influence theory of atonement. The reason for this is clear. If the barrier to salvation is not God's wrath, but merely alienation on humanity's part, then the solution to the problem will necessarily always consist in the adjustment of a wrong attitude on the part of humanity toward an already gracious God. Indeed, this is precisely what Jenson's God delivers. Granted, there is also an objective aspect to his theology. The ultimate goal is for sinful humanity to enter into union with God in Christ through ministry of the objective and very highly visible church. Indeed, this is the goal and purpose of the whole history of creation, irrespective of the problem of sin. Nevertheless, this remains essentially subjective insofar as the problem of sin has to do with the failure of the individual to participate in the new creation offered in Christ and his continuing incarnation in the church.

Secondly, Jenson's claim that God does not need to reconcile himself is flatly false when compared to the biblical authority. The whole of the Bible witnesses to the irreconcilability to between God's holiness and human sin. If one merely examines Romans 1–5 by itself, Paul delineates in extreme detail how Jesus' death saves humanity from the wrath of God made manifest in the natural law and further clarified in the Sinaitic covenant. God's anger and judgment against sin cannot simply be ignored as a factor which atonement must address. For the New Testament, God is gracious, not insofar as he is ready to ignore sin the moment that it is committed. Rather, God's grace consists in his willingness to make payment for the debt of sin himself in the person of Jesus.

Eberhard Jüngel

Among recent German Protestant theologians, Eberhard Jüngel (1934–present) has often been ignored within North American theological circles, despite his significant theological prowess. Although Jüngel considers himself to be a Lutheran, as John Webster rightly observes, he has been heavily influenced by the theology of Karl Barth, and therefore has worked in many ways to extend "many of Barth's concerns . . . in some highly original

Modern Rethinking of Atonement: Radical Revisionists

directions."[50] The following discussion focuses on the major contours of his theological agenda and his doctrine of atonement as it is found in *God as the Mystery of the World*.

Much of *God as the Mystery of the World* focuses on the recent history of Western metaphysics and its relationship to the modern phenomenon of atheism. Jüngel's early life under the oppression of the Communist East German regime created in him an abiding interest in atheism.[51] He locates emergence of the possibility of atheism in the writings of Descartes at the very headwaters of modern philosophy.

Jüngel claims Descartes sought to use God to prop up the rational and autonomous human subject. Descartes viewed God as a "necessary being" in that he was a necessary presupposition of present order of the world. Most importantly, God was a necessary presupposition for the existence of the rational and autonomous self.

For those unfamiliar, in his seminal text, *The Meditations on First Philosophy*, Descartes claims that he can doubt everything, but not that he himself exists as a doubting, and therefore thinking, subject. Hence the famous dictum: "I think, therefore I am" (in Latin, *cogito, ergo sum*). From this, Descartes builds up a theory of knowledge on the basis of his own self-awareness, a pattern followed by much of modern Western philosophy. Descartes notes that he is aware of the idea of God as a supreme being and of other "clear and distinct ideas" (i.e., mathematics, etc.). Because only God could cause the idea of God, God must exist. Since God is perfect and good, he would never want to deceive the human subject. From this, it follows that the clear and distinct ideas in the human mind are a completely valid means for engaging reality.[52]

As can be observed, for Descartes, idea of God is a means of guaranteeing the possibility of human freedom and rationality apart from any divine revelation. The rational and autonomous human subject is supreme, and God comes second as a means of securing the self. From this, Jüngel concludes that, in Descartes's philosophy, the act of "[t]hinking claims that God is necessary in order to be able to secure the continuity of the ego with his help."[53]

---

50. Webster, "Systematic Theology after Barth," 250.
51. Ibid., 251.
52. See Descartes, *The Meditations on First Philosophy*.
53. Jüngel, *God as the Mystery of the World*, 116.

Moreover, Descartes' skeptical subject is able to affirm continuity and existence of the self on the basis of the ability to doubt. It makes itself the ultimate arbitrator of truth and falsehood. God's existence and goodness function as the foundation of rational thought and trustworthy senses.[54] Likewise, it also follows from this that Descartes only succeeds in the "securing of the continuity (unity) of human existence by doubting God." For "[i]f God is really to be able to provide this assurance, which doubt itself cannot provide, then God must be put in doubt and in the process be secured." Indeed, "[t]o that extent, a methodological will to atheism" does belong to this second meaning of the proposition that God must be doubted in order to assure the continuity of human existence."[55]

Ultimately the Cartesian concept of the self and God created several philosophical/theological problems. The first major difficulty was that Descartes pushed the self and its continuity onto center stage, while essentially God became a secondary means of securing the subjective self. The second problem with Cartesian philosophy was that it constructed a philosophical concept of God, whose primary characteristic was his reality as a mind "infinitely superior to the world."[56] In other words, God became merely a larger version of the autonomous and rational self. As a superior version of the autonomous human, God's sovereignty must inevitably push up against the freedom of the human subject. The ultimate result is that the human person must now compete with God in order to secure his own freedom.

According to Jüngel, by the time of Nietzsche, the meaning and autonomy of human existence could only be secured by rejecting the existence of God. Jüngel claims Nietzsche fulfilled the process begun with Descartes, because "Nietzsche understood that the consequence of the Cartesian concept of existence can be emphasized against Descartes only in such a way that the 'ego' which decides existence also decides the divine being"; in the end, "[t]o be able to decide about God means, however, to have made the decision already that there can be only one 'ego' which decides about existence and being, and thus God must be done away with."[57] In Nietzsche's philosophy, the autonomous self becomes God. Morality is merely a power-play by the weak designed to humiliate the strong and self-secure.[58]

54. Ibid., 116–18.
55. Ibid., 122.
56. Ibid., 141.
57. Ibid., 141.
58. For example, see Nietzsche, *On the Genealogy of Morals*.

God then, in the modern period, becomes unbelievable because he stands as a competitor with the human. The self-sufficient, rational, and autonomous human being has already been effectively defined as divine, which calls into question the existence of any other deity. In this regard, John Webster is correct to observe that "[a]theism [in Jüngel's thinking] becomes synonymous with the rejection of one particular tradition of theistic metaphysical doctrine."[59] In other words, according to Jüngel, Western atheism parasitically exists as a rejection of a form of philosophical theism that emerges from the early modern period.

Jüngel's solution to this problem is, in a sense, to agree with the atheists. No one should believe in the artificially constructed God of modern philosophy. He is a false idol with no actual reality. Instead, we must place our faith in the Triune God of the Bible. This God defines himself through the cross and empty tomb. Such a God does not merely prop up the current possibilities of the world, but rather provides eschatological possibilities to the world that transcend its current order. In this, he is not merely a "necessary being," but a "more than necessary being."[60]

Ultimately, in contrast to the God of modern metaphysics, his most significant ontological characteristics are his relationality and loving condescension in the cross.[61] The cross and the empty tomb are a revelation and actualization of eternal divine self-differentiation in history. In other words, God's willingness to be the relational and loving God actualized in the life of Jesus has eternally determined the reality of the Triune God.

In the act of dying on the cross, Jesus, the true Son of God, concretely differentiates himself from the Father. The distinction between the Father and the Son is revealed and actualized in the Father's abandonment of Jesus on the cross.[62] Indeed, "[i]n this sense, God's identification with the dead Jesus implies a self-differentiation on God's part. The being of this dead man defines God's own being in such a way that one must speak of a differentiation between God and God."[63] His simultaneous unity and differentiation is confirmed by the resurrection.[64] The Holy Spirit (in a typically

---

59. Webster, *Eberhard Jüngel*, 82.
60. Ibid., 24.
61. Ibid., 220–23.
62. Ibid., 368–73.
63. Ibid., 363.
64. Ibid., 368–73.

Augustinian fashion[65]) reveals himself to be the bond of love and unity between the Father and the Son when he raises the Son from the dead.[66] This Trinitarian event of redemption both unveils and shapes the eternal relationships among the persons of the Trinity. The biblical God is truly an "event God."[67] The entity that God eternally is, and has in fact decided to be, may be read off its actualization in the earthly life of Jesus through an "Analogy of Advent."[68] God has eternally willed himself to be precisely a God defined by the events of the cross and the empty tomb. There is no room for a "hidden God" (as in Luther) apart from God's loving and redeeming activity.[69] Jüngel's concept of the "Analogy of Advent" possesses many similarities with Karl Barth's concept of the "Analogy of Faith."[70]

Jüngel's belief that the cross is constitutive of God's eternal life as Trinity also shapes his understanding of the redemptive work of Christ. He seeks an overall coherence between the self-actualization of God and Jesus' ministry among sinners. According to Jüngel, Jesus' "proclamation and behavior made the law a problem because he changed the role of the person who is subjected to the demands of the law: the role of the person who is active is changed into the role of the person who first receives. Jesus proclaimed [the gospel] because we had already received from God all things, it was precisely false to attribute anything to our own works." In doing this, "Jesus' freedom with the law was completely defined by the way in which the nearness of God laid claim on him, a nearness which admits of no competition."[71] As the infinitely powerful and loving God, Jesus was able to enter into relationship with sinners and free them from the condemnation of the law.

Therefore, Christ not only proclaimed the gospel, but enacted it by bearing human sin. This, of course, raises the question of the nature of sin. According to Jüngel, the sin that Jesus bears is our "godlessness" and our "God-forsakenness."[72] The essence of sin is the relationless-ness brought to

---

65. See discussion in TeSelle, "Holy Spirit," 434–37.

66. Jüngel, *God as the Mystery of the World*, 374–76.

67. Ibid., 368.

68. Ibid., 285. See general discussion in Ibid., 285–98.

69. Jüngel is, in fact, quite critical of Luther's doctrine of the hidden God. See Jüngel, "The Revelation of the Hiddenness of God," 120–44.

70. See *CD* 1.1.276. For discussion, see Hunsinger, *How to Read Karl Barth*, 6, 8, 20.

71. Jüngel, *God as the Mystery of the World*, 365.

72. Ibid., 367.

expression by both of these adjectives. As the loving and self-donating God, Jesus is ultimately free to enter into this forsakenness and relationless-ness, taking it upon himself, and thereby conquering it.

In Jesus' earthly ministry, he entered into conflict with the law's false promise as a source of life. Indeed, Jüngel notes that "the conflict with the law which he provoked is decided in his own person." Jesus "suffers the death which the law foresees for the godless because he identifies with this godlessness as such." Jüngel argues that it is proper in this sense to call him a substitute for sin, because he took all relationless-ness and godlessness upon himself.[73] This is the "turning point of the world, because God has interposed himself in the midst of fatal God-forsakenness in order to create a new relationship with God." By placing himself in union with these destructive realities, God is able to absorb and conquer them: "The being of love unites love and death in that the event of love goes beyond itself."[74] This destroys human relationless-ness because it integrates humanity into the Trinitarian relatedness, thereby saving humanity from meaninglessness and isolation embodied in the forsakenness of the cross.

Evaluation

When examining Jüngel's writings, one is struck by his skill of analysis and his creativity in dealing with any number of theological topics. One must ultimately admire Jüngel's intellectual gifts, irrespective of whether one ultimately comes to agree with his conclusions. Moreover, there is much to be lauded in his interpretation of modern philosophy and its relationship to the development of theological problems over the last few centuries. That being said, his account of atonement has a number of difficulties from the perspective of the confessional Lutheran paradigm.

First of all, Jüngel is correct that, in the modern period, Enlightenment thinkers posited the autonomous human being in opposition to God. The consequence was for modernity to render the very idea of God unbelievable. Nevertheless, Jüngel's belief that competition between God and the autonomous self is the result of a false conception of God is on different levels of analysis, both correct and mistaken. On the one hand, Jüngel is correct to see that God's love and grace as they are encountered in the crucified and risen Christ enables true human freedom. For this reason,

73. Ibid., 367.
74. Ibid., 222.

contrary to the assumption of many modern thinkers, God, when encountered in the gospel, is in fact the author, and not a threat to true human freedom and dignity. True freedom is freedom from the condemning effect of the law. Because the gospel enables this freedom and allows the creature to interact with God in a new way (as a giver of every good and not as a condemning judge), it grants true and authentic freedom to enjoy the good, both here now, and then later in eternity.

Nevertheless, as God encountered in the condemning effect of the law (apart from his love manifest in Christ) he is most certainly a threat to the autonomous post-Enlightenment individual. This is because, apart from Christ, God condemns all who put themselves in his place by claiming independence from him. God as he is manifest in his hiddenness, law, and wrath must necessarily crush all such attempts at independence, as Paul clearly teaches in Romans 1. As Paul also shows in that same chapter, this condemning activity on God's part simply hardens sinners in their opposition, something that might be discerned in the shift from the deism of the early Enlightenment to the outright atheism of much of the modern period. Therefore, contrary to what Jüngel suggests, from the perspective of the law and hiddenness of God, modern individuals are correct to see God as one who threatens their personal fulfillment and autonomy.

Ultimately, Jüngel should recognize that, because God interacts with the world in two different ways (law and gospel), his wrath apart from Christ forms a necessary presupposition of the gospel. If God defined his relationship to the world as love alone (as Jüngel seemingly claims), what condemning effect can the law have, and therefore, how can it be proclaimed? More problematic, since within this scheme the gospel singularly defines God's relationship with the world, it ceases to offer salvation from the law and its condemnation which remain operative outside of word and sacrament. Rather, it simply describes who God is ("Analogy of Advent") and then invites believers to conform to this reality. Hence, without the juxtaposition of the second use of the law, the gospel itself becomes a new law.[75] Moreover, much like Pannenberg, this distortion of the law and the gospel is largely rooted in a desire to construct an apologetic theology that will justify God before humans, rather than humans before God.

When it comes to the actual description of atonement, Jüngel's account has some merit, but it also remains incomplete. As was observed with

---

75. These and other very similar criticism can be found in Paulson, *Analogy and Proclamation*.

Luther, it is appropriate to think of Christ as having overcome human alienation from God by taking it upon himself. As the Gospel accounts make clear, Jesus suffers the Father's total abandonment and rejection (Mark 15:34). Indeed, by emphasizing the alienation and relationless-ness taken on by Jesus, Jüngel approaches Luther's concept of the "happy exchange." For Jüngel, Jesus overcomes the human situation under sin by appropriating it himself and exchanging for it his relationship with the Father.

Nevertheless, as has been shown in our earlier discussion of Jenson, the account of sin as relationless-ness is incomplete when compared to the account given in the biblical and confessional authorities. Sin is not merely a state of relationless-ness, it is also a transgression against divine commandments and a debt for which someone must pay. This more complete account of sin also has an effect on the nature of faith's appropriation of the work of Christ. Faith places its trust in that which is external to itself in Christ. This means that the locus of the law's fulfillment must be found in Christ, and not in the sinner's inner appropriation of a new relationship with God that Christ offers.

Although it does not seem to be Jüngel's intention, the focus in his doctrine of atonement appears to shift the sinner away from the fulfillment of the law, which stands external to them in Christ and back to the sinner's appropriation of the new relationship of faith. If Christ's function is primarily to overcome relationless-ness, then the focus of redemption ceases to be on Christ's objective fulfillment of the law outside of the sinner. Seemingly, the sinner is reconciled to God to the extent that they conform in the new relationship. Not only does this blur the line between justification and sanctification (i.e., in many ways, justification becomes conceptually indistinguishable from the participation in a new relation with God present in sanctification), but it ultimately draws the sinner back into himself and his ability to appropriate the new divine-human relationship found in Christ. With this, the gospel effectively becomes a new law of relationality.

Conclusion

Having discussed a number of major figures in modern revisionist Lutheran thought, it is clear that the doctrine of substitutionary atonement has had a significant number of detractors. As can be observed, these thinkers largely deviated from the Scriptures (as understood by the confessional writings of the Lutheran Church) it was largely for the sake of philosophical or apologetic reasons. Deviation from the historic Lutheran understanding of atonement rarely resulted from alternative interpretations of specific biblical passages relevant to atonement. More often than not, the author found various reasons to ignore scriptural teaching and/or replace it with a different criterion of truth. Moreover, as has been shown in a number of cases, the rejection of substitutionary atonement (or at minimum, elements of the classical doctrine) endangers or eliminates the doctrine of justification by faith alone.

In the final two chapters, I will examine the theology of Gerhard Forde. Forde demands special attention in light of his popularity among conservative North American Lutherans. Although Forde has made many fine contributions to Lutheran thought by appropriating some important themes in Luther's writings (most notably in Luther's *Bondage of the Will*), his deviations from biblical and confessional teachings regarding atonement seriously imperil the proper proclamation of the gospel.

6

Gerhard Forde's View of the Law

Introduction and Sources

AN EXAMINATION OF GERHARD Forde's view of the law is a necessary precondition to fully understand his doctrine of atonement.[1] Many of Forde's deviations from the confessional Lutheran paradigm can be traced back to his peculiar views on the nature of the law and its relationship to the gospel.

Giving a proper account of Forde's theology requires finding a method of exposition that fits the material. First, it is not necessary to exhaustively study each passage in which Forde deals with the law in order to evaluate his position. Forde's theology changed very little from the early 1980s until his death in August 2005. Furthermore, much of what one finds from this period onward merely sharpens the contours of the basic theological agenda first outlined in his doctoral dissertation, *The Law-Gospel Debate* (1969). This, then, provides the first and foremost source of Forde's theology of the law. I will also analyze some of Forde's later works, including "The Work of Christ" (1984), a contribution to Robert Jenson and Carl Braaten's collection entitled *Christian Dogmatics*. The basic account contained in these works will be supplemented by other writings and essays, especially Forde's short systematic theology entitled *Theology is for Proclamation!* (1990) and a number of smaller essays published posthumously in *A More Radical Gospel* (2004) and *The Preached God* (2007).

---

1. Most of the contents of this chapter were originally published in Kilcrease, "Gerhard Forde's Doctrine of Law," 151–80. The portions here have been reproduced by the permission of the journal publisher.

Sources of Forde's Thought

Forde's thinking on the topics of law, justification, and atonement were significantly influenced by several sources. In his essay entitled, "Examining Sources," James Nestingen (a student, colleague, and friend of Forde) describes a series of major influences on Forde's thinking. According to Nestingen, among the many sources of his thought, Forde was deeply influenced by the theology of the Old Norwegian Synod. In the nineteenth and early-twentieth century, Forde's family was associated with this synod. Forde's father was a Lutheran minister in the synod, and continued in the tradition of the synod's theology throughout his career.[2] This theological tradition was further reinforced by Forde's experience at Luther Seminary in the 1950s. While at seminary, Forde and his friends and classmates Robert Jenson, Roy Harrisville, and Carl Braaten (later the founders of the journal *Dialog*) fell under the influence of Herman Preus.[3] Preus was one of the few major proponents of the synod's traditional theology that remained at Luther Seminary into the mid-twentieth century.[4]

The Old Norwegian Synod largely continued the tradition of Lutheran confessionalism and scholasticism present in certain quarters of the state-church of Norway. One of the defining moments in its history was the American Lutheran "Election Controversy" of the later nineteenth century. During the controversy, the synod joined with the Lutheran Church-Missouri Synod in upholding Luther and the Formula of Concord's teaching regarding election and predestination.[5] According to the teaching of Luther and the Lutheran Confessions, predestination is a real decree of God aimed at saving a specific number of the elect in Christ.[6] Predestination does not consist of a merely passive divine foreknowledge as to the number of believers, who would maintain their faith until their death (*intuitu*

---

2. Burgess and Kolden, "Introduction," 5–6. Also Nestingen, "Examining Sources," 10–11. See comments by Forde himself, largely paralleling those of Nestingen in Forde, "One Acted Upon," 59–61.

3. See the following works: Preus, *The Communion of Saints*; Preus, *A Theology to Live By*.

4. Nestingen, "Examining Sources," 11.

5. Ibid., 10–11.

6. For an outline of the continuity of Luther's position with that of the Formula of Concord, see Kolb, *Bound Choice*.

fidei),[7] as many theologians in the Age of Orthodoxy had in fact argued.[8] This controversy very likely largely accounts for Forde's own strong emphasis on the sovereign electing power of divine grace. Throughout his life, Forde focused his attention on Luther's *Bondage of the Will*.

Linked with Forde's commitment to the confessional Lutheran teaching regarding election was his interest in the theology of Karl Barth. Barth is, of course, not the only mid-twentieth-century Protestant theologian who exercised an influence on Forde. Nestingen also mentions Paul Tillich and Rudolf Bultmann. Nonetheless, states Nestingen, Karl Barth represented for Forde "the most appealing and formidable" of all the twentieth century Protestant dogmaticians. Forde's engagement with Barth's theology continued throughout his career. He did not agree with everything taught by Barth, but found him an interesting and useful dialogue partner.[9] For a child of the election controversy, Barth's Reformed emphasis on the doctrine of election was extremely appealing.

Beyond the aforementioned theological influences, Forde also drew much inspiration from the late-nineteenth-century and early-twentieth-century wave of historical research on Luther's theology. Known as the "Luther Renaissance," this movement began in Germany and also eventually spread to Scandinavia. Among German researchers, Forde respected and drew heavily upon the work of Hans Joachim Iwand.[10] Beyond his Luther research, Iwand was an influential figure in mid-twentieth century German church politics. Though a Lutheran, Iwand developed a strong relationship with Karl Barth and other major theologians of the period. As a result, he worked closely with the Confessing Church to resist the Nazi party during the World War II.[11] A strong emphasis on the dual forensic and effective aspects of justification,[12] as well as the hiddenness and sovereignty of God, were characteristics of Iwand's scholarship. As we shall see below, this later accent is pervasively throughout Forde's own atonement theology, particularly in his appropriation of Luther.[13]

---

7. Gritsch, *A History of Lutheranism*, 196–99. Also see Nelson, *Lutherans in North America*, 313–25.

8. Schmid, *Doctrinal Theology*, 295–313.

9. Nestingen, "Examining Sources," 11.

10. Ibid., 14–16.

11. Ibid., 14.

12. See Iwand, *Righteousness of Faith*.

13. Nestingen, "Examining Sources," 15.

The Doctrine of Atonement

Among mid-twentieth-century German theologians, some have also suggested that Forde is dependent upon the thought of Gerhard Ebeling.[14] This perception may be due to some superficial similarities. For example, Ebeling's concept of the "Word-Event"[15] seems to rhetorically mirror some of Forde's descriptions of the effective nature of the word of God. Nestingen nonetheless see this association as the "academic world's equivalent of village gossip."[16] Nestingen may resist making the connection to Ebeling since some theologians saw it as a means of discrediting Forde. Such a connection would link Forde by proxy with the existentialist approach to theology pervasive in mid twentieth-century Protestant dogmatics. Nestingen notes that Existentialism is presently out of favor in certain circles (notably Post-Liberal and Evangelical Catholic ones[17]) because of its commitment to individualism.[18] Revealing a link with Ebeling makes Forde vulnerable to the same criticisms launched against Ebeling and other Existentialist theologians. Nevertheless, it should be observed that contrary to Nestingen's claims, Forde himself does mention Ebeling as a formative influence.[19] Ultimately, it is not necessary to determine how much Ebeling exercised influence on Forde. Even if Forde's theology is not linked to a particular Existentialist theologian, his work still possesses many existentializing tendencies.

Among Scandinavian Luther scholars and theologians, Forde drew heavily upon the Swedish theologian and church historian Gustaf Wingren, who was discussed in a previous chapter. Nestingen notes that Forde's reception of Wingren was not entirely uncritical. He disagreed with many of the criticisms the great Swedish scholar leveled against Barth's theology.[20] Nevertheless, Nestingen observes that there are many commonalities

---

14. Ibid., 20.
15. See Ebeling, "Word of God and Hermeneutics," 322–31.
16. Nestingen, "Examining Sources," 21.
17. According to a personal correspondence with the author, Nestingen referred to a series of letters exchanged between Robert Jenson and Forde. Jenson accused Forde of being influenced by Ebeling, which Forde denied, claiming that although he found him to be a good Luther scholar, he believed he was a subpar theologian. Jenson responded to Forde's denial by insisting on his accusation all the more strongly (James Nestingen, email message to author, July 2, 2007). Again, as observed above, Forde himself does count Ebeling as a formative influence. See Forde, "One Acted Upon," 60.
18. Nestingen, "Examining Sources," 20.
19. See Forde, "One Acted Upon," 60.
20. Nestingen, "Examining Sources," 21.

between the two theologians. For example, Forde treats issues of law and gospel in a manner similar to that of Wingren.[21] Regarding other similarities, Nestingen is less forthcoming. It might be inferred though that one shared area of emphasis is Forde and Wingren's insistence on the close connection between law and creation. Both also have a common appreciation for living and effective nature of the gospel.

Beyond Wingren, another Scandinavian who strongly influenced Forde was the Finnish Luther scholar Lauri Haikola.[22] In his work *Usus Legis,* Haikola argued that, unlike Philipp Melanchthon, Luther rejected the doctrine of eternal law (in Latin, *lex aeterna*). Although Haikola admitted that Luther used the term, he nonetheless claimed that the Reformer did not mean the same thing by it as did his younger colleague Melanchthon. For Luther law was not an eternal order, but rather a dynamic and flexible phenomenon. According to its first use, the law was merely a just, practical, and intelligent way of adapting to one's historical environment. For example, the law that Adam and Eve had to obey was different from that of Israel, due to differing circumstances.[23] Likewise, Luther writes, in *How Christians Should Regard Moses,* that the Germans of his own day should not attempt to return to the Old Testament law (as the Enthusiasts had claimed), but should rather obey the "*Sachsenspiegel*,"[24] that is, the legal code of Saxony. According to its second use, Haikola argued that Luther had spoken of the law as the sinner's pervasive experience of being accused and rendered guilty within creation. By contrast, Haikola reasoned that Lutheran scholasticism under the influence of Melanchthon had come to accept *lex aeterna*, and with it the doctrine of penal substitution. These two doctrines went hand-in-hand, because the Lutheran scholastics came to the conclusion that the eternal legal order would be undermined if the requirements of the law were not fulfilled in the event of redemption. According to Haikola, since Luther understood the law as more of a dynamic existential relationship, he could use a variety of images to describe atonement. As a result, Luther's doctrine of atonement did not need the law to be fulfilled in order to achieve salvation.[25]

21. Ibid., 11.

22. See the following works: Haikola, *Gesetz und evangelium;* Haikola, *Studien zu Luther;* Haikola, *Usus legis.*

23. Nestingen, "Examining Sources," 17.

24. *LW* 35:167; *WA* 16: 376.

25. Nestingen, "Examining Sources," 17.

Lastly, although Nestingen does not mention him, it seems clear that the nineteenth-century theologian Johannes von Hofmann had a significant influence on Forde.[26] Von Hofmann's impact can be observed in his domination of the first half of Forde's doctoral dissertation, *The Law-Gospel Debate*.[27] Similarly, in light of this fact, it is no accident that much of Forde's account of atonement is very nearly identical with that of von Hofmann's, although Forde does make a number of modifications.[28] In particular, von Hofmann did not conceptualize atonement as an act of substitution whereby God in Christ fulfilled the law. Rather, for both von Hofmann and Forde, atonement was an event wherein sinful humanity opposed God's love, but was eventually conquered by it. In light of these parallels and Forde's undeniable engagement with von Hofmann, it is deeply puzzling that Nestingen does not mention the author. Forde himself makes only one reference to von Hofmann in the endnotes to his contribution to the Jenson-Braaten dogmatics.[29] Nevertheless, it cannot be denied that von Hofmann's thinking, which is presented in a relatively positive light in his early works (with some criticism), effects the formulation of the doctrine of atonement in his later works.

Forde's General Concept of the Law

In *The Law-Gospel Debate*, Forde begins his discussion of the law by critiquing the Lutheran scholastics. Much of his treatment here is based on Haikola's aforementioned work and not directly on the primary sources. Forde has many difficulties with the Lutheran scholastic definition of the law as "the eternal will of God" (that is, "eternal law" or in Latin "*lex aeterna*"). Primarily, he believes that the doctrine of eternal law makes the law into abstract reality existing in God's eternal being and will.[30] Instead, Forde insists that one should define the law as a concrete reality within

---

26. I must thank Mark Mattes for having made me aware of this fact and pointing me in many relevant directions of research.

27. Forde, *Law-Gospel Debate*, 3–69.

28. Forde's position owes much to the theology of von Hofmann. He spends nearly half of his doctoral dissertation discussing him, and his view of atonement is very nearly identical with that of von Hofmann. For scholarship on von Hofmann, see Becker, *The Self-Giving God*.

29. Forde, "The Work of Christ," 1:62.

30. Forde, *Law-Gospel Debate*, 3–11.

human experience. The law should be described as "a general term for the manner in which the will of God impinges on Man."[31] The law can impinge upon humanity through a "bolt of lightning, the rustling of a dry leaf on a dark night, the decalogue, the 'natural law' of the philosopher, or even (or perhaps most particularly) the preaching of the cross itself."[32] In effect, the law is less a set of commandments than a generalized existential dread experienced by human beings in the old, evil age. Scott Murray, in his work on the law in twentieth-century American Lutheran thought, agrees with this characterization of Forde's position: "The Law is merely and entirely a threat to being . . . [T]he person only feels the unease caused by the threat of the Law."[33] As we will see below, Murray's "merely and entirely" may be a bit of an overstatement. Nevertheless, at times, this is certainly the impression that much of Forde's earlier work definitely gives.

Part of Forde's interpretation comes from his re-reading of Luther's disputations against the Antinomians. Luther here describes the law as it relates to the angels and the beatified as an "empty law" (in Latin, *lex vacua*); in other words, a law that cannot accuse or demand and, therefore, has ceased to be law.[34] If one has come into compliance with the law through the death and resurrection of faith, then one is no longer under the law. Law, therefore, according to Forde, only technically refers to the experience of dread proceeding from non-compliance with God's will. Indeed, Forde assumes that law can only function as a positive demand on the human person when he is out of compliance with it. For the law to ask a righteous person to do something would be rather like asking an oak tree to produce acorns. If one is sanctified by faith, then all is fulfilled and the law has ended. With regard to this point, Forde cites Luther: "Where sin ceases, there law ceases, and to that degree sin ceases, to that degree law ceases, so that in the future life the law ought to completely cease, because then it will be fulfilled."[35] According to Forde, Luther understands of the law as merely an interim measure between the fall and the eschaton.[36]

From the perspective of the confessional Lutheran paradigm, Forde's definition of the law as merely the pervasive accusing activity of God is

31. Ibid., 192.
32. Ibid., 177.
33. Murray, *Law, Life and the Living God*, 128.
34. Ibid., 184. See discussion in ibid., 180–87.
35. Forde, *Law-Gospel Debate*, 182. quoting from WA 39.I:431. Forde's translation.
36. Ibid., 178–99.

inadequate. The first problem is that the Formula of Concord defines the law as "the eternal and immutable righteousness of God."[37] For the confessional authors then, the law also designates God's eternal will for humans apart from its temporal effect, which after the fall will necessarily be accusing. The definition offered by the Formula of Concord accurately represents the biblical understanding of God as the eternal and immutable author of the law.[38]

It should of course be emphasized that Forde is correct that in this present evil age the law continuously accuses us through mediums of nature and Scripture. The Formula of Concord favorably quotes Luther's statement that "Anything that preaches concerning our sins and God's wrath, let it be done how or when it will, that is all a preaching of the law."[39] Furthermore, in this age there is no non-accusing law. As Melanchthon writes in the Apology: "the law always accuses."[40] Nonetheless, if one accepts Forde's premise that the law is that which accuses and threatens in this evil age, why cannot the law additionally exist as the eternal will of God? In other words, if God is operative in the masks of his creatures threatening and accusing sinners as Luther states,[41] then would not this activity be an expression of the eternal will of God, which sinful humans are in revolt against? If God is eternally life itself,[42] he must necessarily will the life of his creatures eternally. This becomes condemning after the fall, when creatures have murderous impulses and engage in murder (hence the need of the fifth commandment). Nevertheless, although the content of God's will does not change, one's own existential relationship to it does. If God's will were not eternal, there would be no eternally valid content for the human race to violate.[43]

---

37. FC, SD III; *CT*, 935.

38. Exod 3:14, 20:1–21:1, 24:14; Num 23:19 Deut 32:4; 1 Sam 15:29; Ps 33:11, 46: 1–5 102:25–27; Isa 46:10, 54:10; Lam 3:21–23; Mal 3:6; Heb 6:17, 13:8; Jam 1:16–18; Tit 1:2.

39. FC, SD V; *CT*, 955.

40. Ap III; *CT*, 168.

41. See *LW* 26:95; *WA* 40.I:173.

42. Gen 1–2; John 1.

43. Scaer, "Law and Gospel in Lutheran Theology," 30. David Scaer agrees that we can distinguish between the law's original intent and how it acts upon us in a state of sin: "Sin transformed the law. For example the command not to murder reflects that God is life. This and the other negative assertions of the Commandments do not have an eternal origin in God, but are the positive commands of God reflecting his eternal nature, now transformed and translated into terms which man in the state of sin can understand."

Holding these two aspects of the law together, therefore, is the only logical solution in light of Scripture and the confessional tradition. In fact, the Luther scholar Theodosius Harnack, more than a hundred years ago, attempted to hold both aspects of the law together in Luther's thought by suggesting that Luther made a distinction between the "office" and "essence" (in German: *Amt und Wesen*) of the law. Though in the present age of sin and death, the office of the law is to accuse and condemn sinners through the mediums of God's created masks, the law is nevertheless also a positive good, which expresses the eternal will of God for human beings.[44]

This distinction appears to work well on certain texts of Luther's. For example, in the *Antinomian Disputations*, Luther states that the law is eternal ("the Decalogue is eternal"[45]) and distinguishes its reality as the eternal will of God from the "office of the law" which is "[w]hatever shows sin, wrath, and death."[46] Of course, in the same breath, Luther can also say that "the law and the showing of sin, or revelation of wrath, are synonymous terms as are man and risible and rational."[47] Nevertheless, it does not appear that Luther is succumbing to a completely existential definition of the law. The context suggests that what Luther is rejecting is the notion of the Antinomians, that one could simply eliminate the accusing activity of the law by removing the term "law" from the preaching of the church. Hence, the Reformer writes: "To eliminate the law and retain the revelation of wrath is the same as when you deny that Peter is a man, but affirm that he is risible and rational."[48] Hence, the revelation of divine wrath is objectively real. It is identical with the accusing function of the law. It is irrelevant if one uses the word "law" in relationship to it. At the end of this set of theses, Luther reaffirms the eternity of the law as God's legal will: "*For never will the law be removed in eternity, but it will remain*, either as to be fulfilled in those damned, or as fulfilled in those

---

44. See Harnack, *Luthers Theologie*, 368–401. Of course, Robert Schultz has argued that Harnack's view might be based on some faulty understandings of certain statements of Luther and in one case an inaccurate translation. See Schultz, *Gesetz und Evangelium*, 142. Though some of these criticisms may be valid, it does not discredit the idea of this basic conceptual scheme underlining Luther's thinking on the subject when seen as a whole.

45. Luther, *First Disputation*, 75; WA 39.I: 413.

46. See Thesis 18 in ibid., 80; WA 39.I:348. Emphasis added.

47. See Thesis 20 in ibid., 80; WA 39.I: 348.

48. See Thesis 21 in ibid., 80; WA 39.I: 348.

blessed . . . *true disciples of Satan seem to think that the law is something temporal* that has ceased under Christ, like circumcision."[49]

Likewise, in the Genesis commentary, the Reformer discusses the existence of law before the fall and insists that the claim that the law did not exist before the fall is "full of wickedness and blasphemy."[50] If the law did exist before the fall, then Luther must have believed that the law had an existence apart from its condemning effect and the ensuing sense of human existential dread. This would also suggest that Luther defined the law in an identical fashion to the Formula of Concord, where, as noted above, both aspects of the law are held together.

If God's will threatens humanity, then it logically must do so because human have been disobedient to it. If it has been disobeyed, then it must have existed prior to its violation, and therefore must have an existence apart from sin. As previously observed, Forde assumes this and must admit, at least on some level, that the law is eternal insofar as it is God's will. The law is only abrogated as a threat because the creature comes into compliance with it, and as a result neutralizes its judgment. Nevertheless, it would not follow that the content of the law would cease to exist as God's positive will for his creatures at the moment that it ceased to threaten his fallen creatures. In other words, it is not as if Forde is positing that, after redemption has come, God somehow begins to approve of murder and lying.

Seen from this perspective, Forde has merely reworded the definition of the law by identifying it with the human experience of threat and demand. Since this experience will not persist forever, the law cannot be eternal. Nonetheless, Forde has not eliminated the law as something which objectively and eternally exists as God's will prior to and apart from human sin. He has simply suggested that creatures possess different experiences of this will. In the process, he effectively makes human experience of the law into the definitive theological criterion for describing the reality of the law. He thereby endangers the objectivity of the content of the law, as revealed in nature and Scripture.

On the level of the philosophy of knowledge (epistemology), one suspects that the German philosopher Immanuel Kant's denial that human beings can know "things in themselves" (in German, *ding an sich*) underlines this refusal.[51] According to Kant, humans can only talk about how differ-

---

49. See Theses 47 and 48 in ibid., 81; *WA* 39.I: 350. Emphasis added.
50. *LW* 1:108; *WA* 42:82.
51. See Kant, *Critique of Pure Reason*, 74, 87, 149, 172–73. Robert Preus has noted

ent objects affect our consciousness, but not what they are in themselves. This is because the human mind imposes its own categories of thought and experience on the world. One cannot get around them to see what things actually are apart from the lens of these categories.

Kant's influence was extremely pervasive in modern German theology,[52] which, as was noted, Forde draws upon very heavily. Hence the underlining assumption appears to be that one can only speak of the experience of dread and judgment. For Forde, one cannot get around the experience and recognize reality of God's eternal will itself. Ultimately, by very nearly exhaustively identifying the law with sinner's experience of wrath, Forde nearly reduces the law to a human experience, and tends toward a theological anti-realism.[53] This does not mean that Forde is an outright theological anti-realist. The definitions he presents merely make this an uncomfortable tendency of his thought.

Neither does Forde allow his position to be corrected through Harnack's essence-office distinction. Forde claims that if one accepts Harnack's distinction (and possibly Luther's[54]), we place ourselves above the concrete situation of the law,[55] because to consider the law according to its essence (i.e., as the eternal will of God), apart from its accusing effect on human being, is to "view it in the abstract . . . This allows man to place himself *above* the law and to look at it from God's point of view."[56]

This conclusion seems less than satisfactory. Why would a sinner's recognition of the law as God's eternal will, originally intended for his good, but corrupted by sin, necessarily be placing himself above the law in a realm of abstractions? To say that the law is God's eternal will, and that apart from sin it does not accuse, need not contradict its present accusing effect. It is no more an abstraction to say that the law, at one time, functioned differently (before the fall) than it is to say that the world once existed in a state other than we presently find it. Though such a world is beyond my

---

the tendency of modern concepts of revelation to existentialize and interiorize God's self-disclosure. See Preus, "Doctrine of Revelation," 111–23.

52. See Davidovich, *Religion as a Province of Meaning*.

53. See criticism of this tendency on modern theology in Marquart, "The 'Realist Principle' of Theology," 15–17.

54. We obviously lack the space to argue decisively in favor of this reading of Luther. The least we can say is that the passages that we will cite below seem to strongly suggest this reading.

55. Forde, *Law-Gospel Debate*, 184–85.

56. Ibid., 185.

present experience, it is certainly not unthinkable or a pure abstraction. For example, if within my present experience I am poisoned by cyanide, I can nevertheless recognize that the chemical has a reality apart from its harmful effects on me.[57] I can also recognize that it originally possessed a good use (i.e., as a cleaning agent). In the same way, the Apostle Paul recognized the original intention of the law as something good, without placing himself above it. In the midst of an intense confession of sin, Paul states, "I found that the very *commandment that was intended to bring life* actually brought death" (Rom 7:10, emphasis added).[58] Indeed, what Forde's objection at this point actually demonstrates is his tendency to reduce theological statements to the realm of human existential experience. Thus, any statement which does not directly relate to an existential experience (i.e., positing the eternity of the law) must be jettisoned as a "pure abstraction."

Returning to the question of whether or not law existed before the fall brings up several interesting issues regarding the law's definition and place in the Christian life. If law did exist before the fall, then it does possesses a positive use of regulating creation from the beginning, and cannot be reduced to existential dread or threat. Luther emphasized this point in the passages in the Genesis commentary that deal with the orders of creation.[59] Nevertheless, this does not mean that Luther believed that human beings were bound to something akin to the covenant of works, as in the later Reformed tradition.[60] Humanity did not need to "earn its keep," so to speak.[61] Rather, Luther argues that the law functioned as a needed

---

57. See Scaer, "Law and Gospel," 30. Scaer agrees with my assessment: "Though law appears to man in the state of sin as demanding and punishing, law as it exists in God is neither demanding nor punishing, but it is positive affirmation expressing God's relationship to creation."

58. Hereafter, all biblical citations will be from the ESV version.

59. *LW* 1:104, *WA* 42:79; *LW* 1:115–16, *WA* 42:87–88; *LW* 1:80, *WA* 42:134; *LW* 1:95, *WA* 42:145. For a summary of the points we will make, see Bell, "Man is a Microcosmos," 159–84.

60. For a description, see Heppe, *Reformed Dogmatics*, 281–300.

61. See Scaer, 30. David Scaer agrees with Luther's assessment. He writes: "The law as a positive affirmation was understood by man only during his brief stay in paradise. He knew God as his Creator, accepted his responsibility for creation and procreated. He was prohibited from stepping out of this positive relationship with God. But this prohibition is not arbitrarily superimposed on man to test him, but was simply the explanation or description of what would happen to man if he stepped outside of the relationship with God in which he was created."

"channel"[62] whereby humanity might use its own natural goodness to glorify God[63] and of regulating the created order. This law would therefore also express God's will in accordance with his eternal purpose for creation. Such a purpose comes to express itself in the threat of civil coercion after the fall, but it nevertheless remains true that the law represents God's original intention and relationship to the created order. I will discuss how Forde deals positively with the civil use of the law later. It suffices to say here that the law's original role before the fall is simply not answered, and represents something of a loose end. Implicit in his position is that, before the fall, human beings who were in compliance with the law could never possess the law as a positive commandment. If they did, then by definition they would be out of compliance with it, since law in Forde's thinking can only command in a situation of sin.

This raises the question of how Luther's statement about law ceasing with sin is consistent with his explicit belief that law existed as a positive commandment prior to the fall.[64] It would, of course, be historically irresponsible to try to solve the perceived inconsistency in such a small space. Nevertheless, based on the number of texts that I have examined thus far, it would not be entirely irresponsible to venture one possible answer. It should be noted that Luther is abundantly clear that human beings before the fall had the eschatological destiny of being translated into heavenly existence in the same manner that fallen humans do.[65] In such a final state of consummation, there would doubtless be no need for the command to be "fruitful and multiply," since "people will neither marry nor be given

---

62. To use David Scaer's description of Luther and the Lutheran confessional understanding. See Scaer, "Formula of Concord Aticle VI," 152.

63. Specifically, this is Luther's understanding of command not to eat from the tree of the knowledge of good and evil. See *LW* 1:104 and *WA* 42:79: "But the church was established first because God wants to show by this sign, as it were that man was created for another purpose than the rest of the living beings. Because the church is established by the Word of God, it is certain that man was created for an immortal and spiritual life, to which he would have been carried off or translated without death after living in Eden and on the rest of the earth without inconvenience as long as he wished." Again, we read in *LW* 1:106: "This outward place, ceremonial word, and worship man would have had; and later on he would have returned to his working and guarding until a predetermined time had been fulfilled, *when he would have been translated to heaven with the utmost pleasure*" (emphasis added).

64. Forde, *Law-Gospel Debate*, 182. quoting from *WA* 39.I:431, 6–7.

65. *LW* 1:106; *WA* 42:80; "Later on he would have returned to his working and guarding until a predetermined time had been fulfilled, when he would have been translated to heaven with the utmost pleasure."

in marriage" (Matt 22:30). Similarly, in the final state there would be no need for the preaching of the word of God, since all will see God "face to face"(1 Cor 13:12). The law would then completely cease to regulate human life after humans were translated into heavenly existence, because it would cease to function, even as a means of structuring the estates of the church and the family as they existed before the fall. Read this way, Luther's statement means that he views the law ending not merely with the end of sin, but rather with the end of temporal creational relationships.

If such an understanding can be inferred from Luther's statements, it would be perfectly consistent with the way in which the New Testament authors interpreted creation and eschatology. The author of the Epistle to the Hebrews understood the Sabbath rest as being typological of the eternal rest towards which creation has always been moving (See Heb 3–4). Indeed, Peter Brunner notes that the structure of the week in the primal state in Genesis 1, where work leads to a day of rest and worship, are an image of the history of creation. The movement of history must eventually end in God's eternal rest and the integration of temporal worship into that of the celestial hosts.[66]

Regarding the existence of the law before the fall, it is important to make one final observation. If human beings existed before the fall, then they presumably existed in a state in which the law (i.e., God's commandments) did not threaten or accuse. To claim that they did not creates two major problems. The first problem is the question of how human beings would have guided their moral conduct within the pre-fall order of existence. Genesis chapters 1 and 2 appear to suggest that human beings had a very definite set of commands which they were asked to obey. Forde partially resolved this problem by denying the literal historical truth of the Genesis creation and fall narratives.[67] This nevertheless leaves the most serious problem of all. If the stories of Genesis 1–3 are not to be taken literally, and the world has always been governed by the law of entropy and nature, "red in tooth and claw," then humans would presumably have always been under the threat of the law. Paul clearly states that "The sting of death is sin, and the power of sin is the law" (1 Cor 15:56). Creation would, in effect, then be redeemed by Christ in his death and resurrection, not from the fall, but from its original and actual state of existence. Forde insists in *Theology is for Proclamation!* that we must take the fall seriously as an

---

66. Brunner, *Worship in the Name of Jesus*, 38–41.
67. Forde, *Theology is for Proclamation!*, 50–51.

historical event (somewhere in the recesses of human history, certainly not the literal event recorded in Genesis 3), but then refuses to reconcile this with the presence of death and violence (i.e., the threat of the law) within the biological order prior to human beings evolving reflective consciousness. He suggests that we should accept the modern, scientific worldview as something objective and neutral, and think about sin and death as existential problems recognized by the preaching of the cross.[68] To try to investigate their origins would be purely speculative. Nevertheless, this attitude solves very little and calls into question the entire orthodox Christian story of creation and redemption. Furthermore, the acceptance of the presence of death and, therefore, the curse of the law as something existing from the beginning of creation, places Forde perilously close to the Gnostic heresy of the conflating of creation with the fall.[69]

Forde on the Second Use of the Law

Forde's treatment of the second use of the law[70] logically follows from his general definition of law and his concept of atonement. Although I will give a fuller account of Forde's view of atonement later, in order to fully understand his concept of the second use of the law, it is necessary to give a brief summary here.[71]

Forde starts with the recognition that human beings exist under the law and the hidden God. Having God constantly impinge upon their reality, humans cannot trust God because they recognize him as a mortal threat. In order to overcome this situation, God has sent Jesus into the world in order to forgive, and thereby reverse God's relation to the world from one of hiddenness and law to one of love and forgiveness. This forgiveness is not brought about by the fulfillment of the law or the propitiation of God's wrath. God, as he is actualized in Jesus, simply makes a unilateral decision to forgive without any fulfillment of the law. This action on God's part is completely disruptive of the previous human situation under the law. It is

---

68. Ibid., 51.

69. For the classic study of the subject see Rudolph, *Gnosis*.

70. FC, SD VI; *CT*, 963: "the Law of God is useful . . . that through it men are brought to a knowledge of their sin."

71. I will investigate Forde's two main expositions of the doctrine in Forde, "The Work of Christ." Also see Forde, *Where God Meets Man*, 32–44, as well as Forde, "Caught in the Act," 85–97.

an eschatological event. If God redeemed by fulfilling the law in Jesus, the new age of grace would not properly disrupt the old age of law. Rather, it would simply be a continuation of it. Humans prefer to be under the law because they believe that they can control God with their good works. Their response to being forgiven is to kill Jesus in order to maintain their sense of control. In doing this, they reveal their own sin of unbelief, and they thereby die in their recognition of sin. Jesus was resurrected by God, and his practice of unilaterally forgiving was thereby vindicated. This practice of forgiveness continues in the life of the church. By being confronted with Jesus' act of forgiveness in word and sacrament, we recognize our sin and are killed. We are also resurrected by the same promise, and faith is created. Since faith fulfills the law and sanctifies us, God now looks at the person of faith as righteous and is "satisfied."

As a result of his view of atonement, Forde significantly reshapes how the practice of preaching law and gospel should take place. A direct reassertion of the law by Christ would not disrupt the previous existential situation under the law, but rather prolong it. Nevertheless, if preaching is discontinuous with the law, we necessarily fall into a kind of antinomianism, something that Forde also wishes to avoid.

In fact, it cannot be emphasized enough that Forde rejects antinomianism. He frequently refers to antinomianism as "fake theology." In his essay of the same title, "Fake Theology: Reflections on Antinomianism Past and Present," Forde insists that antinomianism does not take into account the full eschatological nature of the gospel: "The root cause of antinomianism is failure to apprehend the gospel in its full eschatological sense . . . Christ, not theology, is the end of the law to faith, experienced as new life from death, the breaking in of the eschaton."[72] In other words, antinomianism's greatest flaw is that it assumes that, by verbally eliminating the law, it can simply get rid of it. The law, as we have seen, is the persistent experience of existential dread of those out of compliance with it. If the law remains unfulfilled within us, this experience of dread cannot be done away with by merely having someone telling us that everything is actually alright. Forde insists that the law's power only ends by its disruptive execution of judgment upon the sinner in death, and their being brought into compliance with it by the resurrection of faith. The problem for Forde nevertheless remains, concerning how the law is to be proclaimed to the

---

72. Forde, "Fake Theology," 215.

Gerhard Forde's View of the Law

sinner in a manner that does not make the proclamation of the church a mere continuation of the old age of the law.

In order to solve this difficulty, Forde posits more often than not that the law should be proclaimed indirectly through the preaching of absolution. In his essay "Radical Lutheranism" (1987), he describes what he considers to be Paul's understanding of the law: "The law does not end sin, does not make new beings [that is, believing ones]; it only makes matters worse. Where the old continuity is maintained, sin does not end." Further application of the law does not work: "No matter how much religious pressure is applied, sin only grows."[73] There must be courage to unleash the gospel: "There is too much timidity, too much of a tendency to buffer the message to bring it under control." Only through the proclamation of the eschatological gospel of forgiveness can old beings be destroyed, and new beings of faith be created: "Faith comes from hearing. Will the old persist? Will we understand ourselves to be continuously existing subjects called upon to exercise our evanescent modicum of free choice to carve out some sort of eternal destiny for ourselves?"[74] Forde makes a similar observation concerning the dual work of death and resurrection (law and gospel) through the word of absolution in "Absolution: Systematic Consideration." In absolution,

> The sinner is not just changed. Rather, the sinner must die to be made new. The paradigm is death and resurrection, not just changing the qualities of a continuously existing subject. Unconditional absolution is indeed dangerous for the sinner. It means the death of the sinner one way or another. Either the sinner will try to appropriate it on his or her own conditions as a sop to the self, and go to that death which is eternal, or the unconditional absolution will itself put to death the old and raise up the new in faith to new life.[75]

As is evident from this passage, Forde's view of law and gospel parallels his view of atonement. Just as the divine gestures of the cross both executes the divine judgment of guilt and forgives sin, the preacher's word of absolution functions as both law and promise in that it both kills and resurrects. Since the word of absolution presupposes that one is a sinner, it accuses as law while it forgives as gospel. Direct proclamation of individual divine commandments would simply facilitate a continuation of the old age.

---

73. Forde, "Radical Lutheranism," 9.
74. Ibid., 15. Emphasis added.
75. Forde, "Absolution," 162. Emphasis added.

It is therefore somewhat ironic that Forde's attempt at staving off antinomianism brings him uncomfortably close to the pastoral practice of the early Lutheran heretic Johann Agricola. To simplify a complex theological debate, Agricola came to the conclusion in the mid-1520s that, since only faith could bring about works of love, and because true, heartfelt contrition was a work of love, only persons who had faith already could truly repent. Therefore, Agricola also concluded that since faith came from the gospel, only the preaching of the gospel could bring about true repentance.[76] For this reason, only the gospel and not the law should be preached.

During this same period, Philipp Melanchthon attacked this position, by stating that it was necessary for the law to be preached to reveal sin.[77] By the 1530s, Luther himself also began to attack Agricola as well. This was the source of the aforementioned *Antinomian Disputations*. The Reformer completely rejected Agricola's elimination of the preaching of the law and repentance. In "Against the Antinomians" (1539), one of his many disputations against Agricola and his followers, Luther sides with Melanchthon and gives the law and the gospel their proper offices. Luther first agrees that the word of the cross can function as either law or gospel depending on one's own existential relationship to it: "To be sure, I did teach that sinners shall be stirred to repentance through the preaching or the contemplation of the passion of Christ, so that they might see the enormity of God's wrath over sin, and learn that there is no other remedy for this than the death of God's Son." Furthermore, Luther insists that it is impossible to preach the gospel without the law in the form of divine commandment, "When Isaiah 53[:8] declares that God has "stricken him for the transgressions of my people," tell me, my dear fellow, does this proclamation of Christ's suffering and of his being stricken for our sin imply that the law is cast away? What does this expression, "for the transgression of my people," mean? Does it not mean "because my people have sinned against my law and did not keep my law?" By removing the law, then, Satan not only wants to destroy God's commandments, but also "to remove Christ, the fulfiller of the law."[78] What then should our preaching praxis be? Luther asserts that it must take the form of a full elucidation of the biblical message of law and gospel:

---

76. See discussion of Agricola's early position in Wengert, *Law and Gospel*, 84–89. Also see description in Bente, *Historical Introductions*, 161–69. Also see Murray, *Law, Life, and the Living God*, 16–19.

77. Wengert, *Law and Gospel*, 158–59.

78. *LW* 47:109; *WA* 50:471. Emphasis added.

> Preach that sinners must be roused to repentance not only by the sweet grace and suffering of Christ, by the message that he died for us, but also by the terrors of the law. For they are wrong in maintaining that one must follow only a single method of preaching repentance, namely, to point to Christ's suffering on our behalf, claiming as they do that Christendom might otherwise become confused and be at a loss to know which is the true and only way. No, one must preach in all sorts of ways—God's threats, his promises, his punishment, his help, and anything else—in order that we may be brought to repentance, that is, to a knowledge of sin and the law through the use of all the examples in the Scriptures. This is in accord with all the prophets and apostles and St. Paul, who writes in Romans 2[:4]: "Do you not know that God's kindness is meant to lead you to repentance?"[79]

If this sort of preaching does not take place, and the gospel alone is preached without the law (Agricola's teaching), then no one can truly know the gospel itself: "How can one know what sin is without the law and conscience? And how will we learn what Christ is, what he did for us, if we do not know what the law is that he fulfilled for us and what sin is, for which he made satisfaction?"[80]

The Formula of Concord echoes Luther by condemning the heresy of Agricola, and recommends the preaching of the law by way of a clear delineation of God's commandments: "the Spirit of Christ must not only comfort, but also through the office of the Law reprove the world of sin."[81] Chemnitz and the other Concordists go on to point out that the preaching of God's commandments to bring forth repentance has a firmly biblical basis. The practice of the prophets, Jesus, and Paul are cited.

Returning again to Forde, it should be noted in fairness to him that, in spite of some similarities, Forde's position is somewhat different than Agricola's. In Forde's conception, God truly acts through the word of absolution as law in such a way that it "kills" the sinner, rather than in one that only brings about faith and, therefore, a loving desire to repent. This idea in and of itself cannot be viewed as objectionable. As can clearly be seen in both Luther and the Formula of Concord, any accuser possesses the office of the law and, therefore, the word of the gospel can function in that it causes the recognition of sin. In fact, the Apostle Paul appears to suggest that this is

---

79. *LW* 47:111; *WA* 50:472.
80. *LW* 47:111; *WA* 50:472. Emphasis added.
81. FC, SD V; 955.

precisely how he himself came to the recognition of his own inability to earn his salvation.[82] What is objectionable is that Forde appears to totally exclude the preaching of God's commandments and insists that we must wholly rely on absolution to do the work of the law. It is thus Forde's belief that preaching of the promise of the gospel can take over a function of the law that places him in close proximity to Agricola in actual practice.

Forde himself also appears to see this resemblance, and at one point even goes so far as to speak favorably of Agricola at the expense of Melanchthon. According to Forde, Melanchthon and his followers (past and present) "attempt to shore up a sagging enterprise [Luther's concept of the gospel] by various applications of law." Therefore:

> When they discovered in the Saxon visitations the sorry state of affairs and feared that the gospel of justification by faith was just leading to laxity, they faced the question of what to do . . . A great debate ensued, the "antinomian" controversies, which stretched over several decades and took various shapes. . . . Melanchthon, and those who followed him, thought that rigorous proclamation of the law first was the remedy. If folks are abusing the gospel and Christian freedom they must be brought to true and heartfelt contrition and repentance by preaching the law in all its rigor. If they were apprised of the seriousness and consequences of sin, they could be brought to repentance and proper living. . . . there were those (starting with Johann Agricola) who smelled a rat in this method. They held that you cannot really scare people into faith. Repentance that comes from fear of consequences is merely legalistic repentance based on the self's own desire to preserve itself. True evangelical repentance, Agricola held, comes from preaching the gospel. And because he insisted that the law should be banished from the church and the pulpit he earned the title Antinomian. . . . [Agricola taught that] [f]rom the pulpit we preach the gospel alone, and the gospel brings true and heartfelt evangelical repentance.[83]

There are several difficulties with this passage. First, Forde seems to be overstating his position in that (as was shown earlier) he does not entirely approve of what Agricola taught. Elsewhere, it should be noted, Forde speaks negatively of Agricola's teaching.[84] Forde believes that, since the law

82. See Gal 2:17–18 and Phil 3:7–9.
83. Forde, "Lutheran Faith," 202–3. Emphasis added.
84. Forde, "Fake Theology," 216–17. Here Forde describes Agricola as an "overt Antinomian," something he is definitely against. The difficulty over Antinomianism is that

is that which accuses and threatens, it can be present in the preaching of absolution. Also in this statement, Forde fails to mention that Luther approved of Melanchthon's position regarding the preaching of repentance. He approved it to the extent that he went so far as to write the introduction to Melanchthon's articles of visitation, the recommendations of which Forde implicitly criticizes above.[85]

What is most problematic, though, is that Forde continues his practice of moving the law into the realm of a vague abstraction. If one lacks a specific enumeration of their sin by way of the preaching of God's commandments, how are they to recognize in a concrete fashion their reality as a sinner? Forde's answer, that the sinner knows by way of implication through both the practice of absolution and the reaction of sinful humanity to Jesus, finalized in its condemning him to the cross. Nevertheless, this represents an extremely incomplete answer. This incomplete account of the second use of the law appears to have a dual antecedent: Forde's definition of the law and his rejection of the biblical and confessional doctrine of penal substitution.

First, Forde's rejection of the doctrine of eternal law in favor of the law as a generalized existential anxiety makes it impossible for the law to be enumerated in a specific concrete form. Consequently, since the law is a vague, generalized existential anxiety, it can only come to a climax in the cross and the preaching of absolution as something equally vague. The impact of this implication can be felt by the reaction of sinful humanity to Jesus' preaching of absolution. Secondly, because of Forde's rejection of penal substitution, there is, at best, a tenuous connection between the law as God's objective will set forth in divinely given commandments and what Jesus does. As we noted earlier, Luther believed that the law is preachable in relationship to the cross precisely because the cross represents a fulfillment of the law as a set of commandments. If, in fact, this is not the case, then it is not difficult to see why Forde has difficulties with specific divine commandments being preached in relationship to the cross. For Forde, the cross and the law have only a weak connection. Humans bring about the event of the crucifixion because they are out of accord with the law. The law's judgment is existentially executed on humanity in the cross in that they recognize their sin. Nevertheless, Christ does not really contain within himself an objective fulfillment of the law. This makes the connection

---

it tries to realize the end of the law by merely "shouting the law down." Mere verbal rejection of the law cannot end its tyranny.

85. See this introduction in *LW* 40:265; *WA* 26:195.

between the law and the cross merely indirect, thereby also necessitating an indirect relationship between the preaching of God's law and absolution.

There are other problems associated with Forde's claims regarding the knowledge of sin brought about by the cross. Notably, only a very small number of the human race was actually present at the crucifixion. To say to me that, hypothetically, I would have also killed Jesus, may very well be true, but it does not solve the problem of how this sinful attitude is manifest in my own life. Even if, perhaps, I would have joined the mob, how does this relate to my life here and now? In post-modern America, after all, we run into very few Messiahs whom we have an opportunity to call for the death of. Such a hypothetical scenario makes my sin into abstraction, something that Forde is trying to avoid and which he unintentionally achieves with his formulation. Similarly, I might very well (by exercising a kind of purely civil righteousness) not have wished Jesus dead. There are many examples of this in the Gospels: Pilate, Pilate's wife, the disciples, Nicodemus, and perhaps some other members of the Sanhedrin. Can these people be absolved from the judgment of the cross? Certainly not! But Forde's method makes this at the very least a loose end. Again, this problem would be solved by positing an eternal law of God, enumerated in specific divine commandments which Jesus fulfilled, as one finds in the teaching of Scripture, Luther, and the classical confessional tradition. By simply looking at God's commandment in relationship to the cross, I could very easily see what I had caused by not obeying them. Through a specific enumeration of the law and Christ's fulfillment of it, our role as sinners in Jesus' death can become clear. One can, with Luther, see in the flesh of Jesus, "Peter the denier; Paul the persecutor, blasphemer, and assaulter; David the adulterer; the sinner who ate the apple in Paradise; the thief on the cross. In short . . . the person of all men, the one who committed the sins of all men."[86]

Forde on the First and Third Uses of the Law

Although Forde theoretically rejects the third use of the law, he does so only by subsuming it under the first use. For this reason, Forde's doctrine of the first and third uses of the law will be discussed together. The subsuming of the third under the first use has in fact not been an uncommon practice in twentieth-century revisionist Lutheran theology.[87] Unfortunately, this

---

86. *LW* 26:280; *WA* 40.I:437.

87. For example, see Wingren, *Creation and Law*; see also Wingren, *Luther on*

move creates some ambiguities regarding the role of the law in the life of the Christian.

Before proceeding to a discussion of Forde, it is important to understand what the Formula of Concord means by the first and third uses of the law. As noted earlier, following Luther, the Formula of Concord believes that the law is God's eternal and objective will. This will is revealed to his creatures through both nature and Sacred Scripture. Because of the fall, this revelation becomes restraining and condemning. Nevertheless, it is no less a revelation of God's will. According to the sixth article of the Formula of Concord, the law possesses a first use, that "external discipline and decency are maintained by it against wild, disobedient men."[88] Notice that the Formula here specifically defines the first use as applying to non-Christians or at least false ones through coercive authorities (parents, teachers, police, military etc.). It is not meant to instruct or discipline Christians, but non-believers who are "wild and disobedient."

The sixth article of Formula then goes on to define the third use of the law. Although humans are no longer defined and determined in their relationship with God by the condemnation of the law, the law nevertheless still represents God's will for human life: "For the law is a mirror in which the will of God, and what pleases Him, are exactly portrayed, and which should [therefore] be constantly held up to the believers and be diligently urged upon them without ceasing."[89] Such a formulation provokes the question, if faith sanctifies and renews Christians, will they not automatically perform the works of the law? Yes, to the extent that Christians are sanctified, they will perform the works of the law, but "believers are not renewed in this life perfectly or completely."[90] The justified sinner, therefore, is in need of the law to subdue his or her old nature. The Formula of Concord compares the old nature to "an intractable, refractory ass" that "is still a part of them [believers], which must be coerced to the obedience of Christ, not only by the teaching, admonition, force and threatening of the Law, but also oftentimes by the club of punishments and troubles, until the body of sin is entirely put off."[91] Therefore, this use of the law is no less harmless than

---

Vocation.

88. FC, SD VI; *CT*, 963.
89. FC, SD VI; *CT*, 963.
90. FC, SD VI; *CT*, 965.
91. FC, SD VI; *CT*, 969.

any other uses of the law. It cannot rightly be characterized as a pleasant or non-threatening form of the law.

The second point made by the Formula is that justified sinners renewed by sanctification need the law as instruction so that they do not engage in "self-chosen worship, without God's Word and command."[92] In other words, although the regenerate person desires to do good works, he does not automatically know which works are God-pleasing. This strikes a similar note to that of the Augustana with characterization of late medieval Catholicism as encouraging "childish" and "needless"[93] works such as pilgrimages, praying the rosary, etc. God desires specific works, and engaging in works of devotion not commanded by God is useless. The old nature tempts renewed believers to ignore works God has commanded in favor of ones they themselves think are more fitting. This fits very well with Luther's previously examined remarks in both the Genesis commentary and the *Antinomian Disputations*.

Therefore, when the Formula of Concord posits a third use of the law, it is not supplementing a weak connection between justification and sanctification (a charge frequently made[94]). Neither does it attempt to claim that the law has suddenly become friendly and non-threatening to those justified.[95] The Concordists thoroughly agree with the young Melanchthon's assertion that "the law always accuses." In reality, the Formula has attempted to take seriously the fact that the Christian is at the same time saint and sinner. On the one hand, the Christian remains a sinner and lives in the old creation regulated by the law and the orders of creation and, therefore, needs practical instruction in God's will. On the other hand, Christians have already received Christ's alien righteousness and been sanctified by faith. In their inner person, believers have been translated ahead of time into heaven with its "empty law" (lex vacua), while simultaneously, in their

---

92. FC, SD VI; *CT*, 969.

93. CA, XX; *CT*, 53.

94. This is a charge Forde himself makes. See Forde, "Fake Theology," 220: "Nervousness about the effectiveness of the gospel in the confessional generation of Protestantism resulted in the positing of an added function of the law: a 'third use' by the 'reborn Christian.' The gospel does make a difference, supposedly, but only such as to add to the function of the law."

95. Forde also makes this charge. We will discussion this at length late below. See Forde, "Fake Theology," 220: "[By the third use] . . . the function [of the law] is really a watering down and blunting of the impact of the law. Instead of ordering and attacking, law is supposed to become a rather gentle innocuous 'guide.'"

external person they remain on earth within the duties and structures of the divine commandments. To describe this situation in the Apostles Paul's terms, the Christian is sanctified and can say "in my inner being . . . I delight in God's law" (Rom 7:22). At the same time, the Christian does what he "hate[s]" (Rom 7:23). For this reason they must "discipline the flesh" (1 Cor 1:27).

In light of the definition of the Formula, what Forde says about the first and third use of the law is not entirely satisfactory. In his essay "Luther's Ethics," Forde stakes out his position in no unclear terms. The third use cannot be accepted from Forde's perspective, because the law can never be a "friendly guide for the reborn Christian." The law is ever a threat to the Christian. The law always accuses and cannot be "used by us like a friendly pet." What is even more abhorrent to Forde is that "the idea of a third use assumes that the law story simply continues after grace."[96] Forde finishes by concluding that the "law story" is ended by and is subordinate to the "Jesus story."[97]

In response to this, it should first be observed that Forde is not critiquing the doctrine of the third use of the law as found in the Formula of Concord. As was shown earlier, the Formula is quite clear that the law remains a threat and an accuser of the Christian throughout his whole life. Neither does the Formula describe the third use as a "pet" (to use Forde's term) that Christians can be harmlessly use. It is rather compared to a club! On this level, Forde's critiques of the third use are (at least when directed at the definition found in the Formula of Concord) are not relevant. In all fairness to Forde, however, certain interpretations of the third use of the law made since the Reformation have described it as non-threatening and even pleasant.[98] If he means to take aim at those formulations, then, in light of the confessional understanding of the law, he is most certainly correct.

From Forde's perspective, then, how is the Christian to know how to live in the world if there is no teaching of the third use of the law? Scott Murray has questioned whether or not Forde can really account for how the Christian is supposed to live while, at the same time, being saint and sinner.[99] Murray makes this judgment in light of his very strict identification of

---

96. Forde, "Luther's Ethics," 153.

97. Ibid., 154.

98. See Murray's description of the treatment of the third use of the law in *The Abiding Word*; see also Murray, *Law, Life, and the Living God*, 64–67.

99. Forde, "Luther's Ethics," 174.

the first use of the law (based on the definition of the Formula of Concord) as it is used to restrain non-Christians.[100] On the other hand, Forde sees the Christians as still being subject to the first use of the law, insofar as they remain sinners.[101] He defines the first use as being the "political use," but then stops and states that perhaps it would be better to call it "the ethical use."[102] In the essay discussed earlier, at least, Forde subsumes the third use into the first use. Mark Mattes correctly observes that, ultimately, "Forde rejects a third use because he does not see this formulation as offering anything that is not already in the first use."[103] Echoing Wingren, Forde states that faith sees the created order as its arena of ethical activity.[104] The Christian is to be ethically guided by the rewards and punishments that the created realm offers one in return for external adherence to the law: "So it [the first use of the law], most often, by threat, coercion, power social persuasion and/or often just shame."[105] These are phenomena that Christians are subject to as much as non-believers, and as a result they become the basis of Christian ethical action in the world this side of the Last Judgment.[106]

In other words, Forde does not reject the idea that the law can serve as a guide for human beings in the world; rather, because of the dual nature of Christian existence in the old and new ages, he is more comfortable placing this under the first use of the law.[107]

This brings us back to Forde's use of the idea of eschatological disruptiveness as the chief paradigm for understanding law and gospel. For Forde, to the extent that the Christian remains in the flesh, he is subject to the first

---

100. Murray, *Law, Life, and the Living God*, 13.

101. Forde, "Luther's Ethics," 149. There is some wisdom in this. After all, sincere Christians (including the author of this article) still get speeding tickets, and have even been known to run red lights! It is nevertheless hard to imagine a sincere Christian robbing a bank or dealing narcotics.

102. Ibid., 152.

103. Mattes, "Re-Examining the Third Use," 279–80.

104. Forde, "Luther's Ethics," 149. Forde writes that the "arena of ethical activity [is for the Christian] disclosed as creation."

105. Ibid., 152.

106. Ibid., 153.

107. Forde, "Law and Sexual Behavior," 7: "The civil use of law ushers us into a strange and exciting new world, the world of the neighbor. Talk of the end of the law is unfortunately often taken to imply that the door is suddenly open to a certain relaxation and permissiveness. To think so, however, would be a fatal mistake. What the end of the law opens the door to is the world of the neighbor, the world in which the self is turned outward toward the other."

and second uses of the law, but as far as the new regenerate life goes, the law cannot inform the Christian of their non-existent duty. The new person has fulfilled the law by faith and, therefore, has no need of it. Because faith inspired by the event of the cross and the empty tomb fulfills the law, the law has become empty and reaches its eschatological fulfillment. If that is the case, then the law, having been fulfilled, cannot stand over against the Christian any longer. If one remains faithless, the law will simply persist forever until it is fulfilled.[108] This goes hand in hand with Forde's claim that the law lacks reality apart from sin. Nevertheless, to the extent that the new person needs the law as a specific "channel" (to use Scaer's term noted earlier) to express his regeneration, they are already provided with such a channel by the ethical structures present in their specific historical situation.

This conflation of vocation and law is another reason why, in *The Law-Gospel Debate*, Forde so strongly affirms Haikola's rejection of the concept of eternal divine law.[109] Law as positive directive is new every day and merely what human beings discern regarding how best to fulfill their vocation in the kingdom of the world at any given moment. For this reason, it cannot be eternal since it is temporal and highly mutable.[110] Forde approvingly summarizes Haikola's interpretation of Luther: "God has not revealed his absolute will to man even in paradise [according to Luther]. The will of God is not made known in once-for-all fashion, least of all can man capture this will in the form of an eternal principle." On the contrary, "man must learn to know God's will anew in each situation."[111] Returning to the essay "Luther's Ethics," Forde even appears to posit that the divine will as law can be read off of and learned from the rewards and punishments that society gives the human person: "it [the law] can also work by persuasion, conditional promise, by a kind of seduction or bribery. You eat your spinach, you

---

108. Forde, "Law and Sexual Behavior," 4: "A faith that knows of the true end of law in the double sense of goal and cessation will at the same time 'establish the law,' that is, allow the law to stand just as it is. In the light of the end one can gain some understanding of how God puts the law to its proper uses. Indeed, knowing the end, faith supports the law until the end is given. If the end is given and assured, there is no need to try to 'make the law of no effect.' That happens only when faith is lost. Without faith, that is, there is no hope. There is no end in sight. Law just goes on forever."

109. Forde, *Law-Gospel Debate*, 176–77.

110. This is not necessarily a cogent argument. If the law is eternal, it can still manifest itself differently in different historical situations without changing in principle.

111. Forde, *Law-Gospel Debate*, 177.

get your pudding . . . . [if] [y]ou do your work well, you get your bonus! So it [the law] works, politically, ethically."[112]

The main difficulty here is that this creates a great deal of ambiguity regarding the specific content of the law. Here, the Augustana's prohibition of "childish" works (noted above) is instructive. God wishes that human beings perform certain concrete acts of worship and obedience and exclude other acts. It is irrelevant how sincere the motivation underling them may be (think of the sacrifices of King Saul). Part of the difficulty here is that Forde has little appreciation for the law as a concrete and specific set of commandments revealed by God in Scripture. He is rather more inclined towards the notion that God's will is read off of creation by human practical reason. For this reason, the law as taught by Scripture cannot be final.

Although following Psalm 19, and Romans 1–2, we must certainly agree that humanity can, to a certain extent, read the Decalogue of the structure of creation in our fallen state, and humans are still in need of the law's clarification through a specific act of special revelation. Humans this side of the eschaton must have God's commandments clarified and taught to them so that the sinful nature does not tempt them into self-chosen works, which are a particular problem in the contemporary church.[113] In both cases, the church's full proclamation of the law and its work as a ministry of reconciliation (2 Cor 2–3) have been sidelined for other concerns.

In Forde's case, the danger of self-chosen works for the church is less acute, in that he emphasizes the church's role as a ministry of forgiveness. Nevertheless, with regard to the kingdom of the left, Forde's ethics do not give a clear criterion regarding what social norms are to be regarded as reflecting God's will for creation and which are not. It is, of course, correct to ask whether or not a particular commandment applies to our situation, as Luther notes.[114] Nevertheless, it goes without saying that human beings have a tendency of fitting the law to their own desires, and not everything that our society wishes us to do is God-pleasing. Even if one emphasizes

---

112. Forde, "Luther's Ethics," 152.

113. Regarding the later, Forde must be praised for having resisted the temptation of many in the ELCA to accept homosexual practice. See the aforementioned "Law and Sexual Behavior." Also see a positive assessment of his thought in relationship to other ELCA theologians in Pless, "The Use and Misuse of Luther," http://www.logia.org/index.php?option=com_content&view=article&id=77&catid=39:web-forum&Itemid=76;.

114. *LW* 35:170; *WA* 16:385: "It is not enough simply to look and see whether this is God's word, whether God has said it; rather we must look and see to whom it has been spoken, whether it fits us."

with Forde the positive role of vocation in shaping ethics, it is clear that one cannot accept every vocation assigned to us by our culture as salutary. The vocations of prostitute or drug dealer would undoubtedly be against the law of God. Neither does vocation automatically contain within itself an outline of how that vocation might be fulfilled in a God-pleasing manner. A soldier who fights for the Nazis or Soviets is clearly violating God's law, whereas one who fights for a marginally just government in a just war is not. In both cases, it is not the description of the vocation itself which outlines the individual's ethical praxis within it, but rather God's commandments.

Overall, the main problem here appears to be ambiguity regarding the content and criterion of the law regarding the Christian life. Forde often agrees that the content of the law cannot be changed: "Under the guise of the concern for ethics, morality, and justice, law is watered down and blunted to accommodate our fancies."[115] Nevertheless, on some issues he seems to think that certain aspects of the law can be abrogated, while others not. This is nowhere more apparent than when Forde, in his essay "Law and Sexual Behavior," insists that homosexual behavior cannot be accepted or promoted by the church, because we cannot change the goals (procreation) and structures of the order of marriage. Nevertheless, he also goes on to claim that it was legitimate to change them with regard to divorce and the ordination of women: "Some in the church like to argue also that since the church has changed its mind on matters like divorce or ordination of women it seems consequent that it could change its stance on sexual behavior as well. But in questions of the civil use of law it is not legitimate to argue that one example of change justifies another. Each case has to be argued individually."[116] This response, however, comes off as more of a dodge than an answer to the question of the changeability of the law.

As Forde argues, love of neighbor must of course be the ultimate criterion as to how the law is applied (Matt 22:36–37).[117] Nevertheless, one must have the divine word of guidance to tell us what form that love should take. It should also be emphasized again that Scriptures suggests this even before the fall, Adam needed a word from God to know how to establish true worship and proper governance of Eden. This was true, even though

---

115. Forde, "Fake Theology," 220–21.

116. Forde, "Law and Sexual Behavior," 6.

117. Ibid., 5. "Thus the purpose of the civil use of law is to take care of God's creation and God's creatures. To be sure, law is not therefore to be imposed as an absolute which must be obeyed for its own sake."

he was still uncorrupted by sin and therefore desired to love his neighbor in the purest way possible.

Overall, Forde's definition of law as the experience of dread, threat, and demand, tends to undermine enumeration-specific commandments Christians should obey. Much of this appears to be tied to Forde's opposition to law defined as the eternal content of the divine will, and his insistence that law can only coexist with sin. Obviously, Forde does believe that Christians should work within the created order in order to promote the love of neighbor, but the specifics of that love are left less than satisfactorily defined.

Conclusion

As can be observed from the discussion above, Forde's concept of the law and the gospel tend to be very highly existential. This existentializing tendency, present throughout his work, will strongly define his treatment of the article of the work of Christ. As will be shown, it is for this reason they are so highly problematic in light of the Scriptures and historic confessions of the Evangelical Lutheran Church.

7

Gerhard Forde's View of Atonement and Justification[1]

Introduction and Sources

AS PREVIOUSLY NOTED, FORDE's theology changed very little from the early 1980s until his death in August of 2005. Therefore, in discussing Forde's doctrines of atonement and justification, roughly the same sources will be drawn upon that were used to investigate his understanding of the law. Nevertheless, more central to the present investigation will be Forde's systematic treatment of the doctrine of atonement and justification in his contribution to the Jenson-Braaten dogmatics, "The Work of Christ" (1984). Secondarily, I will also draw upon his essay "Caught in the Act," written in the same year.

Forde's Use of Scripture

In "The Work of Christ," Forde commences his discussion by describing the historical and biblical basis for the doctrine of the work of Christ. As Forde correctly notes, the Christian church has only come into existence because of the life and actions of the historical Jesus.[2] According to Forde, the narrative of Jesus' life as it has come down to us is simple and relatively un-

---

1. Much of the contents of this chapter originally appeared in a slightly different form as Kilcrease, "Gerhard Forde's Theology," 269–94. The portions here have been reproduced by the permission of the journal publisher.

2. Forde, "The Work of Christ," 2:11.

complicated. During his life, Jesus forgave sins and announced the coming of the kingdom of God, and as a result, he was killed.[3] The death that Jesus suffered was absolutely brutal. Within the Roman world, it was a death suffered primarily by slaves and political insurgents.[4] On a psychological level, the crucifixion must have been absolutely devastating for the earliest Christian community that gathered around Jesus. Nonetheless, God raised his Christ from the dead, thereby putting his stamp of approval on Jesus' practice of unilateral and unconditional forgiveness.[5]

Forde claims that this no-frills account of the life and significance of Jesus constitutes the original core of the New Testament teaching. In order to justify this assertion, Forde appeals to the Apostle Peter's Pentecost sermon at the beginning of Acts. He claims that this account represents the earliest strain of tradition we find in the New Testament. According to this tradition, Jesus is understood as being a prophet of the kingdom whom God had vindicated. There is nothing in Peter's speech that suggests that Jesus' death was a substitution for sin.[6]

There are several problems with this assertion. First, Peter's speech in Acts 2 is neither an exhaustive theological treatise on the death of Jesus, nor does it give the author's (or the Apostle Peter's[7]) full view of the work of Christ. Turning to his earlier Gospel, Luke certainly does approve citing the words of Jesus at the Last Supper, that his blood would be "shed for you" (Luke 22:20). Similarly, in Acts 8:26–40, we find Philip teaching an Ethiopian eunuch about the significance of Jesus by using the Fourth Servant Song (Isaiah 53). This passage speaks of Isaiah's Servant as a substitute for sin. Similarly, Paul describes the church as having been "obtained with his [God's] own blood" (Acts 20:28).[8] All this suggests a considerably more complex atonement theology of substitution. Neither does Jesus' portrayal

---

3. Ibid., 2:11.

4. Ibid., 2:12.

5. Ibid., 2:12.

6. Ibid., 2:12–13.

7. Peter's full view can be found in his letter: "He [Jesus] himself bore our sins in his body on the tree, that we might die to sin and live to righteousness. By his wounds you have been healed" (1 Pet 2:24). Of course, Forde would doubtless reject Petrine authorship of this letter based on his acceptance of the historical-critical method.

8. Though it should be acknowledged that there is a textual variant here, many scholars consider this to be the best reading, not least the translators of the ESV. Regardless of whether or not this is the correct reading, Luke certainly teaches substitutionary atonement elsewhere.

as a vindicated prophet in Peter's sermon necessarily contradict the idea of his life and death functioning as a sacrifice for sin. Since references to both ideas can be found throughout the Synoptic Gospels, there is no reason to think that the earliest Christians should have found the two ideas contradictory. On the level of logical coherence, neither is there any reason to view the two ideas as mutually incompatible.

Moreover, although Luke's report regarding Pentecost certainly should not be marginalized as an historical account,[9] the letters of the Apostle Paul provide us with an even earlier first-hand account of the atonement theology of the original Christian community. Writing in the mid-50s AD,[10] Paul explicitly states, in describing the significance of Jesus' death, "I delivered to you as of first importance what I also received: that *Christ died for our sins in accordance with the Scriptures*" (1 Cor 15:3, emphasis added). Forde acknowledges Paul's use of these traditions, but suggests that they came from Hellenistic sources and not from the original Palestinian community.[11] Not only is this a mere assertion without any reliable basis for verification, it makes little sense in light of Paul's own claim that he had received this teaching from the original community of Jesus' disciples. In examining 1 Corinthians 15:1–11, Paul begins by referring to the tradition that he has received that Christ died as a sacrifice for sin. He then proceeds to speak of it within a body of traditions that refer to Jesus' appearances to the original disciples. Paul ends by affirming the unity of his proclamation with that of the original disciples by stating, "Whether then it was I or they, so we preach and so you believed" (1 Cor 15:11). Therefore, Paul himself clearly asserts that his proclamation of Christ's substitutionary death for sin was both received from and is in agreement with the earliest apostolic community.

Beyond these claims, Forde also makes other arguments in favor of his minimalist understanding of the original apostolic teaching concerning the work of Christ. Among others, he notes that some scholars (whom he does not directly name) reject the authenticity of the words of institution.[12] This argument is a necessary support of Forde's belief that substitutionary

---

9. See arguments in favor of the historical reliability of the book of Acts in the following: Barnett, *Is the New Testament Reliable?*, 145–58.

10. Ehrman, *The New Testament*, 262. Even a liberal critic like Ehrman concedes this very early date to the letters of Paul.

11. Forde, "The Work of Christ," 2:16.

12. Ibid., 2:13.

atonement was not part of the original apostolic teaching insofar as the words of institution clearly attest to Jesus' understanding of his own death as a sacrifice for sins. Not only does Jesus state that this death will work the forgiveness of sins (Matt 26:28), but he specifically describes his flesh and blood as something separated in his death.[13] As the Old Testament makes clear, for Israel, atoning sacrifice was always the act of separating body from blood (Lev 17:11). Likewise, Jesus spoke of his flesh and blood as something that had been separated. Therefore, in the words of institution, Jesus presented his person as something that had been sacrificed for sins.

Historically speaking, the claim that the words of institution are not authentic is highly problematic. The first difficulty lies in the fact that the Apostle Paul attests the words in 1 Corinthians, which is one of the oldest pieces of Christian literature. Beyond this, the veracity of Paul's own witness to these words and the narrative of institution in 1 Corinthians 11:23–26 cannot be doubted. As is attested in 1 Corinthians 15, Galatians 1–2, and Acts, the Apostle clearly knew Jesus' original followers; that is to say, those persons who had been in Jesus' own presence when he spoke the words of institution. Unless one is to believe that the original disciples intentionally lied to Paul about what Jesus had said at the Last Supper, the words must be understood as historical. Consequently, Jesus undoubtedly understood his death as a sacrifice for sins.

Moreover, beyond Paul's own witness to the words of institution, they are also attested by the Synoptic tradition. The Synoptic Gospels record the words in a nearly identical form to those of Paul. There is some variation, but this is not surprising. Such variation is doubtless due to the words having been translated differently from the original Aramaic. Jesus' words may also have been stylized by their liturgical usage in the early church. Nevertheless, what is important is that this dual witness to the words of institution reinforces their veracity through multiple attestation. Multiple attestation is generally one of the criterion used by liberal scholars to test the veracity of the words of Jesus.[14] Therefore, using even this highly skeptical criterion, the data shows that the words of institution must be considered

---

13. Jeremias, *The Eucharistic Words of Jesus*, 222. Jeremias writes that Jesus "is applying to Himself terms from the language of sacrifice . . . [e]ach of the two nouns ['body' and 'blood'] presuppose a slaying that has separated flesh and blood. In other words: Jesus speaks of himself as a sacrifice."

14. See good discussions in Meier, *A Marginal Jew*, 174–75, 218–21.

historical, and therefore Jesus must have considered his death a priestly act of sacrifice for sin.[15]

Besides the historical truth of the words of institution, Forde also rejects the authenticity of other aspects of the Synoptic tradition.[16] Not unlike many contemporary scholars,[17] Forde insists that Jesus' predictions of his own passion must necessarily have been invented by the later church.[18] He also rejects the arguments in favor of the authenticity of Jesus' predictions advanced by scholars like Oscar Cullmann. Cullmann argued that the idea of Jesus' death as a substitution for sin resonated within the first-century Jewish cultural milieu, because texts like Isaiah 53 might very well have been interpreted in a Messianic fashion.[19] Forde correctly points out that there is little evidence that the Jews at the time interpreted Isaiah 53 as messianic. While acknowledging the theology of substitution present in texts like 4 Maccabees, he insists that substitution cannot be properly understood as a Palestinian Jewish idea. Instead, the idea of substitution emerged from a Hellenistic influence on the early church. For this reason, Forde argues that it could not have been part of Jesus' self-understanding, or even that of the earliest Palestinian community.[20]

Beyond historically inaccurate division between Judaism and Hellenism (after all, Palestinian Jews had been under Hellenistic domination and influence for many centuries before the time of Christ[21]), Forde's claims about the antecedents to the idea of atonement in early Christianity are inaccurate. In addition to the proof offered by the words of institution, the Gospels provide other historical evidence in support of Jesus' own belief

---

15. Against Crossan, *The Historical Jesus*, 360–67.

16. Forde, "The Work of Christ," 2:13.

17. See the following: Borg, *Meeting Jesus Again*, 128–33; Crossan, *The Historical Jesus*, 354–95; Fredriksen, *Jesus of Nazareth*, 241–59; Funk, *Honest to Jesus*, 219–41; Theissen and Merz, *The Historical Jesus*, 100, 571–72.

18. Forde, "The Work of Christ," 2:13.

19. See Cullmann, *Christology of the New Testament*, 52–109.

20. Forde, "The Work of Christ," 2:15.

21. See a strong argument for this historical point in Hengel, *Judaism and Hellenism*. Forde's remarks seem to reflect more of the "History of Religions" school, into vogue in the mid-twentieth century, when he received his theological education. Nevertheless, the claims of this school were becoming extremely outdated even when he wrote this piece in the mid-1980s. The division between "Judaism" and "Hellenism" goes primarily back to the early nineteenth century with F. C. Baur and the Tübingen school of the 1830s. It rests on Baur's Hegelian theory of the origins of Christian dogma. See Baur, *History of Christian Dogma*.

in his death as a substitionary payment for sin. For example, N. T. Wright has pointed out that it cannot credibly be believed that the early church invented Jesus' prayer in Gethsemane that his vocation of dying might be changed (Mark 14:32–42, Matt 26:36–46, Luke 22:39–46).[22] Rather, it seems likely that they would have invented scenes where Jesus heroically embraced his death without visible fear. In support of this, there is fairly good evidence that the Gospels' portrayal of Jesus stands in rather stark contrast to the images of heroic martyrdom found elsewhere in ancient and classical writing. For example, one might point to Josephus' description of the binding of Isaac in the *Antiquities of the Jews*.[23] One could also point to Eusebius' source for the martyrdom of Saint Polycarp.[24] In both of these histories, the hero goes unflinchingly to his death and does not ask God for a reprieve. Josephus tells us that it "pleased" Isaac to hear of his impending death. Raymond Brown has made a similar comparison of Jesus to the brave and stoic martyrs of 2 Maccabees.[25]

For this reason, it is highly implausible that the early church invented Jesus' Gethsemane prayer. If they had, they would have broken with the cultural ideal of heroic martyrdom for absolutely no discernible reason. Likewise, they would have made Jesus look weak and un-heroic to many of their contemporaries. Furthermore, since this scene is therefore clearly historically accurate, it demonstrates that Jesus believed his mission was to die. Combined with the authenticity of the words of institutions, this data all appears to point to the fact that Jesus understood his death to be a sacrifice for sins.

Moreover, it should be noted that Jesus' belief that it was his vocation to die as a sacrifice for sins was not unprecedented, but possesses close parallels in Second Temple Jewish apocalypticism. As Wright has shown, the idea of the necessity of Israel's eschatological suffering for sin as a prelude to the final judgment was a staple of apocalyptic Jewish thought.[26] Furthermore, that this suffering could take on a vicarious and representative character has also been attested among a variety of Jewish apocalyptic texts, including the literature of Qumran.[27] Both Ben Witherington III

---

22. Wright, *Christian Origins*, 2:606.
23. Josephus, *The Works of Josephus*, 43–44.
24. Eusebius, *The Church History*, 145–52.
25. Brown, *The Death of the Messiah*, 218.
26. Wright, *Christian Origins*, 1:277–79.
27. Whitherington, *The Christology of Jesus*, 252. Whitherington also discusses 4

Gerhard Forde's View of Atonement and Justification

and, more recently, Brant Pitre, have demonstrated that Jesus' claim to be the bringer and embodiment of the kingdom was closely tied up with the idea of vicarious and representative suffering.[28] Within certain strands of the Jewish apocalyptic worldview, being the agent of the kingdom would have necessitated Jesus' suffering of what have been typically referred to as "the Messianic woes."[29] Pitre makes this judgment after surveying a large number of Second Temple Jewish eschatological texts that refer to representative and atoning suffering as a necessary perquisite to the kingdom.[30]

For this reason, Forde's rejection of substitution on the grounds that it is a deviation from the original teaching of Jesus and the apostles cannot be sustained. Moreover, it reveals Forde's attempts to interpret statements within the New Testament that speak of Christ dying "for us" as meaning "for our good"[31] in a broad existential sense, as a highly implausible. Within the worldview of apocalyptic Judaism, it is hard to see why these statements would have anything other connotation than that Christ's death being a sacrifice for sin closely tied up with the fulfillment of God's purposes in history.

Moving beyond the Synoptic tradition and turning to the letters of the Apostle Paul, Forde admits that there are frequent confessional formulas acknowledging that Jesus' death was a sacrifice for sin. Nonetheless, Forde asserts that Paul simply repeats such formulas, and that he did not consider them important.[32] Forde again asserts that these early confessions of faith are due to the influence of Hellenism.[33] This, of course, raises the question: if Paul did not consider these confessional statements important, then why did he repeat it so frequently? Forde insists that Paul's main understanding of atonement is that the cross is simply a divine act, whereby the old age is

---

Maccabees and does not consider its references to vicarious, salvific suffering to be a product of Hellenism. Wright also makes reference to this belief in the Qumran. According his reading, the Essenes believed that the righteous suffering of the "Teacher of Righteousness" pointed ahead to the community's own eschatological suffering. Such suffering would be atoning for sin. See Wright, 2:581–82.

28. See the aforementioned Pitre, *Jesus, the Tribulation*.

29. Whitherington, *The Christology of Jesus*, 123.

30. Pitre, *Jesus, the Tribulation*, 41–127.

31. Forde, "The Work of Christ," 2:16. This is an argument borrowed from von Hofmann. See von Hofmann, *Der Schriftbeweis*, 2.1:115–40. When read against the historical background that I have discussed above, von Hofmann's argument in this regard comes as a form of special pleading as much as Forde's does.

32. Forde, "The Work of Christ," 2:17–18.

33. Ibid., 2:16.

negated. In a word, the cross was an event of "crisis," whereby the old was destroyed and the new was created. The cross and its preaching were the end of all old pretensions and the creation of a new situation of grace. Unlike other New Testament authors, Paul never blunted the raw, stark reality of the cross with the obfuscations of a Hellenizing or Judaizing theology of substitution.[34]

Although Paul never gave into the temptation to submerge the death of Jesus under abstractions, other New Testament authors did. Books like the Epistle to the Hebrews (one might also point to the Gospel of John and the Book of Revelation), which strongly connect Jesus' death to the Levitical cult, were "no doubt an attempt to deal with the stark offensiveness of the cross with the biblical materials themselves: where Jewish thought had almost insurmountable difficulties, one used Jewish means to try to overcome them."[35] Therefore, the explicit use of the idea of Jesus as a sin offering in these works must be rejected, because they are an attempt to plaster over the brutal and gritty reality of the cross.

One of Forde's central beliefs is that the cross cannot be forced into conceptual schemes. The raw, gritty, and offensive nature of the cross must be allowed to stun the believer with its violent existential impact. Nevertheless, insofar as any event occurs in a particular context and within a particular horizon of meaning, it is impossible to interpret the cross without a conceptual scheme. Therefore, the real question is not whether the New Testament authors or contemporary theologians interpret the cross within a particular interpretive grid, but whether or not that grid is the correct one.

If, indeed, Jesus was the fulfillment of the Old Testament (as the New Testament and the mainstream of the orthodox Christian tradition has always claimed), then why is the interpretation of him on the basis of prophecies, and types of the old dispensation illegitimate? Insofar as the Old Testament has always been confessed by the Christian church to be God's word, it is impossible from the perspective of historic orthodoxy to answer in the negative. In fact, if one does not hold that the Old Testament is the proper lens for understanding Jesus and his redemption, then it is difficult to see how one does not fall into the early Christian heresy of Marcionism which advocated the rejection of the Old Testament. Moreover, as will be shown in the coming sections, Forde himself is not free from the influences

---

34. Ibid., 2:18.
35. Ibid., 2:16.

of modern philosophies such as existentialism,[36] or German Protestant theology as it has been influenced by Immanuel Kant.[37] In many respects these modern philosophical schemes (rather than notions of sacrifice and prophecy taken over from the Old Testament) serve as his interpretative grid through which he understands the person and work of Christ. For this reason, one might say that Forde's own criticisms may be legitimately directed back at himself.

Forde's Critique of Previous Theologies of Atonement: Penal Satisfaction

Of all the doctrines of reconciliation that Forde discusses, it would seem that he dislikes none more than penal satisfaction. Forde's negative judgment upon this view of atonement first took shape in his doctoral dissertation *The Law-Gospel Debate*, which largely colors his view of the doctrine his subsequent writings.

In this early work, prior to discussing the doctrine law and atonement in the theology of Johannes von Hofmann, Forde enters into a short critique of the doctrine of reconciliation as expounded by the Lutheran scholastics. As observed in the previous chapter, Lutheran scholasticism held that there was an eternal law (i.e., the holy and eternal statutory will of God), which was reflected both in natural law and Sacred Scriptures. Since the law is the eternal will of God, it must be fulfilled in order for redemption to take place.[38] To put the matter succinctly, in redeeming creation, God simply cannot ignore his own original legal will for creation.

As it pertains to the nature of atonement, Forde primarily registers his dislike of the doctrine of eternal law (*lex aeterna*) because it seems to place redemption within the structure of the law.[39] According to Forde, if the gospel only comes about as a result of the fulfillment of the law, then the gospel is necessarily subsumed under the form of the law. As a result, the law becomes God's primary reality, and the gospel is, at best, merely derivative and, at worst, something of an afterthought.

---

36. Murray, *Law, Life and the Living God*, 129. Scott Murray finds existentialism to be a particularly strong influence on Forde's thinking.

37. See Davidovich, *Religion as a Province of Meaning*.

38. Forde, *Law-Gospel Debate*, 4–6.

39. Ibid., 6.

Forde's second objection to penal substitution touches on the eschatological nature of salvation. According to our author, conceptualizing redemption as the fulfillment of the law by Christ does not make atonement a maximally disruptive eschatological act. Forde divides the human relationship to God between an old age of law and a new age of the gospel. If the law was fulfilled in the gospel, then the new age of grace would, in fact, represent an unactualized potency latent in the old age of law.[40] Much of Forde's treatment here appears to be dependent on interpretations of New Testament eschatology proposed by such figures as Albert Schweitzer[41] and Rudolf Bultmann[42] in the early-to-mid-twentieth century. These treatments argued that the advent of the kingdom of God in Jesus and Paul's preaching represented a total reversal of previous reality of the old age.

Lastly, in *The Law-Gospel Debate*, Forde dislikes the idea of substitutionary atonement because it describes reconciliation as an act that simultaneously fulfills God's justice and mercy. Forde feels that atonement is best thought of as a fulfillment of God's unilateral love, without any attempt to balance out love with justice. According to Forde, in contrast to this, the Lutheran scholastics "attempted to understand the nature of the divine act in Christ in terms of an equivalence between wrath and love."[43] Therefore, for Forde, the Lutheran scholastic doctrine of atonement makes the grace of redemption less authentic, because it insists on the need for the satisfaction of justice.

In his treatment of the subject in the Jenson-Braaten dogmatics, Forde expands the criticisms first offered in *The Law-Gospel Debate*. Having described Anselm's theory of atonement,[44] Forde asks "But what of God? Can God not simply forgive?"[45] In other words, not only is God's sovereignty constrained by the concept of the eternal law, but the doctrine of substitution represents God as an ogre, who can only forgive as a result of Jesus' death. Ultimately, according to Forde, for God's mercy to truly be merciful, it must be the result of spontaneous forgiveness. A God who demands

---

40. Ibid., 200–16.

41. See his most famous work: Schweitzer, *The Quest for the Historical Jesus*.

42. See his most famous works: Bultmann, *Die Geschichte*; Bultmann, *Theologie des Neuen Testaments*.

43. Forde, *Law-Gospel Debate*, 131.

44. See discussion of Anselm's doctrine of atonement in the following works: Aulén, *Christus Victor*, 84–92; Deme, *The Christology of Anselm of Canterbury*, 175–208; Evans, "Anselm of Canterbury," 94–101.

45. Forde, "The Work of Christ," 2:21.

that sin be punished would actually not be merciful, since by definition mercy is relenting from judgment, not a pardon resulting from judgment's fulfillment. Therefore, Forde states, "The question remains: If God has been satisfied, where is God's mercy?"[46]

Of course, it should be noted that this is Forde's own artificially created criterion of mercy. He is not drawing on the scriptural definition of mercy and forgiveness, which, in both the Old and New Testaments presupposed the necessity of sacrificial atonement as a payment for sins (Lev 17, Rom 5:9, Eph 1:7, etc.).

"Subjective" or "Moral Influence" Theories of Atonement

After having discussed substitionary atonement, Forde moves on to a discussion of "subjective" theories of atonement and their theological strengths and weaknesses. Subjective, or what are frequently described as 'moral influence' theories of atonement, fare somewhat better in Forde's appraisal than the class of theories described in the previous section. Forde's assessment is more favorable on several fronts. First, Forde appreciates[47] many of the critiques of penal satisfaction offered by Abelard[48] and by the later Socinians,[49] particularly with regard to issues of rational coherence.[50] Secondly, according to Forde, those who advocate subjective theories of atonement understand the gratuity of divine love. The recognition that divine love is a love that does not need to be "bought off,"[51] which was, and remains, the main contribution of those who advanced this theory of atonement. This particular insight is very strongly represented in nineteenth-century Liberal Protestant theologies of atonement. In his treatment of this class of atonements theologies, Forde mainly focuses on the figures of Friedrich Schleiermacher and Albrecht Ritschl.[52]

---

46. Ibid., 2:23.

47. Ibid., 2:24.

48. See Abelard, "Exposition of the Epistle to the Romans," 276–87. Also see summary in the following: Aulén, *Christus Victor*, 95–98; Bromiley, *Historical Theology*, 185–88.

49. Forde, "The Work of Christ," 2:24. Regarding the Socinian theory of atonement, see the following: Socinus, *The Racovian Catechism*, 297–320.

50. Forde, "The Work of Christ," 2:24.

51. Forde, *Where God Meets Man*, 11.

52. Forde, "The Work of Christ," 2:29–31. See the following works by Schleiermacher,

Ultimately though, Forde does not find these theories of atonement to be without fault either. To begin with, he observes that both Schleiermacher and Ritschl identified Jesus' work with the communication of his peculiar religious experience to the church. The vocation of the church is then, in turn, to communicate this consciousness to the world.[53] In Schleiermacher, this consciousness consists of divine sovereignty (i.e., "absolute dependence"), whereas in Ritschl, it is primarily that of divine love. For the liberal theologians, these experiences were not meant to contradict previous or normal human experiences of the divine, but rather to fulfill and complete them.

For Forde, herein lies the difficulty with these theories. According to him, the eschatological nature of atonement necessitates that the work of Christ be a wholesale reversal of all that had come before. The gospel cannot be identified with an activation or supplementation of the possibilities already present in the old age. This is true whether these possibilities or potencies are to be identified with an eternal law or a particular description of universal religious experience. The continuity of the old creation represents the continuity of the law. If the law's continuity is unbroken, then the condemnation and demand of the law will never be broken. Therefore, the cross must be something brutal, harsh, and utterly disruptive, smashing to pieces all previous realities. It is the end of all human attempts at controlling God, including the attempt to force God into the straightjacket of human conceptual schemes, which ultimately serve a death-dealing legalism.

In discussing the feminist strain of the liberal theological tradition and its challenge to the Christian idea of atonement, Forde makes many of the same criticisms. In his late essay, "In Our Place," Forde argues that the feminist theological critique that the Anselmic doctrine of atonement represents cosmic child abuse is unfair. After all, even within the Anselmic scheme, Jesus was an adult and gave up his life freely.[54] Nevertheless, such a critique on the part of feminist theologians (and other liberals) certainly does correctly expose the legalism of penal substitution, as well as the

---

The Christian Faith. For the theology of Albrecht Ritschl, see the following: *Die christliche Lehre.*

53. Forde, "The Work of Christ," 2:30.

54. Forde, "In Our Place," 103. No date for this essay is given. It appears to have been written for a conference at Luther Seminary in the late 1990s. The article that Forde is referring to is the aforementioned Brown and Parker, "For God so Loved the World?", 1–29.

tyrannical view of God which it presupposes (i.e., one who demands sacrifice in exchange for forgiveness).[55]

That being said, the feminist theologians have the same problem that the larger liberal tradition does. In rejecting legalism, they set up a new law of personal fulfillment and social justice in order to replace it. Although they believe that such goals mean liberation from the tyranny of the law (i.e., an antinomianism that seeks to disestablish heteronomous authorities), such theological proposals degenerate into a new legalism. In effect, they simply set up a new law of personal liberation and therefore perpetuate the law's oppression.[56] If one posits that the goal of human existence is personal liberation, then one must live up to that goal, and the demanding character of the law has simply reappeared in a new form. Since the human person is viewed as the innocent victim of oppressors, one is prevented from understanding oneself as a sinner. Without the death-dealing revelation found in the cross, one will simply persist within the sphere of the old creation and its legalism. Likewise, one will never be resurrected through divine grace and have the law fully established within one by faith. In feminist theology, then, the old medieval interpretative method of "moral tropology"[57] is revived and Christ becomes primarily an exemplar of the continuity of the legal scheme and not a redeeming sacramentum of death and resurrection.[58]

Hence, when liberal theologians claim that Christ went to the cross merely to demonstrate his loyalty to his mission of communicating his God-consciousness or perhaps uphold his belief in the liberating truth of social justice, the harsh, brutal, and eschatological disruption of the cross was obscured and obfuscated. Ultimately, this does little better than serve as a means for sinful humanity to protect itself from the brutal negation presented before its eyes in the crucified Jesus. Therefore, Forde writes, "The bleakness and disaster of the cross are covered by all the theological roses. Jesus is rescued from death by theology, so any further resurrection is largely superfluous."[59] As a result, legalism is unbroken by the disruptive event of the cross and human conceptual schemes are allowed to put a limitation on God's grace.

55. Forde, "In Our Place," 102–3.
56. Ibid., 105–9.
57. Ibid., 102–5.
58. Ibid., 109–13.
59. Forde, "The Work of Christ," 2:31.

"Classical" or "Conquest" Theories of Atonement

Finally, Forde discusses the "classical," or what is often called the "conquest," theory of atonement. This theory of atonement primarily views the work of Christ as the conquest and destruction of demonic forces (i.e., sin, death, the devil, etc.). In describing this model of atonement, Forde draws heavily on the scholarly findings of the previously discussed Swedish Lutheran theologian Gustaf Aulén in his classic work *Christus Victor: An Historical Study of the Three Main Types of the Idea of Atonement* (1931). After reviewing the various versions of this motif in patristic theology,[60] Forde discusses what he considers to be weaknesses and strengths of the theory. Among the strengths, Forde argues that the conquest theory represents "a protest against any legalistic rationalization that oversimplifies the human problem and ends with a God who is either a vindictive bookkeeper [penal substitution] or an overindulgent lover [subjective theories]."[61]

In this, Forde appears to largely adopt Aulén's own interpretation. For Aulén, the conquest motif was the most fitting description of atonement because it represented a movement of God towards humanity, rather than a movement of humanity to God.[62] In both the satisfaction and moral influence theories, he detected an often latent and sometimes not-so-latent legalistic and anthropocentric impulse.[63] Beyond this, Aulén viewed the conquest motif as representing an important negation of what he considered to be the rationalization of theological discourse found in scholasticism and post-Reformation theology.[64] As mythological and anthropomorphic as the theories of conquest offered by the church fathers were, they nevertheless functioned as accurate narrative representations of the event of redemption.[65] The event of redemption in Christ transcended normal human categories of rationalization and, therefore, the actual mechanism of redemption is best left undescribed.[66] The most Aulén believed that one could say is that atonement was a unilateral movement of

---

60. Ibid., 2:37–39.
61. Ibid., 2:41.
62. Aulén, *Christus Victor*, 145–46.
63. Ibid., 146–47.
64. Ibid., 156–58.
65. Ibid., 58–60.
66. Ibid., 153, 156–58.

the Second Person of the Trinity towards the created realm in order to save it from the snare of demonic forces.[67]

According to Forde, the difficulty with the view of Aulén and the church fathers is that the gritty reality of the cross once again becomes obscured. For the Greek Fathers in particular, Jesus' humanity is invested with divine glory in order to overcome and conquer where previously Adam had failed. Does this not, asks Forde, come perilously close to the Gnostic idea that Christ did not actually die?[68] Does not his redemption therefore reside in his hidden glory and not his death? Moreover, taken to its logical conclusion, the true battle of redemption for the church fathers occurs not in the concrete reality of the cross, but in the unseen realm of demonic forces. In looking for redemption in Christ, the believer is therefore asked to look past the actual and concrete reality of the cross to something invisible beyond it. Ultimately, "the dramatic-dualistic imagery can also misdirect our attention away from the Jesus who was crucified for us under Pontius Pilate to a mythic figure who was paying a ransom to the Devil"[69] The cross is therefore transcended, and its existential force is blunted through mythological and cosmological speculation. Indeed, yet again, "roses still obscure the truth."[70]

Forde's Treatment of Luther's Theology of Atonement

Forde's earliest treatment of Luther's doctrine of atonement may be found in his popular work *Where God Meets Man* (1972). Here our author gives more or less a truncated version of his interpretation of Luther's atonement theology that one later finds in the Jenson-Braaten dogmatics.[71] In discussing Luther's theology of atonement, Forde attempts to argue that penal substitution is simply inconsistent with other aspects of the Reformer's thought. In making this argument, Forde offers little textual evidence for this judgment. While acknowledging the presence of the substitutionary atonement in many of Luther's writings, he attempts to downplay or dismiss these passages.[72] Forde states that Luther could not really have believed in

67. Aulén, *The Faith of the Christian Church*, 204.
68. Forde, "The Work of Christ," 2:40.
69. Ibid., 2:41.
70. Ibid., 2:40.
71. Forde, *Where God Meets Man*, 32–44.
72. Ibid., 41.

the doctrine because the Reformer did not believe that God was one who could be "bargained with."[73] In other words, according to Forde, works righteousness assumes that human beings can control God with their good works. According to the doctrine of penal substitution, Jesus fulfills the law in the place of humans. Hence, Jesus merely becomes an extension of works righteousness and the human impulse to control God with their good works. Thereby, the basic Lutheran claim that the works of the law do not justify is contradicted.

Although it is certainly true that human beings cannot bargain with God or control him with their good works (see Deut 10:17), this is in fact precisely what the doctrine of substitutionary atonement teaches. According to the doctrine, it is not humans who control God with their good works, but God himself in the person of Christ who pays the debt of sin in order to maintain his faithfulness to his word of the law. The overall argument that Forde makes in this piece is extremely weak. His ultimate claim is that, although he cannot account for the presence of the doctrine of penal satisfaction in Luther's writings, Luther could not have really believed in what he said regarding it because Forde's inaccurate description of the doctrine conflicts with the Reformer's conception of the divine-human relationship. This is not only tortured logic, but bad history.

Moving onto Forde's piece in the Jenson-Braaten dogmatics, he acknowledges the two main traditions of Luther interpretation described earlier at the beginning of the second chapter. He first discusses Aulén and his attribution of the victory motif to Luther. Although Forde does not find himself in total agreement with Aulén's interpretation, he is nevertheless minimally critical of his views. According to Forde, Aulén's genius was that it was he above others who saw that Luther had not just appropriated the victory motif, but given it new depth. He did this by not only seeing the law and wrath of God as one of the many tyrants overcome by the Messiah, but as his chief opponents.[74] Aulén rightly perceived that divine wrath could not simply be "bought off" with some sort of "abstract payment." God's wrath, judgment, and hiddenness could only be conquered by the actualization of his love in the person of Christ.[75]

Forde next moves to discuss modern interpreters who read Luther as an advocate of the doctrine of penal substitution. Forde's discussion

---

73. Ibid., 42.
74. Forde, "The Work of Christ," 2:48.
75. Ibid., 2:48.

Gerhard Forde's View of Atonement and Justification

here is initially focused on Paul Althaus, but then enters into a more general polemic against this interpretation. He largely dismisses this scholars' finding and claims that they must "admit the picture is by no means unambiguous."[76] In order to support this claim of ambiguity, Forde musters a series of citations from Luther's writings. He believes that it is possible to prove from these citations that the Reformer "often and explicitly attacks the idea of satisfaction as at best too weak and at worst an abomination and the source of all error."[77] The first citation he uses is as follows:

> Even if one wants to retain the word satisfaction and say thereby that Christ has made satisfaction for our sins, nevertheless it is too weak and says too little about the grace of Christ and does not sufficiently honor Christ's suffering. One must give them higher honor because he did not only make satisfaction for sin but also redeemed us from death, the devil, and the power of hell, and guarantees us an eternal kingdom of grace as well as the daily forgiveness of subsequent sins, and so becomes for us (as St. Paul, 1 Cor 1:1 says) an eternal redemption and sanctification.[78]

To begin with, what is most problematic about his use of the passage is that Luther explicitly states that Christ satisfied the law. In some ways, it is extremely puzzling that Forde would appeal to a passage that so directly contradicts his thesis. Secondly, the passage does not criticize the idea of Christ's satisfaction per se, but rather says that, in addition to satisfying the law, Christ's death and resurrection also saved humanity from the demonic powers of the old creation and brought eternal life. As was demonstrated earlier, this by no means denigrates the satisfaction as the primary instrument, whereby humanity is saved from divine wrath. Since all creatures are God's masks, satisfaction of the law and the wrath of God also necessarily neutralize the dark powers of the old creation as manifestations of God's judgment.

Regarding his claim that satisfaction is "the source of all errors," Forde cites a passage in which Luther states that the idea of satisfaction in the medieval sacrament of penance was the "beginning, origin, and entrance to all the abominations."[79] But Luther is not referring to the work of Christ in

---

76. Ibid., 2:49.

77. Ibid., 2:49.

78. Ibid., 2:49. Quoting from *WA* 21:264, 27. Forde's translation. Emphasis added.

79. Forde, "The Work of Christ," 2:49. Quoting from *WA* 51:487, 29. Forde's translation.

this passage, but rather speaks of the activity of penitents. If we return again to the Galatians commentary (1531/1535), the Reformer makes it clear that his main objection to the medieval system of merit and penance is that it transfers satisfaction of the law from Christ to human beings: "for as long as they seek to be justified through the merit of congruity or through their own works and afflictions, or through the Law, they nullify the grace of God and Christ.... This [the teaching of merit and satisfaction] is ample testimony that Christ has died to no purpose, and that grace is vain and useless."[80]

Forde then moves to describe what he considers to be Luther's actual view of atonement. First, he suggests that the two main traditions of Luther's interpretation are, in a sense, wrong, because they both presuppose that Luther did not make a radical break with the previous tradition of Christian atonement theology.[81] In studying Luther, states Forde, one must follow the Reformer's method of dealing with the actual situation of sinners and God's action towards them. Theologians of glory (i.e., those who attempt to justify themselves by seeing into God's eternal being[82]) traffic in the abstractions of God hidden in his majesty, rather than looking to what is "Actual."[83] Forde correctly observes that Luther perceived the human situation after the fall as one in which humanity suffers the unending wrath of the hidden God. Luther saw through both the victory and penal substitution motifs, because they represent an insufficient break with humanity's existence under divine wrath. Both ultimately preserve the continuity of human existence, and for this reason simply continue divine-human relationship as regulated by the law. For atonement and reconciliation to occur, "there must be a reversal of direction."[84] Forde suggests that, for Luther, God reversed his relationship with humanity as defined by wrath and law by unilaterally surrendering himself to humanity in the person of Christ. By doing this, God not only changes his relationship to humans, but also human beings as well. Hu-

---

80. *LW* 26:181; *WA* 40:303.

81. Forde, "The Work of Christ," 2:49–50.

82. The terms "theologian of glory" and "theologian of the cross" come from the *Heidelberg Disputation*, which can be found in the following: *LW* 31:35–70; *WA* 1:350–74. See also the following sources: Althaus, *The Theology of Martin Luther*, 25–35; Forde, *On Being a Theologian*; Loewenich, *Luthers Theologia Crucis*; McGrath, *Luther's Theology of the Cross*; Ngien, *The Suffering of God*; Prenter, *Luther's Theology of the Cross*; Sasse, "The Theology of the Cross," 35–45.

83. Forde, "The Work of Christ," 2:95.

84. Ibid., 2:50.

manity is changed and becomes pleasing to God when "God succeeds in creating faith, love, and hope [in them]."[85] Similarly, Forde writes that God "gives himself in such fashion as to create a people pleasing to [himself] . . . a people no longer under law or wrath, a people who love and trust God. When God succeeds in that, God is 'satisfied.'"[86]

Forde attempts to render credible his assertions concerning Luther's view of atonement by referring to some of the Reformer's writings. Much like the earlier Luther quotations, Forde's references do little to bolster his case. For example, in one Luther citation, he attempts to prove that it is the faith and subsequent moral regeneration of the believer, rather than the substitutionary work of Christ that God counts as righteous. In this passage, we read:

> God's majesty is greater than the blood of the whole world and the merits of all the angels are able to placate. The Body of Christ is given and his blood is shed and just so is it placated. Indeed it is given and shed for you, just as it is said, "for us." Why "for us" except to placate the wrath of God which threatens our sins? Moreover, the wrath of God is placated when sins are forgiven. That is, as it is said, "Given and shed for the remission of sin." For unless it is given and poured out the wrath will be retained. So you see that the work of satisfaction or sacrificial placation is worth nothing except by faith alone.[87]

Again, notice that this passage explicitly teaches that Christ fulfilled the law on behalf of sinners and thereby placated the wrath of God. The "ambiguity" that Forde spoke of earlier is utterly missing in this passage, in that it clearly and unequivocally teaches penal substitution. Moreover, the reference to the importance of faith in this citation simply suggests that the alien righteousness of Christ is appropriated by faith, not that the attitude of faith actually renders a person righteous in themselves before the judgment seat of God. Commenting on Forde's treatment of Luther, Burnell Eckardt observes, "Perhaps Forde's treatment [of Luther's atonement theology] is the most annoying [among various scholars] because it is most clearly an effort to put words into Luther's mouth, words which are in fact more convincing of Forde's antagonism towards the Anselmian view than his accuracy in

---

85. Ibid., 2:50–51.

86. Ibid., 2:51.

87. Ibid., 2:51. Quoting from *WA* 8:442. Forde's translation and emphasis.

representing Luther here."[88] In other words, Forde has simply read his own theological opinions into them. He is ultimately unable to muster a single text in Luther's writings to support his interpretation.

Forde then moves on to discuss various passages from Luther's writings, particularly the Galatians commentary (1531/1535). In some respects, Forde's description of the contents of the Galatians commentary is similar to our own in an earlier chapter. Nonetheless, one major difference is the fact that he assiduously avoids mentioning the ubiquitous references to Christ's satisfaction of the law. Forde agrees that Christ, of his own free will, enters into the place of sinful humanity in a radical sense, and was subject to the wrath of God.[89] On the cross, God's wrath and the dark powers of the old creation attacked him, but they could not destroy him because of his omnipotent righteousness.[90] Since, according to Forde's own description, Christ was able to overcome death and divine wrath by his righteousness; does this not suggest that he has fulfilled the law in the place of humanity? Forde does not seem willing to draw this conclusion. The overall picture that Forde gives here is one in which Christ simply persists as divine love and power without the law and wrath of God being able to overcome him. In many ways, his reading of Luther on this point is more reminiscent of Aulén's own theology of atonement than what we have discovered in our own investigation of the writing of the Reformer.

Human Existence Under the Hidden God

For Forde, Christ's work of reconciliation should be understood primarily as God's response to humanity's bondage to the power of unbelief. He therefore primarily constructs his theory of atonement around the moral influence and conquest atonement motifs. Put succinctly, Forde holds that God overcomes human bondage to unbelief by way of the grand existential gesture of the cross and the empty tomb.

Forde begins the exposition of his doctrine of atonement by describing the human situation under the power of sin and God's wrath. Similar to Luther in *Bondage of the Will*,[91] Forde describes God's wrath as manifesting

---

88. Eckardt, *Anselm and Luther on Atonement*, 6.
89. Forde, "The Work of Christ," 2:52–53.
90. Ibid., 2:53.
91. *LW* 33; *WA* 18:551–787. See Forde's excellent and unfortunately somewhat incomplete commentary on *Bondage of the Will* in Forde, *The Captivation of the Will*.

itself primarily in his act of concealing his eternal being. As hidden, God is not concrete, but rather frighteningly abstract. He is everywhere and nowhere. By the power of his electing will, he relentlessly works all things. Because of human unbelief in his goodness and grace, his electing and all-determining nature becomes an unbearable threat. As Forde writes:

> It is time now to take the final step. The fact is that we simply cannot reconcile ourselves to God. Why? Just because God is God. We cannot bear that. God is the almighty Creator of heaven and earth. God rules over all things, and God's will ultimately will be done. That is too much. Furthermore, according to the Scriptures, God is an electing God. God chooses. "I will have mercy on whom I will have mercy" is virtually God's name. The very thought of such a God is a threat to us.[92]

As we observed in the last chapter, relying on several remarks Luther made in his *Antinomian Disputations*,[93] Forde identifies the hidden God's threatening activity with the law. In his earlier work, *The Law-Gospel Debate*, Forde writes that the law must be broadly understood as "a general term for the manner in which the will of God impinges on Man."[94]

Because the God of the Bible has revealed and identified himself as the almighty and electing creator, we cannot get around his unrelenting accusing and demanding activity by appealing to secondary causes, human autonomy, or by trying to weaken him with metaphysical tricks. All these acts are, according to Forde, attempts by sinful humans to justify themselves against God and his law. In a similar fashion, contemporary theologies whose goal is to develop a theodicy represent little more than human attempts at self-justification. Ultimately, all such theologies are infantile attempts at intellectualizing away the self-evident threat posed by the hidden God to humanity. God's law, wrath, and hiddenness cannot be escaped by way of clever intellectual theories.[95]

Whether consciously or unconsciously, all human beings recognize these truths and, therefore, rightly perceive the hidden God as a threat. This is why the human will is bound to the power of unbelief and sin. Humanity is incapable of loving or trusting in a God who wills its annihilation. Therefore, Forde writes,

---

92. Forde, "The Work of Christ," 2:65.
93. Luther, *Only the Decalogue is Eternal*, 359–584.
94. Forde, *Law-Gospel Debate*, 192.
95. Forde, *Theology is for Proclamation!*, 19–20.

> God is a threat and a terror to the alienated. Faced with the threat of God and especially with the mere idea of God's election, I can only say, "No." In defiance of God and all the logic of the case, I must simply assert my own freedom so as to have some say about my own destiny. So, I must take over God's role. I must say to God, in effect, "God, I do not know what you plan to do; I cannot trust you. Therefore I must take my destiny into my own hands because I believe I can better decide such things."[96]

A God who is neither touched nor seen, and who relentlessly works all things in his wrath, cannot be trusted. Deluding itself into the fantasy that it can rely on its own power of self-determination, humanity must eventually deny God's existence itself. Forde writes: "To put it bluntly, our so-called freedom cannot stop until it has done away with God altogether."[97]

The only solution to this situation is for God to become a God who in a tangible manner relents from his wrath and becomes a God of love and grace. In a word, it is for God surrender himself in the person of Jesus and thereby to reverse his previous negative existential relationship to humanity.[98] This action will entail the event of atonement and justification, to which we will now turn.

The Actualization of Atonement and Justification: The Ministry, Death and Resurrection of Jesus

As previously observed, Forde holds that one cannot start from a preexistent scheme or an abstract theory about God's nature in order to attain correct theological knowledge. Therefore, invoking the Roman Catholic theologian Karl Rahner's famous distinction between Christology from "below and above,"[99] he begins his atonement essay "Caught in the Act" (1984) by stating that a proper understanding of the work of Christ must necessarily begin "from below."[100] What this means in practice is that the starting point of all theological reflection must involve what Forde refers

---

96. Forde, "The Work of Christ," 2:66.
97. Ibid., 2:68.
98. Ibid., 2:67–69.
99. Rahner, "The Two Basic Types of Christology," 213–23.
100. Forde, "Caught in the Act," 93.

to as the "actual narrative"[101] found in the Gospels.[102] According to Forde's reading of this "actual narrative," Jesus did not come teaching a particular atonement theology or an abstract theory about the nature of God. Rather, Jesus simply traveled around Palestine, spontaneously and unilaterally forgiving sinners. Regarding this, Forde writes,

> Why could not God just up and forgive? Let us start there. If we look at the narrative about Jesus, the actual events themselves, the "brute facts" as they have come down to us, the answer is quite simple. He did! Jesus came preaching repentance and forgiveness, declaring the bounty and mercy of his "Father." The problem, however, is that we could not buy that. And so we killed him. And just so we are caught in the act. Every mouth is stopped once and for all. All the pious talk about our yearning and desire for reconciliation and forgiveness, etc., all our complaint against God is simply shut up. He came to forgive and we killed him for it; we would not have it. It is as simple as that.[103]

For Forde, this "actual narrative" therefore provides a more correct rationale for the crucifixion than either traditional theology, or even the New Testament authors themselves, ever could.[104] Jesus died because the legalistic opposition of sinful humanity ran headlong into the gracious and forgiving will of God. In point of fact, humanity, enthralled under the power of legalism, prefers not to be forgiven so that it can maintain its illusory control over God with its good works. In this regard, Forde writes, "But why did we kill him? It was, I expect we must say, as a matter of 'self-defense.' Jesus came not just to teach about the mercy and forgiveness of God but actually came to do it, to have mercy and to forgive unconditionally . . . [this] shatters the 'order' by which we must run things here."[105] Another analogy Forde uses to describe the crucifixion is that of an "Accident." Jesus' death is not unlike a man who throws himself in front of a moving truck and is killed while attempting to save a child playing in the road.[106] In this

---

101. Ibid., 91.

102. This emphasis probably owes much to Barth's so-called "Actualism." See discussion in CD 2.257–321 and in Hunsinger, *How to Read Karl Barth*, 30–32. For Barth's influence on Forde, see the following: Nestingen, "Examining Sources," 11.

103. Forde, "Caught in the Act," 90–91.

104. Again, oddly enough, Forde argues that the authors of the New Testament misunderstood the work of Jesus. See Forde, "The Work of Christ," 2:11–19.

105. Forde, "Caught in the Act," 92.

106. Forde, "The Work of Christ," 2:88–89.

analogy, sinful humanity is driving the truck and the man killed is Christ. Humanity drives the truck insofar as they participate in the legalistic order of the present evil age.

In spite of Forde's analogy of a car accident, Jesus' death is not, in a literal sense, accidental. It was, in point of fact, a quite integral part of God's own plan of redemption. Forde asserts that God willed that Jesus be "crucified by the [sinful and legalistic] order itself, so to bring a new order."[107] By killing Jesus, sinful humanity comes to recognize its bondage. In rejecting Jesus and his mercy, humanity is truly made conscious of its root sin: opposition to God's grace. God allows himself to be killed by us, states Forde, in order to "make it plain that 'all have sinned and fall short of the glory of God' (Rom 3:23)."[108] Therefore, Jesus did not die to fulfill the law or suffer the punishment for our sins. Rather, he died in order to reveal fallen humanity's sin of self-justification and opposition to God's grace.

Ultimately, Jesus is victorious over the old sinful order by the power of his resurrection. In the resurrection, God not only negated the present evil age, but has also vindicated Jesus and his practice of unconditional forgiveness of sinners. Therefore, writes Forde, "The resurrection is his [Jesus'] vindication against us. Therefore, it is vindication against death, the power of death resident in our legalism (see 2 Cor 3). It is the proof that he was right and we are wrong. God has made him Lord. God has now said what he has to say."[109]

For this reason, the death and resurrection of Jesus is an utterly disruptive eschatological event. It is the breaking point between the old age and the new, the death of the old being of sin and the re-creation of the new person of faith.[110] In that we are made conscious of our sin by the death of Jesus, we quite literally die.[111] Nevertheless, by the power of the resurrection, God validates Jesus' forgiveness and, therefore, creates new beings of faith.[112] Having succeeded in inculcating trust in his grace, God is "satisfied," not by Jesus' death and righteousness, but by our own righteousness actualized by faith. In this regard, Forde comments,

---

107. Ibid., 2:91.
108. Ibid., 2:90.
109. Ibid., 2:92.
110. Ibid., 2:93.
111. Ibid., 2:94.
112. Ibid., 2:95.

When faith is created, when we actually believe God's unconditional forgiveness; then God can say, "Now I am satisfied!" God's wrath ends actually when we believe him, not abstractly because of a payment to God "once upon a time." Christ's work, therefore, "satisfies" the wrath of God because it alone creates believers, new beings who are no longer "under" wrath. Christ actualizes the will of God to have mercy unconditionally in the concrete and thereby "placates" God.[113]

As is clear from what was said above, Forde's rejection of the confessional Lutheran understanding of atonement also causes a significant deviation from the historic Lutheran teaching regarding justification. For this reason, Forde's view of justification is not in accordance with the Formula of Concord's definition of justification as the forgiveness of sins and the imputation of righteousness.[114] In traditional Lutheran doctrine, Christ's positive act of obedience and his negative act of suffering the judgment of sin are imputed to the believer and received by faith.[115] For Forde, the role of the imputation of passive righteousness is taken over by the divine act of forgiveness by fiat (i.e., forgiveness without a payment for sin), whereas the role of active righteousness is taken over by the positive righteousness of the new being of faith. Hence, faith saves not because it receives Christ's imputed righteousness, but rather partially because it receives God's act of forgiveness in Christ, and partially because it recreates the believer as righteous in themselves through faith.[116] Because of this, justification ceases to

113. Forde, "Caught in the Act," 97.

114. FC Ep. III; *CT*, 793. "Accordingly, we believe, teach, and confess that our righteousness before God is [this very thing], that God forgives us our sins out of pure grace, without any work, merit, or worthiness of ours preceding, present, or following, that He presents and imputes to us the righteousness of Christ's obedience, on account of which righteousness we are received into grace by God, and regarded as righteous."

115. FC Ep. III; *CT*, 793. "Christ is our Righteousness neither according to the divine nature alone nor according to the human nature alone, but that it is the entire Christ according to both natures, in His obedience alone, which as God and man He rendered to the Father even unto death, and thereby merited for us the forgiveness of sins and eternal life, as it is written: As by one man's disobedience many were made sinners, so by the obedience of One shall many be made righteous."

116. See Forde, "Forensic Justification and the Christian Life: Triumph or Tragedy?", 114–36. Forde appeals to Luther's teaching in the Romans commentary of 1516 over against the teaching of the Lutheran scholastics. He appears to assume that Luther's teaching on this point was different than Melanchthon's forensic concept of justification present in the Lutheran confessional writings. This view goes back to Karl Holl and the Luther Renaissance, and is heavily influenced by his Swabian Pietism. See discussion

be wholly outside of the sinner and is only in the most tenuous sense for the sake of Christ.

A Confessional Lutheran Assessment and Response

In turning to an assessment of Forde's teaching from the perspective of the confessional Lutheran paradigm, the first and most important issue to tackle in this evaluation is the nature of atonement and its inner relationship to the central article of justification. What Forde's interpretation of the doctrine of atonement makes clear is that there is a necessary relationship between the article of the work of Christ and that of justification. In other words, if one rejects the notion of Christ's vicarious satisfaction of the law (both actively and passively), the entire forensic nature of justification is lost.[117] Put succinctly, if Christ does not fulfill the law on our behalf, then someone else must, and that someone is necessarily us.[118] This is evidenced by the fact that, without fail, those who reject vicarious satisfaction (for example, the aforementioned Abelard and Socinians) posit the fulfillment of the law by believers in some sort of watered-down form. In Forde's case, the believer does not fulfill the law by his own efforts, per se, but rather is recreated by God's effective address as one who has fulfilled the law by faith. God is thereby "satisfied" and his wrath is silenced. In this formulation, Forde wishes to describe atonement and justification as expressions of the dynamic character of God's word.

Nevertheless, beyond the brute fact that Forde's description of justification is in total disagreement with the confessional and biblical authorities,[119] his teaching lacks coherence with his own theological pre-

---

in Green, *How Melanchthon Helped Luther*, 31–45 and Boehme, "Tributaries into the River JDDJ," 1–16. Boehme helpfully gives the following essays that deal with Holl's work on justification in Luther: Holl, "Die Rechtfertigungslehre," 1:111–54; Holl, "Die *justitia dei*," 3:171–88; Holl, "Die Rechtfertigungslehrein," 3:525–57; Holl, "Was hat die Rechtfertigungslehre dem modern Menschen zu sagen?" 3:558–67. For evidence of Forde's influence by the Luther Renaissance, see Nestingen, "Examining Sources," 14–16.

117. This is a point that several theologians at Erlangen (specifically Gottfried Thomasius and Theodosius Harnack) made against von Hofmann. See Thomasius, *Das Bekenntniss*.

118. See similar argument in Pieper, *Christian Dogmatics*, 2:361–72.

119. See in particular CA III; *CT*, 45. We read: "Also they teach that the Word, that is, the Son of God, did assume the human nature in the womb of the blessed Virgin Mary, so that there are two natures, the divine and the human, inseparably enjoined in one Person, one Christ, true God and true man, who was born of the Virgin Mary, truly suffered, was

suppositions in at least two ways. First, in his discussion of penal substitution, Forde registers much distain for the idea that God needs bloody sacrifice in order to save. Ultimately, though, within Forde's own doctrine of atonement, God does apparently need the law to be fulfilled, or divine wrath will never cease. Forde's own critique of the antinomianism present in the feminist theology presupposes this. The sinner is never free from the law until the law is fulfilled. For Forde, the redemptive fulfillment of the law is simply moved from an external location (in Christ) to an internal one (within the believer).

Moreover, despite Forde's attacks on the Lutheran scholastic doctrine of atonement, the structure of the fulfillment of the law in his theology and their own remains roughly the same. In other words, the Lutheran scholastic doctrine of active and passive righteousness[120] assumed that two things needed to be accomplished for salvation to be realized: Negatively, guilt needed to be dealt with and sin judged. The imputation of sin to Christ and his suffering of God's judgment against sin on the cross (passive righteousness) fulfilled this aspect of reconciliation. In Forde, such a negative judgment does not occur on the cross, but through the cross. Internally, the believer suffers the judgment of their old being through the existential encounter with the reality of their own rejection of God and his grace actualized on the cross. Secondly, in addition, positive righteousness before the judgment seat of God (active righteousness) needed to be actualized in the form of Christ's perfect adherence to the law. In Forde, faith fulfills the law, and therefore "satisfies" God. The new creature of faith is positively righteous before God, and God's wrath is neutralized. Consequently, the role of Christ's active righteousness is replaced by the transformation of the sinner through the efficacy of the word of God.

Though space does not allow for us to explore the sources of Forde's thought within this context, perhaps it is not too bold to suggest that here one might detect here a lingering preference (discussed in the last chapter in connection with the German philosopher Immanuel Kant) to limit one's self to a discussion of things as they are experienced over things as they exist in themselves. As was observed in an earlier chapter, Kant's influence is to be felt throughout modern German Protestant dogmatics, which Forde

---

crucified, dead, and buried, that *He might reconcile the Father unto us, and be a sacrifice, not only for original guilt, but also for all actual sins of men*" (emphasis added). Also see Isa 53, Rom 3:25, Cor 5:21, 1 Pet 2:24.

120. See summary in Schmid, *Doctrinal Theology*, 352–56.

drew so heavily upon.[121] As the reader may recall, for Kant, one cannot know "things in themselves" (in German: "*ding an sich*"[122]) and therefore we can only know the effects of an entity on us, rather than its actual reality in itself. Likewise, for Forde, positing the existence of an objective eternal law is too abstract, and we must therefore focus on the existential impact of the law alone.[123] Correspondingly, he considers the idea of vicarious satisfaction to represent a mere "abstract payment,"[124] rather than the more-concrete fulfillment of the law actualized internally through the existential impact of the cross on the consciousness of the believer.

This leads us to the second area of difficulty, namely, the consequences for the preaching of justification. Since Forde's account of reconciliation internalizes the basis of righteousness before the judgment seat of God, it is not difficult to recognize that, on a pastoral level, such an account will ultimately have the opposite effect that he intends. Forde is, of course, correct to identify the problem of human nature as it exists after the fall as self-centered trust and self-justification. It is for this reason that his understanding of justification is so problematic. If one is told that the basis of his righteousness before God is not outside of one's self, but rather that one becomes righteous in oneself through faith, the problem of the inward gaze of the sinner's eye will simply be exacerbated. Forde is correct to emphasize the effective nature of the word of the gospel for both justification and sanctification.[125] Nevertheless, his desire to give an account of justification that effectively and completely de-centers the self is ultimately blunted by his false understanding of the righteousness of faith.

Moving beyond issues directly pertaining to atonement and justification, another major area of concern and difficulty is Forde's underling understanding of the relationship between the old and new creations. As

---

121. See Davidovich, *Religion as a Province of Meaning*.

122. Kant, *Critique of Pure Reason*, 74, 87, 149, 172–73.

123. Forde, *Law-Gospel Debate*, 185. In response to Theodosius Harnack's *Amt-Wesen* (in English: "essence/office") distinction, Forde rejects the whole notion of speech about the law apart from its existential impact in stating that such a description of the law makes sinful humans "view it [God's law] in the abstract . . . This allows man to place himself *above* the law and to look at it from God's point of view." For the *Amt-Wesen* distinction see Harnack, *Luthers Theologie*, 1:368–401

124. Forde, "The Work of Christ," 1:48.

125. See Forde, *Justification By Faith*, 36. Forde writes: "[t]he old argument about whether justification is "only" forensic or also "effective" is transcended. . . . It is, to be sure, "not only" forensic, but that is the case only because the more forensic it is, the more effective."

is clear from my earlier discussion (particularly with regard to penal substitution), Forde is absolutely adamant that the relationship between the old and new beings must be thought of as a wholly disruptive death and resurrection. For him, atonement and justification are apocalyptic events that annihilate the old being of sin and replace it with a new being of faith. Sinful humanity resists this movement of death and resurrection because it wishes to maintain continuity with the old being and its autonomy through death-dealing legalism.[126]

In one of his later books, *Justification by Faith: A Matter of Death and Life*, Forde quite specifically attacks the idea of a purely forensic justification on these grounds.[127] Much as penal substitution allows for the expression of God's merciful saving will to stand in an internal coherence with his holiness, so too a purely forensic account of justification (the "legal metaphor" as he puts it) allows the old being under the condemnation of the law to stand in continuity with the new creature of faith. Since the idea of imputed righteousness presupposes that the person of faith is the same subject as the one who once stood under the power of sin, a purely forensic justification allows the sinner to forgo the total death-dealing apocalyptic break of the cross.[128] In speaking forth the word of the gospel, God wishes to bring about something completely new, and not simply a dressed-up version of the old creation. In light of this, the imputation of righteousness is simply unnecessary if the old sinful subject has ceased to exist and been replaced. As a side note, it should not go unnoticed that this account of the human subject's discontinuity is almost nearly identical with that of Immanuel Kant's own conception of justification.[129]

---

126. This emphasis can also be found in Forde's students. See Mattes, "Beyond the Impasse," 278. Mattes writes: "there is no continuity between old and new beings. This is because the new being lives from faith in Jesus Christ alone."

127. Forde, *Justification By Faith*, 18–19.

128. Ibid., 13.

129. See discussion in Kant, *Gesammelte Schriften*, 6:74–75. Also see McGrath, *Iustia Dei*, 340. Though I do not have the space in this article to cite the whole passage, McGrath (within whose writing I discovered the above citation from *Religion Within the Limits of Reason Alone*) notes that Kant holds that because substitution is impossible, the repentant and renewed human person must be conceptualized as simply having replaced the old person before God. Otherwise, they would not be able to escape the reality of guilt and the past. Note that Forde agrees with Kant in his rejection of the biblical principle of representation and substitution (see Forde, "The Work of Christ," 2:24). As any historian worth their salt knows, influence is extremely difficult to prove. Nevertheless, it can be suggested that because the two authors have similar premises, they come to similar conclusions.

The Doctrine of Atonement

From this, much of the difficulty with Forde's doctrine of justification and atonement becomes evident from the perspective of the article of creation. According to Forde's description, what appears to be the case is that creation is not so much redeemed, but is in fact replaced.[130] The old creation is not purified and redeemed by the cleansing blood of Christ, but rather is annihilated. This also seems to raise the logical problem concerning why, if the old and new creatures are totally discontinuous, forgiveness is necessary in the first place. If I am not the same subject who was guilty, then why is it necessary that must I be forgiven?

Though it is certainly not his intention to impugn the goodness of the created order, by using the language of radical discontinuity Forde seems to place himself perilously close to Flacius' similarly unintended heresy that after the fall sin was the "substance" of human nature and not a mere "accidental quality."[131] After all, such an account of the relationship between the old and new creation would appear to assume the very thing that Flacius asserted, namely, that sin is the substance of human nature after the fall and not merely an accident adhering in it.

In order to combat this charge, Forde would likely appeal to the sometimes-rather-hazily defined concept (common in many late-twentieth-century Lutheran theologians, notably Gerhard Ebeling[132]) of "relational ontology."[133] According to this manner of thinking, the true nature of a thing or person is not constituted by an unchanging essence within, but rather by the relationships they enter into, the most fundamental of which is their relationship to God.[134] Therefore, claiming a total discontinuity

---

130. I thank Reverend David Ramirez for this particular way of expressing the problem with Forde's description of redemption.

131. FC, SD, I; *CT*, 859–81. FC, Ep. I; *CT*, 779–85. For sources on Flacius and his misstatement regarding original sin, see the following: Bente, *Historical Introductions*, 144–45; Klann, "Original Sin," 115–17.

132. See Ebeling, *Dogmatik*; Ebeling, *Lutherstudien*; Ebeling, *The Nature of Faith*; Ebeling, *Wort und Glaube*.

133 Forde credits Ebeling as formative influence: Forde, "One Acted Upon," 60. By contrast, James Nestingen states that the claim that Forde was influence my Ebeling was a pernicious rumor. See Nestingen, "Examining Sources," 20–21. Also note Forde's endorsement of the concept of relational ontology. See Keifert et al., "A Call for Discussion," 226–27. Note that the authors view the difference between Lutherans and Catholics on the issue of justification as specifically pertaining to substance versus relational ontology.

134. See Ebeling, *Dogmatik*, 3:195–200. Ebeling describes the movement of justification from a state of non-being (*Nichtsein*) to being (*Sein*). Also see Joest, *Ontologie*, 14, 37, 362.

between the old and new beings is not somehow to assert that the substance of a creature is evil and therefore needs to be replaced by a new substance. Rather, it is to claim that, through the effective address of the gospel, a total and wholesale reversal of the existential relationship between God and the sinner occurs.[135]

On one level, Forde's insight here is something that confessional Lutherans should heed. The relationship of the sinner to God is not one of degrees, but of kind. The divine-human relationship constituted by the condemnation of the law is the very opposite of that of grace and justification. The life-orientation of the sinner is precisely the opposite of that of the person of faith. Lutherans should not be lulled (as some in fact have[136]) into accepting a Thomistic account of divine grace completing nature.[137] God's power, present and active in the preached word, completely turns the sinner around. Divine grace does not work to activate the sinner's hidden potencies.

Nevertheless, Forde's rhetoric of total discontinuity fails on another level. First, his choice of language often seems to suggest that the creature's total being is constituted by the relationship of sin and condemnation. In fact, Forde often boldly speaks of his wholesale contempt for the notion that we are "continuously existing subjects,"[138] i.e., that there is any continuity between the old and new beings. Nonetheless, if indeed, we are not continuously existing subjects, what becomes of our status as God's good creatures, of which as the Formula of Concord states, sin is merely an accident disruption?[139] If essence of humanity is conceptualized relationally, must it not be defined at an even more fundamental level by the creator-creature relationship and not merely by the relationship of sin and condemnation? Indeed, as the history of the fall suggests, this more fundamental relational status as God's good creatures is precisely what defines us as sinners. As Luther at the very least strongly implies in his description of the first article of

---

135. For this reason, Forde's proposal should not be confused with the debate within Lutheran scholasticism regarding the question of whether the created world would be completely annihilated or renewed. All parties involved assumed the continuity of the human subjects in creation, redemption, and the eschaton. See discussion in Schmid, *Doctrinal Theology*, 655–56; and also Pieper, *Christian Dogmatics*, 3:542–43.

136. See description in Mattes, "The Thomistic Turn," 65–100.

137. See description in Maritain, *Integral Humanism*, 291–308.

138. Forde, "Radical Lutheranism," 15.

139. FC Ep. I; *CT*, 779–85.

the creed,[140] sinful humanity perpetually receives itself as God's ever good creation, but nevertheless remains untrusting and ungrateful.

Beyond its inability to coherently maintain the creator-creature relationship in light of redemption, Forde's rhetoric of wholesale disruption fails in other regards as well. Chiefly, the rhetoric of total reversal stands disconcertingly out of step with God's trustworthiness as it is proclaimed and revealed in the gospel. In other words, if God's redemptive act destroys creation, rather than redeems and purifies it from its negative relationship of sin and condemnation, then has he not been faithless to that which has come before? If he acts in such a way as to be faithless to his original creation by simply replacing it, why would the believer expect God to be faithful in his promise of the gospel?

The problematic nature of Forde's fixation on the paradigm of discontinuity also manifests itself in his understanding of the relationship between forgiveness and the law. As was observed earlier, for Forde, God spontaneously forgives sinners by an act of fiat. God may, it appears, simply abandon his word of law and its clearly articulated threats of retribution present throughout Sacred Scripture (Deut 27:26; 32:35; etc.). Nevertheless, what assurance does the believer possess that God will not abandon his word of gospel just as he did his earlier word of law? Seen from this perspective, Christ's fulfillment of the law in traditional confessional Lutheran theology is neither an abstract nor a mechanical legal transaction. It is part and parcel of the coherence of the creedal faith that sees God's dynamic activity in the first article (creation and law) as faithfully fulfilled in the second and third articles (atonement, justification, and sanctification).

Part of the answer to this question is that Forde tends to subsume the idea of the law as commandment into the larger reality of the law as negative existential relationship.[141] If God so chooses, he may reverse this relationship, and thereby abrogate the law in favor of the new relationship of grace. Moreover, as I have previously shown, despite his rhetoric to the

140. SC II.1; *CT*, 543. Luther writes: "I believe that God has made me and all creatures; that He has given me my body and soul, eyes, ears, and all my limbs, my reason, and all my senses, and still preserves them; in addition thereto, clothing and shoes, meat and drink, house and homestead, wife and children, fields, cattle, and all my goods; that He provides me richly and daily with all that I need to support this body and life, protects me from all danger, and guards me and preserves me from all evil; and all this out of pure, fatherly, divine goodness and mercy, without any merit or worthiness in me; for all which I owe it to Him to thank, praise, serve, and obey Him. This is most certainly true."

141. See summary description in Forde, *Law-Gospel Debate*, 192. See my own discussion of this fact in Kilcrease, "Gerhard Forde's Doctrine," 151–80.

contrary, God ultimately really does need the law to be fulfilled in order to save.

Nevertheless, neither answer is sustainable from the perspective of the Scripture and the confessional writings of the Evangelical Lutheran Church. As is abundantly clear from these authorities, God has two separate words of law and gospel. Through his redemptive work of atonement and justification by the blood of Jesus, God reveals his trustworthiness by fulfilling the threats and promises of both. Indeed, as the Apostle Paul puts it, by his act of redemption in the cross and the empty tomb, God revealed "his righteousness . . . [as the one who is both] just and the justifier of the one who has faith in Jesus" (Rom 3:26).

In light of the biblical and confessional authorities, perhaps a better way of conceptualizing the relationship between the old and new creations might be on the basis of an analogy of the fifth ecumenical council's description of the relationship between the two natures in Christ. According to this council, Christ's divine person is a proper center of identity or person (in Greek, *hypostasis*) within which his non-personal humanity (in Greek, *anhypostasis*), which is incorporated and subsists.[142] From this, it follows that the man Jesus is not an independent entity, but finds the center of his identity in the pre-existent person of the Son of God. In a similar manner, as David Scaer has correctly observed,[143] God's new act of redemption always incorporates within itself that which has come before. Hence, the new creation and its relationship with God's grace is (as Forde insists) something completely new. The new creation is not somehow the fruit of the activation of hidden potencies in the old creation (i.e., the Thomistic "grace completing nature"). Rather, the new creation is its own independent and complete reality, in a similar manner to the divine person of Christ. Ultimately, though, because God is faithful to his previous words and works, he always incorporates his previous act into his new one. For this reason, the new creation becomes the proper center of identity for the old creation.[144] Throughout the Scripture one can see this in any number

---

142. For the text of the fifth ecumenical council see Denzinger, *Sources of Catholic Dogma*, 85–90. See discussion in Meyendorff, *Christ in Eastern Christian Thought*, 38–40, 59–64.

143. See Scaer, "Sacraments as an Affirmation," 241–63.

144. See *LW* 34:139; *WA* 39.I:177. Luther himself comments in *The Disputation Concerning Man* (1536): "Therefore, man in this life is the *simple material of God for the form of the future life*. . . [j]ust as the whole creation which is now subject to vanity [Rom. 8:20] is for God *the material for its future glorious form*" (emphasis added).

of instances. In becoming incarnate, Jesus took upon himself the flesh and condemnation of Adam in order to redeem. In the resurrection, his corpse was incorporated into his body of glory (see 1 Cor 15:35–38). Similarly, the sacraments of the new creation contain within themselves the elements of the old creation (bread, wine, water). Lastly, and most importantly, the law is contained within and ultimately fulfilled in the gospel (Rom 3:26, 8:3–4).

This being said, although it is important to recognize the unity of the old and new creations, Forde must be nonetheless commended for insisting that the Bible describes the advent of the new creation as not coming about apart from eschatological judgment. Although the old creation is by no means abrogated by the new, in being purified from sin it does not escape God's judgment. For this reason, in the incarnation of the second Adam, God the Holy Spirit purified the flesh he took from Mary from the sin of the first Adam. In the crucifixion, God concentrated all sin in the flesh of Christ and reduced him to a corpse in order to redeem the whole world (Isa 53:4, 2 Cor 5:21, 1 Pet 2:24). Nevertheless, this judgment does not annihilate, but rather cleanses creation from the accidental vitiation of sin. Jesus' body, which bore the burden of human sin, becomes (for those who have faith) the medium through which we die and are resurrected into a new and infinitely abundant divine life. For this reason, our bodies, though vitiated by sin, will not be destroyed, but will be glorified by "putting on incorruptibility" (1 Cor 15:53).

Conclusion

In developing a theology of atonement and justification, it is absolutely essential that the Christian theologian think in terms of the internal coherence of the creedal faith as attested by Scripture. God's faithfulness in redemption must not trump his faithfulness to his creation and law. In spite of Forde's good intention, much of his theology of redemption can serve as a warning against drawing too sharp a line between the first article of the creed and the second and third. If God is truly the faithful God of the gospel, his identity as such will be revealed, as well as his faithfulness and what he has commanded, to that which he has created. Although it was not Forde's goal to undermine the article of creation or law, his description of the gospel and the new creation as something wholly discontinuous strongly implies a lack of faithfulness on God's part to the realities established in the first article.

In response to this, I have argued that, in Scripture, when God speaks forth his new creation through the gospel, he does so in a way that incorporates the reality of the old creation into the wholly new creation that he brings about. He does this by purifying the old realities from sin and the negative relationship of judgment that sin entails.

Ultimately, the coherence of God's action in creation and redemption serves the certainty of the chief article of the gospel. In that God is faithful to the old creation and the law, he can be trusted to fulfill his promises in the gospel. Christ's righteousness gives sinners new life and the assurance of God's favor, which they can live out in their everyday lives. All this is dependent on Christ's substitutionary work, which redeems the old creation and breaks the control of legalism over human existence. Alternative accounts of atonement and justification do not do this. Without fail, they send sinners back to their own works, and thereby to their own self-trust.

Bibliography

Abelard, Peter. "Exposition of the Epistle to the Romans." In *A Scholastic Miscellany: Anselm to Ockham*. Translated and edited by Eugene R. Fairweather, 276–87. Philadelphia: Westminster, 1966.
Adam, Karl. *The Spirit of Catholicism*. Translated by Justin McCann. New York: Crossroads, 1997.
Addis, Mark. *Wittgenstein: A Guide for the Perplexed*. New York: Continuum International, 2006.
Althaus, Paul. *The Theology of Martin Luther*. Translated by Robert Schultz. Philadelphia: Fortress, 1966.
Anderson, Deland. *Hegel's Speculative Good Friday: The Death of God in Philosophical Perspective*. Missoula: Scholar's, 1996.
Anselm of Canterbury. "Cur Deus homo?" In *A Scholastic Miscellany: Anselm to Ockham*, translated and edited by Eugene R. Fairweather, 100–183. Philadelphia: Westminster, 1966.
Arand, Charle. "Luther and the Creed." In *The Pastoral Luther: Essays on Luther's Practical Theology*, edited by Timothy Wengert, 147–70. Grand Rapids: Eerdmans, 2009.
Athanasius. "On the Incarnation of the Word." In *The Christology of the Later Fathers*. Translated and edited by Achidbald Robertson, 55–110. Philadelphia: Westminster, 1954.
Aulén, Gustaf. *Christus Victor: An Historical Study of the Three Main Types of the Idea of Atonement*. Translated by A.G. Hebert. New York: Macmillan, 1969.
———. *The Faith of the Christian Church*. Translated by Eric H. Wahlstrom. London: SCM, 1960.
Barnett, Paul. *Is the New Testament Reliable?* Downer's Grove, IL: InterVarsity, 2003.
Barth, Karl. "Gospel and Law." In *Community, State and Church: Three Essays*, edited by Will Herberg, 71–100. New York: Doubleday, 1960.
———. *The Theology of the Reformed Confessions, 1923*. Translated by Darrell Guder. Louisville, KY: Westminster John Knox, 2002.
Baur, F. C. *History of Christian Dogma*. Translated by Peter Hodgeson and Robert Brown. New York: Oxford University Press, 2014.
Bavel, Tarsicus van. "Church." In *Augustine through the Ages: An Encyclopedia*, edited by Allan Fitzgerald, 170–71. Grand Rapids: Wm. B. Eerdmans, 1999.
Bayer, Oswald. "Die Reformatorische Wende in Luthers Theologie." *Zeitschrift fur Theologie und Kirche* 66 (1969) 115–50.

Bibliography

———. *Martin Luther's Theology: A Contemporary Interpretation*. Translated by Thomas Trapp. Grand Rapids: Eerdmans, 2008.
Becker, Matthew. *The Self-Giving God and Salvation History: The Trinitarian Theology of Johannes von Hofmann*. New York: T & T Clark International, 2004.
Bell, Theo. *Divus Bemhardus: Bernhard von Clairvaux in Martin Luthers Schriften*. Mainz, Germany: Philipp von Zabern, 1993.
———. "Man is a Microcosmos: Adam and Eve in Luther's Lectures on Genesis 1535–1545." *Concordia Theological Quarterly* 69, no. 2 (April 2005) 159–84.
Bente, Friedrich. *Historical Introductions to the Book of Concord*. St. Louis: Concordia, 1965.
Bertram, Robert. "How Our Sins Were Christ's: A Study in Luther's Galatians (1535)." In *The Promising Tradition: A Reader in Law-Gospel Reconstructionist Theology*, edited by Edward Schroder, 7–21. St. Louis: Seminex, 1974.
Boehme, Armand J. "Tributaries into the River JDDJ: Karl Holl and Luther's Doctrine of Justification." *Logia* 18, no. 3 (2009) 1–16.
Borg, Marcus. *Meeting Jesus Again for the First Time: The Historical Jesus and the Heart of Contemporary Faith*. San Francisco: HarperSanFrancisco, 1994.
Bornkamm, Heinrich. *Luther's World of Thought*. Translated by Martin H. Bertram. St. Louis: Concordia, 1965.
Braaten, Carl. *No Other Gospel: Christianity among the World's Religions*. Minneapolis: Fortress, 1992.
Bromiley, Geoffrey. *Historical Theology: An Introduction*. Grand Rapids: Eerdmans, 1978.
Brown, Dee. *Bury My Heart at Wounded Knee*. New York: Holt, Reinhart & Winston, 1970.
Brown, Joanne Carlson, and Rebecca Parker. "For God so Loved the World?" In *Christianity, Patriarchy, and Abuse: A Feminist Critique*. Edited by Joanne Carlson Brown and Carole Bohn. New York: Pilgrim, 1989.
Brown, Raymond. *The Death of the Messiah, From Gethsemane to the Grave: A Commentary on the Passion Narratives in the Four Gospels*. Vol. 1. New York: Doubleday, 1994.
Brunner, Peter. *Worship in the Name of Jesus*. Translated by M. H. Bertram. St. Louis: Concordia, 1968.
Bultmann, Rudolf. *Die Geschichte der Synoptischen Tradition*. Göttingen, Germany: Vandenhoeck und Ruprecht, 1957.
———. *Theologie des Neuen Testaments*. 2 vols. Tübingen: Mohr, 1953.
Burgess, Joseph A. and Marc Kolden. "Introduction: Gerhard O. Forde and the Doctrine of Justification." In *By Faith Alone: Essays on Justification in Honor of Gerhard O. Forde*, edited by Joseph A. Burgess and Marc Kolden, 3–10. Grand Rapids: Eerdmans, 2004.
Calvin, John. *The Institutes of the Christian Religion*. Translated and edited by John T. McNeill and Ford Lewis Battles. 2 vols. Philadelphia: Westminster, 1967.
Carlson-Brown, Joanne, and Rebecca Parker. "For God so Loved the World?" In *Christianity, Patriarchy, and Abuse: A Feminist Critique*, edited by Joanne Carlson Brown and Carole Bohn, 1–29. New York: Pilgrim, 1989.
Chemnitz, Martin. *Examination of the Council of Trent*. Translated by Fred Kramer. 4 vols. St. Louis: Concordia, 1971–1986.
———. *The Two Natures in Christ*. Translated by J. A. O. Preus. St. Louis: Concordia, 1971.

BIBLIOGRAPHY

Congar, Yves. "Regards et réflexions sur la Christologie de Luther." In Vol. 3 of *Das Konzil von Chalkedon: Geshichte und Gegenwart*. Edited by Aloys Grillmeier and Heinrich Bacht, 488–89. 3 vols. Würzburg, Germany: Echter Verlag, 1953–1954.

Crisp, Oliver. "Robert Jenson on the Pre-existence of Christ." *Modern Theology* 23, no. 1 (2007) 27–45.

Crossan, John Dominic. *The Historical Jesus: The Life of a Mediterranean Jewish Peasant*. San Francisco: HarperOne, 1993.

Cullmann, Oscar. *Christology of the New Testament*. London: SCM, 1963.

Davidovich, Adina. *Religion as a Province of Meaning: The Kantian Foundations of Modern Theology*. Minneapolis: Fortress, 1993.

Deme, Daniel. *The Christology of Anselm of Canterbury*. Burlington, VT: Ashgate, 2003.

Denzinger, Heinrich. *The Sources of Catholic Dogma*. Translated by Roy Deferrai. St. Louis: B. Herder, 1954.

Descartes, Rene. *The Meditations on First Philosophy*. Translated by Donald Cress. Indianapolis: Hackett, 1993.

Ebeling, Gerhard. *Dogmatik des Christlichen Glaubens*. 3 vols. Tübingen, Germany: Mohr Siebeck, 1979.

———. *Lutherstudien*. 3 vols. Tübingen, Germany: Mohr Siebeck, 1971–1989.

———. *The Nature of Faith*. Translated by Ronald Smith. London: Collins, 1961.

———. "Word of God and Hermeneutics." In *Word and Faith*, translated by James Leitch, 305–32. Philadelphia: Fortress, 1960.

———. *Wort und Glaube*. Tübingen, Germany: Mohr Siebeck, 1960.

Eckardt, Burnell. *Anselm and Luther on Atonement: Was It Necessary?* Lewiston, NY: Edward Mellen, 1992.

Ehrman, Bart. *The New Testament: A Historical Introduction to the Early Christian Writings*. New York: Oxford University Press, 2000.

Elert, Werner. *The Christian Ethos: The Foundations of the Christian Way of Life*. Translated by Carl Schindler. Philadelphia: Muhlenberg, 1957.

———. *Law and Gospel*. Translated by Edward Shroeder. Philadelphia: Fortress, 1967.

———. *The Structure of Lutheranism*. Translated by Walter Hansen. Vol. 1. St. Louis: Concordia, 1961.

Eusebius. *The Church History: A New Translation with Commentary*. Translated by Paul Maier. Grand Rapids: Kregel, 1999.

Evans, G. R. "Anselm of Canterbury." In *The Medieval Theologians*, edited by G. R. Evans, 94–101. Oxford: Blackwell, 2001.

Forde, Gerhard. "Absolution: Systematic Considerations." In *The Proclamation in Word and Sacrament*, edited by Mark Mattes and Steven D. Paulson, 152–64. Grand Rapids: Eerdmans, 2007.

———. *The Captivation of the Will: Luther vs. Erasmus on Freedom and Bondage*. Edited by Steven Paulson. Grand Rapids: Eerdmans, 2005.

———. "Caught in the Act: Reflections on the Work of Christ." In *A More Radical Gospel: Essays on Eschatology, Authority, Atonement, and Ecumenism*, edited by Mark Mattes and Steven D. Paulson, 85–97. Grand Rapids: Eerdmans, 2004.

———. "Fake Theology: Reflections on Antinomianism Past and Present." In *The Proclamation in Word and Sacrament*, edited by Mark Mattes and Steven D. Paulson, 214–24. Grand Rapids: Eerdmans, 2007.

BIBLIOGRAPHY

———. "Forensic Justification and the Christian Life: Triumph or Tragedy?" In *A More Radical Gospel: Essays on Eschatology, Authority, Atonement, and Ecumenism*, edited by Mark Mattes and Steven D. Paulson, 114–36. Grand Rapids: Eerdmans, 2004.
———. "In Our Place." In *A More Radical Gospel: Essays on Eschatology, Authority, Atonement, and Ecumenism*, edited by Mark Mattes and Steven Paulson, 101–13. Grand Rapids: Eerdmans, 2004.
———. *Justification By Faith: A Matter of Death and Life*. Milifinton, PA: Sigler, 1999.
———. "Law and Sexual Behavior." *Lutheran Quarterly* 9, no. 1 (1995) 3–22.
———. *The Law-Gospel Debate: An Interpretation of Its Historical Development*. Minneapolis: Augsburg, 1969.
———. "Lutheran Faith and American Freedom." In *The Proclamation in Word and Sacrament*, edited by Mark Mattes and Steven D. Paulson, 195–203. Grand Rapids: Eerdmans, 2007.
———. "Luther's Ethics." In *A More Radical Gospel: Essays on Eschatology, Authority, Atonement, and Ecumenism*, edited by Mark Mattes and Steven Paulson, 137–58. Grand Rapids: Eerdmans, 2004.
———. *On Being a Theologian of the Cross: Reflections on Luther's Heidelberg Disputation, 1518*. Grand Rapids: Eerdmans, 1997.
———. "One Acted Upon." *Dialogue* 36, no. 1 (Winter, 1997) 54–61.
———. "Radical Lutheranism." In *A More Radical Gospel: Essays on Eschatology, Authority, Atonement, and Ecumenism*, edited by Mark C. Mattes and Steven D. Paulson. Grand Rapids: Eerdmans, 2004.
———. *Theology is for Proclamation!* Minneapolis: Fortress, 1990.
———. *Where God Meets Man: Luther's Down-To-Earth Approach to the Gospel*. Minneapolis: Fortress, 1972.
———. "The Work of Christ." In Vol. 2 of *Christian Dogmatics*, edited by Robert Jenson and Carl Braaten, 11–104. Philadelphia: Fortress, 1984.
Fredriksen, Paula. *Jesus of Nazareth, King of the Jews: A Jewish Life and the Emergence of Christianity*. New York: Alfred A. Knopf, 2000.
Funk, Robert. *Honest to Jesus: Jesus for a New Millennium*. San Francisco: HarperSanFrancisco, 1997.
Gerhard, Johann. *Confessio Catholica*. 2 vols. Jena, Germany: n.p., 1634–1637.
———. *On the Person and Office of Christ, Theological Commonplaces: Exegesis IV*. Translated by Richard Dinda. St. Louis: Concordia, 2009.
Green, Lowell. *The Erlangen School of Theology: Its History, Teaching, and Practice*. Fort Wayne, IN: Lutheran Legacy, 2010.
———. *How Melanchthon Helped Luther Discover the Gospel: The Doctrine of Justification in the Reformation*. Fallbrook, CA: Verdict, 1980.
Grenz, Stanley. *Reason for Hope: The Systematic Theology of Wolfhart Pannenberg*. Grand Rapids: Eerdmans, 2005.
Gritsch, Eric. *A History of Lutheranism*. Minneapolis: Fortress, 2010.
Gunton, Colin. "Creation and Mediation in the Theology of Robert W. Jenson: An Encounter and a Convergence." In *Trinity, Time, and Church: A Response to the Theology of Robert W. Jenson*, edited by Colin E. Gunton, 80–93. Grand Rapids: Eerdmans, 2000.
Haga, Joar. *Was there a Lutheran Metaphysics? The Interpretation of Communicatio Idiomatum in Early Modern Lutheranism*. Göttingen, Germany: Vandenhoeck & Ruprecht, 2012.

Bibliography

Hägglund, Bengt. *History of Theology*. Translated by Gene Lund. St. Louis: Concordia, 1963.

Haikola, Lauri. *Gesetz und Evangelium bei Matthias Flacius Illyricus: Eine Untersuchung zur Lutherischen Theologies vor der Konkordienformel*. Lund, Sweden: Gleerup, 1952.

———. *Studien zu Luther und zum Luthertum*. Uppsala, Sweden: Lundequistska Bokhandeln, 1958.

———. *Usus legis*. Uppsala, Sweden: Lundequistska, 1958.

Hamann, Henry. "The Righteousness of Faith before God." In *A Contemporary Look at the Formula of Concord*, e dited by Robert Preus and Wilbert Rosin, 137–62. St. Louis: Concordia, 1978.

Hamm, Berndt. "Wie mystisch war der Glaube Luthers?" In *Gottes Nahe unmittelbar erfahren· Mystik im Mittelalter und bei Martin Luther*, edited by Berndt Hamm and Volker Leppin, 237–87. Tübingen, Germany: Mohr Siebeck, 2007.

Harnack, Theodosius. *Luthers Theologie mit besonderer Beziehung auf seine Versöhnungs- und Erlösungslehre*. 2 vols. Amsterdam: Rodopi, 1969.

Hart, David Bentley. *Beauty of the Infinite: The Aesthetics of Christian Belief*. Grand Rapids: Eerdmans, 2003.

Hegel, G. W. F. *Faith and Knowledge, or the Reflective Philosophy of Subjectivity in the Complete Range of Its Forms as Kantian, Jacobian, and Fichtean Philosophy*. Translated by Walter Cerf and H. S. Harris. Albany: SUNY Press, 1977.

Hengel, Martin. *Judaism and Hellenism: Studies in Their Encounter in Palestine During the Early Hellenistic Period*. Eugene, OR: Wipf & Stock, 2003.

Heppe, Heinrich. *Reformed Dogmatics Set Out and Illustrated from the Sources*. Translated by G. T. Thomson. London: Allen and Unwin, 1950.

Hirsch, Emanuel. *Die Theologie von Andreas Osiander und ihre Geschtlichen Voraussetzugen*. Göttingen, Germany: Vanderhoeck und Ruprecht, 1919.

Hochstraten, Jacob. "Iacobi Hoochstrati Disputationes contra Lutheranos." In *Bibliotheca reformatoria Neerlandica*, edited by F. Pijper, 3:609–10. The Hague, Netherlands: n.p., 1905.

Hoenecke, Adolf. *Evangelical Lutheran Dogmatics*. Translated by Joel Fredrich, James L. Langebartels, Paul Prange, and Bill Tackmier. 4 vols. Milwaukee: Northwestern, 1999–2009.

Hoffman, Bengt. *Luther and the Mystics: A Re-Examination of Luther's Spiritual Experience and His Relationship to the Mystics*. Minneapolis: Augsburg, 1976.

Holl, Karl. *Gesammelte Aufsatze zur Kirchengeschichte*. 3 vols. Tubingen, Germany: Mohr Siebeck, 1928.

Hunsinger, George. *How to Read Karl Barth*. New York: Oxford University Press, 1991.

———. "Truth as Self-Involving: Barth and George Lindbeck on Cognitive and Performative Aspects of Truth in Theological Discourse." *Journal of the American Academy of Religion Journal* 61, no. 1 (1993) 41–56.

Hütter, Leonard. *Compendium Locorum Theologicorum Ex Scripturis Sacris et Libro Concordiae: Lateinisch-Deutsch-Englisch*. Translated by Henry Jacobs. 2 vols. Stuttgart-Bad Cannstatt: Friedrich Frommann, 2006.

Irenaeus of Lyons. *On Apostolic Preaching*. Translated by John Behr. New York: St. Vladimir Seminary Press, 1997.

Iserloh, Erwin. "Luther und die Mystik." In *The Church, Mysticism, Sanctification and the Natural in Luther's Thought*, edited by Ivar Asheim, 60–83. Philadelphia: Fortress, 1967.

BIBLIOGRAPHY

Iwand, Hans Joahim. *The Righteousness of Faith According to Luther*. Translated by Randi Lundell. Eugene, OR: Wipf & Stock, 2008.

Jenson, Robert. *Systematic Theology*. 2 vols. New York: Oxford University Press, 1997-1999.

Jeremias, Joachim. *The Eucharistic Words of Jesus*. London: SCM, 1966.

Joest, Wilfried. *Ontologie der Person bei Luther*. Göttingen, Germany: Vandenhoeck & Ruprecht, 1967.

John of Damascus. *John of Damascus: The Writings*. Translated by Fredric H. Chase. New York: Fathers of the Church, Inc., 1958.

Josephus. *The Works of Josephus*. Translated by William Whiston. Peabody, MA: Hendrickson, 1995.

Jüngel, Eberhard. *God as the Mystery of the World: On the Foundation of the Theology of the Crucified One in the Dispute between Theism and Atheism*. Translated by Darrell Guder. Grand Rapids: Eerdmans, 1983.

———. "The Revelation of the Hiddenness of God: A Contribution to the Protestant Understanding of the Hiddeneness of Divine Action." In Vol. 2 of *Theological Essays*, 120–44. Edinburgh, UK: T & T Clark, 1994.

Junius, Francis. *A Treatise on Truth Theology*. Translated by David Noe. Grand Rapids: Reformation Heritage, 2015.

Kähler, Martin. "The So-called Historical Jesus and the Historic Biblical Christ." Philadelphia: Fortress, 1964.

Kant, Immanuel. *Critique of Pure Reason*. Translated by Norman Kemp Smith. New York: St. Martin's, 1958.

———. *Gesammelte Schriften*. 22 vols. Berlin: Druck und Georg Reimer, 1902–1942.

Keifert, Pat, et al. "A Call for Discussion of the 'Joint Declaration on the Doctrine on Justification.'" *Dialog* 36, no. 3 (Summer, 1997) 226–27.

Kilcrease, Jack. "The Bridal-Mystical Motif in Bernard of Clairvaux and Martin Luther." *The Journal of Ecclesiastical History* 65, no. 2 (2014) 263–79.

———. "Gerhard Forde's Doctrine of Law: A Confessional Lutheran Critique." *Concordia Theological Quarterly* 75, no. 1–2 (2011) 151–80.

———. "Gerhard Forde's Theology of Atonement and Justification: A Confessional Lutheran Response." *Concordia Theological Quarterly* 76, no. 3–4 (2012) 269–94.

———. *The Self-Donation of God: A Contemporary Lutheran approach to Christ and His Benefits*. Eugene, OR: Wipf & Stock, 2013.

———. "Thomas Aquinas and Martin Chemnitz on the Hypostatic Union." *Lutheran Quarterly* 27, no 1 (2013) 1–32.

Klann, Richard. "Original Sin." In *A Contemporary Look at the Formula of Concord*, edited by Robert Preus and Wilbert Rosin, 103–21. St. Louis: Concordia, 1978.

Kolb, Robert. *Bound Choice, Election, and the Wittenberg Theological Method: From Martin Luther to the Formula of Concord*. Grand Rapids: Eerdmans, 2005.

———. "Historical Background of the Formula of Concord." In *A Contemporary Look at the Formula of Concord*, edited by Robert Preus and Wilbert Rosin, 12–87. St. Louis: Concordia, 1978.

———. *Martin Luther: Confessor of the Faith*. Oxford: Oxford University Press, 2009.

Kuhn, Thomas. *The Structure of Scientific Revolutions*. Chicago: The University of Chicago Press, 1970.

Lawrenz, Carl. "On Justification, Osiander's Doctrine of the Indwelling of Christ." In *No Other Gospel: Essays in Commemoration of the 400th Anniversay of the Formula of

BIBLIOGRAPHY

Concord, 1580–1980, edited by Arnold Koelpin, 149–74. Milwaukee: Northwestern, 1980.

Liefeld, David. "Killing to Make Alive: Cruciform Proclamation in the Writings of Gerhard O. Forde." *Logia* 9, no. 4 (2000) 45–51.

Lienhard, Marc. *Luther: Witness to Jesus Christ, Stages and Themes of the Reformer's Christology*. Translated by Edwin Robertson. Minneapolis: Augsburg, 1982.

Lindbeck, George. *The Nature of Doctrine: Religion and Theology in a Post-Liberal Age*. Philadelphia: Westminster, 1984.

Loewenich, Walther von. *Luthers Theologia Crucis*. Munich, Germany: Kaiser Verlag, 1954.

Lohse, Bernhard. *Martin Luther's Theology: Its Historical and Systematic Development*. Edited and translated by Roy A. Harrisville. Minneapolis: Fortress, 1999.

Lonergan, Bernard. *Method in Theology*. Toronto: University of Toronto Press, 1990.

Loughlin, Gerhard. *Telling God's Story: Bible, Church, and Narrative Theology*. Cambridge, UK: Cambridge University Press, 1996.

Louth, Andrew. *St. John Damascene: Tradition and Originality in Byzantine Theology*. New York: Oxford University Press, 2002.

Luther, Martin. *American Edition of Luther's Works*. Edited by Jaroslav Pelikan and Helmut Lehmann. 55 vols. Minneapolis: Fortress, 1957.

———. *First Disputation Against the Antinomians*, Argument 34. In *Only the Decalogue is Eternal: Martin Luther's Complete Antinomian Theses and Disputations*. Edited and translated by Holger Sontag. Minneapolis: Lutheran, 2008.

———. *Only the Decalogue is Eternal: Martin Luther's Complete Antinomian Theses and Disputations*. Edited and translated by Holger Sontag. Minneapolis: Lutheran, 2008.

———. *D. Martin Luthers Werke: Kritische Gesammtausgabe*. 120 vols. Weimar, Germany: H. Bohlaus Nachf, 1883–2009.

Manning, Henry Edward. *Why I Became a Catholic, Or Religio Viatoris*. Sulphur, LA: Secret of the Rosary, 2004.

Mannrmaa, Tuomo. *Christ Present in Faith: Luther's View of Justification*. Translated by Kirsi Sjerna. Minneapolis: Fortress, 2005.

Maritain, Jacques. *Integral Humanism*. Translated by J. Evans. Notre Dame: University of Notre Dame Press, 1968.

Marquart, Kurt. "The 'Realist Principle' of Theology." *Logia* 5, no. 3 (Holy Trinity, 1996) 15–17.

Marx, Karl. *Critique of Hegel's Philosophy of Right*. New York: Cambridge University Press, 1982.

Mathison, Keith. *The Shape of Sola Scriptura*. Moscow, ID: Canon, 2001.

Mattes, Mark C. "Beyond Impasse: Re-examining the Third Use of the Law." *Concordia Theological Journal* 69, no. 3–4 (July–October 2005) 271–92:

———. "Gerhard Forde on Revisioning Theology in Light of the Gospel." *Lutheran Quarterly* 13, no. 4 (1999) 373–93.

———. *The Role of Justification in Contemporary Theology*. Grand Rapids: Eerdmans, 2004.

———. "The Thomistic Turn in Evangelical Catholic Ethics." *Lutheran Quarterly* 16 (2002) 65–100.

McGrath, Alister. *The Genesis of Doctrine: A Study in the Foundations of Doctrinal Criticism*. Cambridge: Basil Blackwell, 1990.

Bibliography

———. *The Intellectual Origins of the European Reformation*. Oxford: Wiley-Blackwell, 2003.

———. *Iustia Dei: A History of the Christian Doctrine of Justification*. Cambridge, UK: Cambridge University Press, 1998.

———. *Luther's Theology of the Cross: Martin Luther's Theological Breakthrough*. New York: Basil Blackwell, 1985.

———. *Reformation Thought: An Introduction*. New York: Wiley-Blackwell, 2012.

———. *A Scientific Theology: Nature*. Vol. 1. New York: T & T Clark, 2001.

McSorley, Harry. *Luther: Right or Wrong? An Ecumenical Theological Study of Luther's Major Work, The Bondage of the Will*. Minneapolis: Augsburg, 1969.

Meier, John P. *A Marginal Jew, Rethinking the Historical Jesus: The Roots of the Problem and the Person*. Vol. 1. New York: Doubleday, 1991.

Melanchthon, Philipp. *Melanchthon on Christian Doctrine: Loci Communes 1555*. Translated by Clyde Manschreck. New York: Oxford University Press, 1965.

Meyendorf, John. *Christ in Eastern Christian Thought*. New York: St. Vladimir's Seminary Press, 1975.

Möhler, Johann Adam. *Symbolism: Exposition of the Differences between Catholics and Protestants as Evidence by Their Symbolic Writings*. Translated by James Burton Robinson. New York: Crossroads, 1997.

Muller, Richard. *Prolegomena to Theology*. Vol. 1 of *Post-Reformation Reformed Dogmatics: The Rise and Development of Reformed Orthodoxy, ca. 1520 to ca. 1725*. Grand Rapids: Baker Academic, 2003.

Murray, Scott. *Law, Life and the Living God: The Third Use of Law in Modern American Lutheranism*. St. Louis: Concordia, 2001.

Nelson, E. Clifford. *The Lutherans in North America*. Philadelphia: Fortress, 1975.

Nestingen, James. "Examining Sources." In *By Faith Alone: Essays on Justification in Honor of Gerhard O. Forde*, edited by Joseph A. Burgess and Marc Kolden, 10–21. Grand Rapids: Eerdmans, 2004.

Ngien, Dennis. *The Suffering of God According to Martin Luther's "Theologia Crucis."* Vancouver, BC: Regent College Publishing, 2005.

Nietzsche, Friedrich. *On the Genealogy of Morals and Ecce Homo*. Translated by Walter Kaufmann. New York: Vintage, 1989.

Oberman, Heiko. *Luther: Man Between God and the Devil*. Translated by Eileen Walliser-Swarzbart. New York: Image, 1992.

———. "*Quo Vadis Petre?* Tradition from Irenaeus to *Humani Generis*." In *The Dawn of the Reformation: Essays in Late Medieval and Early Reformation Thought*. 269–98. Grand Rapids: Eerdmans, 1992.

———. *The Two Reformations: Journey from the Last Days to the New World*. New Haven: Yale University Press, 2003.

Origen. *On First Principles*. Translated by Henri De Lubac. Glouster: Peter Smith, 1973.

Osborn, Eric. "Irenaeus of Lyons." In *The First Christian Theologians: An Introduction to Theology in the Early Church*, edited by G. R. Evans, 121–26. Malden, MA: Blackwell, 2004.

Ozment, Steven. *The Age of Reform, 1250–1550: An Intellectual and Religious History of Late Medieval and Reformation Europe*. New Haven: Yale University Press, 1981.

———. *A Mighty Fortress: A New History of the German People*. San Francisco: Harper Collins, 2005.

Bibliography

Pannenberg, Wolfhart. *Jesus: God and Man*. Translated by Lewis Wilkins and Duane Priebe. Philadelphia: Westminster, 1977.

———. *Systematic Theology*. Translated by Geoffrey W. Bromily. 3 vols. Grand Rapids: Eerdmans, 1991–1993.

Pannenberg, Wolfhart, et al. *Revelation as History*. Translated by David Granskou. New York: MacMillian, 1968.

Pauck, Wilhelm, ed. *Melanchthon and Bucer*. Philadelphia: Westminister, 1959.

Paulson, Steven. *Analogy and Proclamation: The Struggle over God's Hiddenness in the Theology of Martin Luther and Eberhard Jüngel*. Unpublished dissertation, Lutheran School of Theology, 1992.

Pecknold, C. C. *Transforming Postliberal Theology: George Lindbeck, Pragmatism, and Scripture*. New York: T & T Clark International, 2005.

Peters, Albrecht. *Commentary on Luther's Catechisms: Creed*. Translated by Thomas Trapp. St. Louis: Concordia, 2011.

Pieper, Francis. *Christian Dogmatics*. 3 vols. St. Louis: Concordia, 1951.

Pinomaa, Lennart. *Faith Victorious: An Introduction to Luther's Theology*. Translated by Walter J. Kokkonen. Philadelphia: Fortress, 1963.

Pitre, Brant. *Jesus, the Tribulation and the End of Exile: Restoration Eschatology and the Origins of Atonement*. Grand Rapids: Baker Academic, 2005.

Pless, John T., "The Use and Misuse of Luther in Contemporary Debates on Homosexuality: A Look at Two Theologians." http://www.logia.org/index.php?option=com_content&view=article&id=77&catid=39:web-forum&Itemid=76.

Posset, Franz. *Pater Bernhardus: Martin Luther and Bernard of Clairvaux*. Kalamazoo: Cistercian, 1999.

———. *The Real Luther: A Friar at Erfurt and Wittenberg*. St. Louis: Concordia, 2011.

Prenter, Regin. *Luther's Theology of the Cross*. Philadelphia: Fortress, 1971.

Preus, Herman. *The Communion of Saints: A Study of the Origin and Development of Luther's Doctrine of the Church*. Minneapolis: Augsburg, 1948.

———. *A Theology to Live By: The Practical Luther for the Practicing Christian*. St. Louis: Concordia, 1977.

Preus, Robert. "The Doctrine of Revelation in Contemporary Theology." *Bulletin of the Evangelical Theology Society* 9, no. 3 (1966) 111–23.

Rahner, Karl. *Foundations of Christian Faith: An Introduction to the Idea of Christianity*. Translated by William V. Dych. New York: Seabury, 1978.

———. "The Two Basic Types of Christology." In Vol. 13 of *Theological Investigations*, 213–23. New York: Seabury, 1975.

Ritschl, Albrecht. *A Critical History of the Christian Doctrine of Justification and Reconciliation*. Translated by John Black. Edinburgh, UK: Edmonton and Douglas, 1872.

———. *Die Christliche Lehre von der Rechtfertigung und Versöhnong*. 3 vols. Bonn, Germany: A. Marcus, 1895–1903.

Ritschl, Otto. *Dogmengeschichte des Protestantismus*. 4 vols. Göttingen, Germany: Vandenhoeck and Ruprecht, 1927.

Rudolph, Kurt. *Gnosis: The Nature and History of Gnosticism*. Translated by Robert McLachlan Wilson. San Francisco: HarperSanFrancisco, 1987.

Sasse, Herman. "The Theology of the Cross." In *We Confess Anthology*, translated by Norman Nagel, 35–45. St. Louis: Concordia, 1998.

Bibliography

Scaer, David. "Law and Gospel in Lutheran Theology." *Logia* 3, no. 1 (Epiphany, 1994) 27–34.

———. "Sacraments as an Affirmation of Creation." *Concordia Theological Quarterly* 57, no. 4 (1993) 241–63.

———. "The Solid Declaration of the Formula of Concord Article VI: The Third Use of the Law." *Concordia Theological Quarterly* 42, no. 2 (April 1978) 145–55.

Schaller, John. *Biblical Christology: A Study in Lutheran Dogmatics*. Milwaukee: Northwestern, 1981.

Schleiermacher, Friedrich. *The Christian Faith*. Translated by H. R. Mackintosh and J. S. Stewart. New York: T & T Clark, 1999.

Schmid, Heinrich. *The Doctrinal Theology of the Evangelical Lutheran Church*. Translated by Charles A. Hays and Henry E. Jacobs. Minneapolis: Augsburg, 1961.

Schroeder, H. J., trans. *The Canons and Decrees of the Council of Trent*. Rockford, IL: TAN, 1978.

Schultz, Robert. *Gesetz und Evangelium in der Lutherischen Theologie des 19. Jahrhunderts*. Berlin: Lutherisches Verlagshaus, 1958.

Schweitzer, Albert. *The Quest for the Historical Jesus*. Translated by John Bowden. Minneapolis: Fortress, 2001.

Seeberg, Erich. *Luthers Theologie: Christus, Wirklichkeit und Urbild*. Vol. 2. Stuttgart, Germany: W. Kohlhammer, 1937.

Seeberg, Reinhold. *Text-Book of the History of Doctrines*. Translated by Charles Hay. 2 vols. Grand Rapids: Baker, 1977.

Shults, F. LeRon. *The Postfoundationalist Task of Theology: Wolfhart Pannenberg and the New Theological Rationality*. Grand Rapids: Eerdmans, 1999.

Siggins, Ian D. Kingston. *Martin Luther's Doctrine of Christ*. New Haven: Yale University Press, 1970.

Simpson, Gary M. *Critical Social Theory: Prophetic Reason, Civil Society and Christian Imagination*. Minneapolis: Fortress, 2002.

Socinus, Faustus. *The Racovian Catechism*. Translated by Thomas Rees. London: Paternoster Row, 1818.

Steinmetz, David. *Luther in Context*. Bloomington: University of Indiana Press, 1986.

———. *Luther and Staupitz: An Essay in the Intellectual Origins of the Protestant Reformation*. Durham: Duke University Press, 1980.

———. *Misericordia Dei: The Theology of Johannes von Staupitz in its Late Medieval Setting*. Leiden, Netherlands: Brill, 1968.

Strehle, Stephen. *The Catholic Roots of the Protestant Gospel: Encounter between the Middle Ages and the Reformation*. Leiden, Netherlands: Brill, 1995.

Tertullian. *Tertullian: Treatises on Penance and Purity*. Translated and edited by William P. Lesaint. Westminster, UK: Newman, 1959.

TeSelle, Eugene. "Holy Spirit." In *Augustine through the Ages: An Encyclopedia*. Edited by Allan Fitzgerald, 434–47. Grand Rapids: Eerdmans, 1999.

Theissen, Gerd, and Annette Merz. *The Historical Jesus: A Comprehensive Guide*. Translated by John Bowden. Minneapolis: Fortress, 1998.

Thomasius, Gottfried. *Das Bekenntniss der Lutherischen Kirche von der Versöhnung und die Versöhnungslehre D. Chr. K. v. Hofmann's: Mit einem Nachwort von Th. Harnack*. Erlangen, Germany: Theodor Bläsing, 1857.

BIBLIOGRAPHY

Vainio, Olli-Pekka. *Justification and Participation in Christ: The Development of the Lutheran Doctrine of Justification from Luther to the Formula of Concord (1580).* Leiden, Netherlands: Brill, 2008.

Vanhoozer, Kevin. *The Drama of Doctrine: Canonical-Linguistic Approach to Christian Theology.* Louisville: Westminster John Knox, 2005.

von Hofmann, Johannes. *Der Schriftbeweis.* 1st edition. 2 vols. Nördlingen, Germany: C. H. Becker, 1852–1855.

———. *Encyclopädie der Theologie.* Nördlingen, Germany: C. H. Becker, 1879.

Watson, Philip. *Let God Be God! An Interpretation of the Theology of Martin Luther.* Philadelphia: Fortress, 1970.

Webster, John. *Eberhard Jüngel: An Introduction to his Theology.* Cambridge, UK: Cambridge University Press, 1986.

———. "Systematic Theology after Barth: Jüngel, Jenson and Gunton." In *The Modern Theologians: An Introduction to Christian Theology Since 1918.* Edited by David F. Ford and Rachel Muers, 249–64. New York: Blackwell, 2005.

Wengert, Timothy. *Defending Faith: Lutheran Response to Osiander's Doctrine of Justification, 1551–1559.* Tübingen, Germany: Mohr Siebeck, 2012.

———. *Law and Gospel: Philip Melanchthon's Debate with John Agricola of Eisleben over Poenitentia.* Grand Rapids: Baker, 1997.

Whitherington, Ben, III. *The Christology of Jesus.* Minneapolis: Fortress, 1990.

Wicks, Jared. *Man Yearning for Grace: Luther Early Spiritual Teachings.* Washington, DC: Corpus, 1968.

Wingren, Gustaf. *Creation and Law.* Translated by Ross McKenzie. Philadelphia: Muhlenberg, 1961.

———. *Gospel and Church.* Translated by Ross MacKenzie. Edinburgh, UK: Oliver and Boyd, 1964.

———. *Man and the Incarnation: A Study in the Biblical Theology of Irenaeus.* Translated by Ross Mackenzie. Edinburgh, UK: Oliver and Boyd, 1959.

———. *The Living Word: A Theological Study of Preaching and the Church.* Translated by Victor C. Pogue. Philadelphia: Fortress, 1960.

———. *Luther on Vocation.* Translated by Carl C. Rasmussen. Philadelphia: Muhlenberg Press, 1957.

Wittgenstein, Ludwig. *The Blue and Brown Books.* New York: HarperTorch, 1965.

———. *Philosophical Investigations.* Malden, MA: Wiley-Blackwell, 2009.

Wright, N. T. *Christian Origins and the Question of God.* 4 vols. Minneapolis: Fortress, 1992–2013.

Yeago, David. "The Catholic Luther." *First Things* (March 1996) 37–41.

Ziegler, Roland. "The New English Translation of *The Book of Concord* (Augsburg/Fortress 2000): Locking the Barn Door After..." *Concordia Theological Quarterly* 66 (April 2002) 145–65.

www.ingramcontent.com/pod-product-compliance
Lightning Source LLC
Chambersburg PA
CBHW071450150426
43191CB00008B/1301